HANDBOOK FOR SALES, PROJECTS AND FINANCE EXECUTIVES

HANDBOOK FOR SALES, PROJECTS AND FINANCE EXECUTIVES

S. SATYA MURTHY

ATLANTIC PUBLISHERS AND DISTRIBUTORS

Published by
ATLANTIC PUBLISHERS AND DISTRIBUTORS
B-2, Vishal Enclave, Opp. Rajouri Garden, New Delhi-27
Phones : 5413460, 5429987

Sales Office
4215/1, Ansari Road, Darya Ganj, New Delhi-110 002
Phones : 3273880, 3285873, 3280451
Fax : 91-11-3285873
e-mail : info@atlanticbooks.com
web : www.atlanticbooks.com

ISBN 81-269-0005-9

Typeset at
APD Computer Graphics, Delhi

Printed in India at
Nice Printing Press, Delhi

PREFACE

The book is a detailed study of sales and execution of contracts and projects, statutory and legal aspects of commercial terms, estimation, costing, pricing, budget, audit, inspection, inventory, export and import, customer service, communication, monitoring projects using latest techniques renovation, modernization, expansion and diversification of products and projects. The book is meant for executives, managers and staff working in the areas of sales, projects, finance, purchase, management, inspection, planning, production, technologists, users of projects etc. and also students of undergraduate and postgraduate courses in management.

S. SATYA MURTHY

CONTENTS

1

Sales : A Preamble

Sale is one of the most common important and major activities of man. In the ultimate analysis each and every human activity in a way invariably reels around some kind of sales activity. Generally, sales can be classified under the three heads :

1. Type of commodities sold or services rendered
2. Type of customers
3. Whether the transaction is a simple and direct transaction or whether it involves several processes, procedures and agencies.

1. Type of commodities

Commodities are categorized as (1) Basic goods, (2) Capital goods, (3) Intermediate goods, (4) Consumer goods, (5) Consumer non-durables and (6) Consumer durables.

1.1. Basic goods

These are goods, which are used to make other kinds of goods. These are required in abundant quantities. These have to be available all round the year and at the easy reach of customers.

Example of these goods are basic Food articles, vegetables, fruits, flowers, milk and milk products, poultry items, fish and marine items, meats of different kinds, commodities to make beverages like tea, coffee, cocoa, tobacco, basic raw-materials like rubber, jute, wood, cotton, woolen, silk, synthetics items like Pvc, resins, gases like oxygen, nitrogen, carbon monoxide, acetylene, water, coke, coal, electricity, petroleum and natural gas products, all metal items, paper, cement, various chemicals and synthetic materials.

1.2 Capital goods

Capital goods are those goods, which use basic goods to manufacture other variety of goods. These are generally big, costly and sophisticated equipment. These form primary tools for producing other category of goods.

Example of these commodities are machine tools, which are manual, semi automatic, automatic, computer operated, some times using latest technologies such as advanced computers, lathes, cutting, planning, drilling, boring, general purpose machines, welding equipment, presses, lifts, hoists, excavators, cranes, trolleys, haulers, dumpers, conveyors, equipment used for construction of buildings, roads, bridges, such as cement and bitumen mixers, laying machines, leveling machines, road rollers, bulldozers, equipment used for construction of highways, dams, canals, bridges, flyovers, tanks, public utilities such as educational buildings, sports pavilions, industrial sheds, factories, godowns, railways, shipyards, Hydro electric, atomic and other power installations, communication equipment, defence equipment, space equipment, big hotels, water supply, drainage installations, transport equipment including automobiles, like cars, vans, jeeps, trucks, buses, trolleys, trailers, agricultural equipment such as tractors, threshers, pumps, on shore and off shore oil rigs, big auditoriums, theaters, commercial complexes, large motors, fans, compressors, blowers, furnaces, equipment used in mining process plants, refineries, heavy machinery, infrastructure for information technology, films etc.

1.3 Intermediary goods

These are goods, which are made from basic goods and are intermediary commodities between consumer goods and capital goods. These are used to make saleable end products.

These are items like pipes, fittings, all types of material used for water supply, drainage, electricity supply, communication, oils, gases, steam, porcelain fittings, sheets made up of all sorts of material like, zinc, rubber, asbestos, rods, beams, angles, channels, etc. Metal and synthetic material goods, such as yarn, rubber material, foundry material, small tools, gauges, containers for storing food, milk, oil, water, gases, meters, sophisticated material like handicrafts, cottage industries, fabricated wood like, plywood, decolam, fabricated bricks, slabs, agricultural implements, cables, paints, varnishes, resins, medicine, pharmaceutical items, chemicals, fiberglass, insulators and insulating material, typewriters, duplicators, telephone and telegraph items, all patterns, various sizes of springs, gears, rubber tyres for automobiles etc.

1.4 Consumer goods

These are goods of every nature other than capital goods, which are used by all persons in their daily life. These are needed in abundance always and at easy physical reach of all people.

Examples of these items are all food articles including, fruits, vegetables, food grains such as wheat, rice, ragi, jowar, suji, sugar, atta, bread, butter, ghee, edible oils, dhals, all other provisions, processed food, including poultry and marine food, meat products, flowers, synthetic materials, milk and milk products, coke, coal, metals of common use, paper and stationery items, cement, petroleum products, wood and wood based products, chemicals, soaps, detergents, medicines, toiletries, all varieties of cloth, all verieties of cosmetics, aesthetic items, items used for religious purposes, all gases, jewellery items, tobacco, coir, jute, musical instruments, entertainment items, various kinds of beverages, radios, TVs, all varieties of batteries, washing machines, mixies, grinders, heaters, ovens, air coolers and other air-conditioners, different furniture articles, construction items, water, sheep, cattle, electricity, sewage system items, various electricity fittings, cables, communication items, such as telephones, telegraph, fax and computer items and equipment, leather, resins, fertilizers, chemicals, insecticides, pesticides, farm equipment etc.

1.5 Consumer non-durables

These are goods, which are used by people based on their discretion of requirement. These are not cheap and are made in several brands, generally, they are having long life and do not need frequent replacement, as they give more service depending on the use.

Examples of these commodities are Radios, TVs, washing machines, water heaters, water purifiers, refrigerators, costly furniture and upholstery, mixers, grinders, two and four wheelers, leather and other types of suitcases, iron presses, ovens, sewing machines, cookers, air-conditioners, fans, handicrafts, aesthetic items, communication equipment, gas stoves, hair driers, vacuum cleaners etc.

The trend in the use of various commodities in our country with 1993-94 as base is enumerated below to give an idea of break up of commodities, which are needed and produced.

SKETCH

COUNTRY'S TREND OF COMMODITY CONSUMPTION

Use base classification

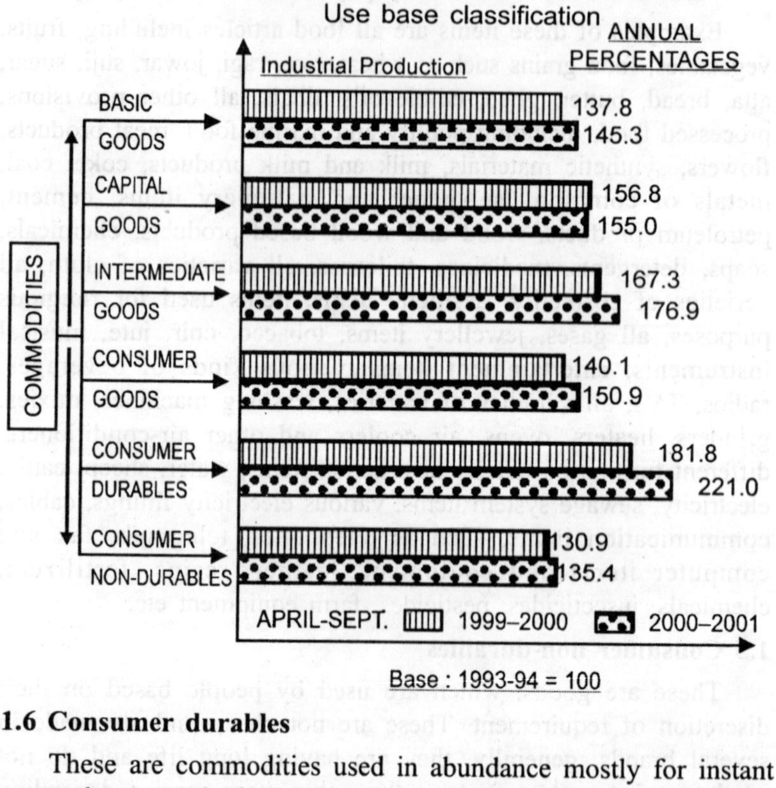

Base : 1993-94 = 100

1.6 Consumer durables

These are commodities used in abundance mostly for instant use and are required at easy reach of people all the time. These are generally cheaper and branded items. These generally have less shelf life and need frequent replacement depending on use and necessity.

Examples of these items are all varieties of food articles, fruits, vegetables, flowers, milk and other dairy products, meat and meat products, soaps, detergents, petroleum products, including lubricants, sanitary items, cosmetics, perfumes, all clothing's, foot-wear, cooking gas, electricity, water, beverages, paints, varnishes, resins, stationery, industrial consumables which are generally non core items, all processed food, tobacco products, insecticides, pesticides, medicines, chemicals of daily use, coke, coal, etc.

2. Type of customers

The second important factor in sales is the type of customer who buys the various commodities and their categorization. The category of customers buying each of the commodities can be any of these or combination of them together :

- Private Individuals
- Private sector
- Cooperative sector
- Joint sector
- Public sector
- State, Central Government's departments and local bodies.

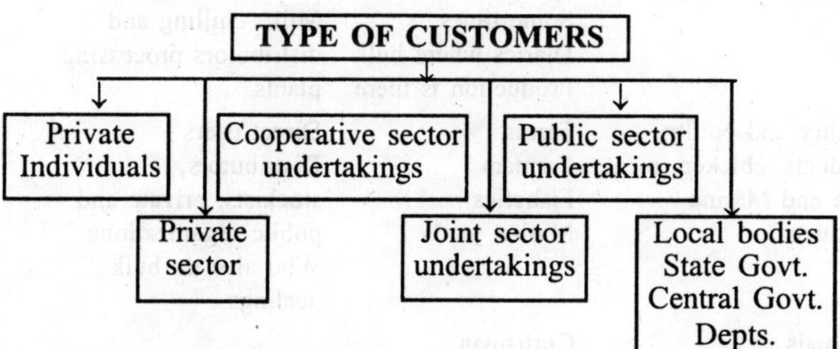

3. Type of sales

3.1 Primary or direct sales

3.2 Secondary, through intermediaries

3.1 Primary sales

In this transaction the deal is simple and direct, right between producer and consumer. Here the producer need not go to a purchaser all the time. Further the buyer also comes to producer directly and buys. Seller need not depend or go through intermediate agencies. Here the commodities are also directly made and sold and user who happens to be buyer can use the commodities directly without doing any major work on it. Here basic activities like storage, transportation, packing and distribution will be the minimum activities done, which are generally simple in nature.

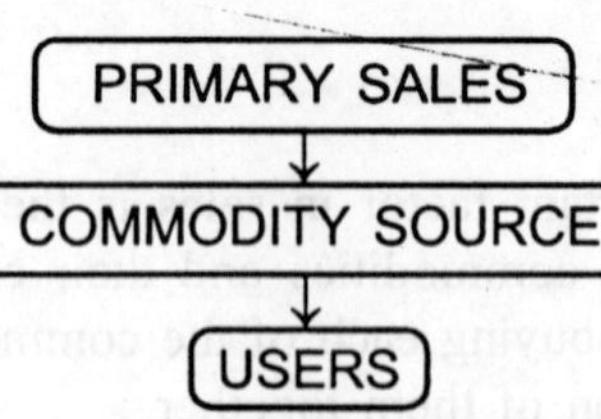

Example of this sale is illustrated below :

Commodity	Source	User
Flowers, fruits, vegetables	Farmers Farms Market yards	Direct users who buy straight away or through agencies, stockists or distributors
Milk and milk products	Farmers, Farms Some times Diaries where bulk Production is there	Direct users Milk chilling and distributors processing plants
Poultry and poultry products, chicken, meat, Fish and Marine products	Farms Farmers Fisheries Market yards	Direct users Distributors, stockists, private and public organizations Who also do bulk dealings
Animals Handicrafts Cottage industry items	Craftsman Small entrepreneurs	

3.2 Secondary sales

Here, generally intermediaries procure the items from the source, they stock it, send to processing plants, Factories, where certain end products are made. The sales of these products generally take place through a big set up depending on the commodity, market location etc. This is a big complicated processes, involves in addition to huge capital, big establishments and commercial implications. Major trade and commerce is in this sector.

Model for Normal Sale of Simple and Branded Varieties of Commodities

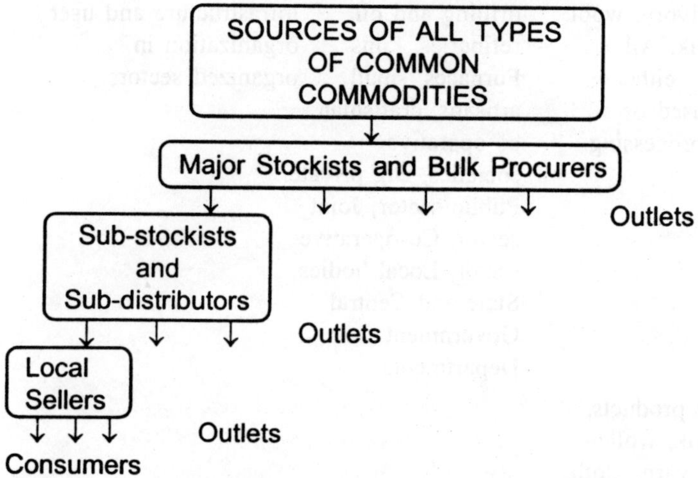

The examples of the commodities and various processes including sales are detailed below in the sketch :

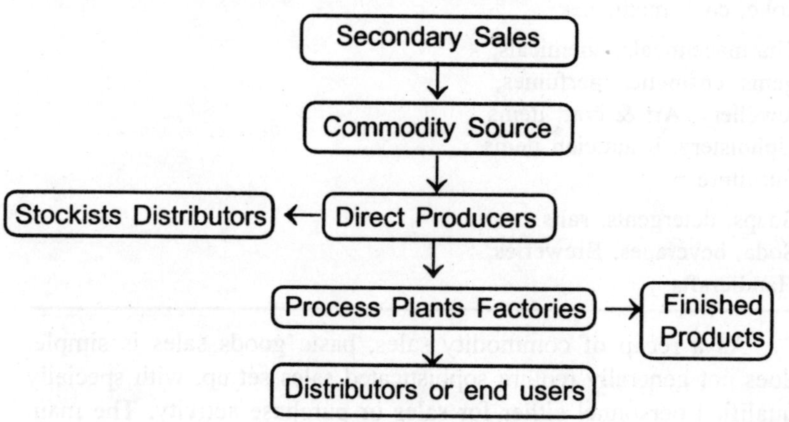

Commodities	Source of these commodities	Users of these commodities
Wheat, Rice, Jowar, Suji, Ragi, Sugarcane, Dhals, oilseeds, Tea, coffee, cocoa, jute, rubber, coir, wood, tobacco, ivory, wool, cotton, silk. All provisions either directly used or through processing plants.	Farmers, Farms, cottage industries, light, medium and big industries processes plants, drilling and oil refineries, kilns Furnaces, small artisans, craftsman, co-operative societies, Big private, Public sector, Joint sector, Co-operative sector, Local bodies, State and Central Government Departments.	Distributors, stockists, Individuals, Hotel and catering organization, processing plants, factories, owners of infrastructure and user organization in organized sectors.
Synthetic products, cotton, silk, wollen, synthetic yarn, cloth, cement, paper,		
Metals and non-metals, coke, coal, medicines		
Pharmaceuticals, chemicals, gems, cosmetics, perfumes, jewellery, Art & craft items, Upholstery, beautician items, Furniture		
Soaps, detergents, salts, Soda, beverages, Breweries, Handicrafts.		

As a recap of commodity sales, basic goods sales is simple, does not generally require sophisticated sales set up, with specially qualified personnel either for sales or purchase activity. The main consideration is money.

In case of capital goods, sellers and buyers need, best sophisticated intelligent and trained staff and set up. People experienced in respective jobs will do best jobs. These goods are generally very highly capital intensive in nature, equipments are complicated requiring specialists in all areas. The cycle of procurement and utilization is long, some times ranging from 6 months to 3 or 4 years. People need knowledge of equipment, performance, production procedure in a very exceptional way. Clarity of procedures of sale and procurement is necessary with good proficiency. Help of experts, consultants, collaborators, financial agencies are taken by sellers and buyers. Since stakes are very high, clarity and expertise at every stage is necessary without any ambiguity as for as practicable. Cost and quality are of utmost importance. Proven experience is necessary in every functional area. The atmosphere will be sophisticated and knowledge oriented. Legal, commercial, technical feasibility are fully evaluated. These are done with precision and care. The sellers capability and competence is weighed by users/buyers, before entrusting jobs to them. Financial soundness of seller and buyer is quite necessary.

In case of intermediate goods, almost the same care as for capital equipment is taken both by seller and user. One consideration is, the value will be lesser in the transactions, compared to the capital equipment. All care and precautions are taken, expert advise is sought in these transactions also, by buyers and sellers. Brand names are of very great significance, as they reflect the organizations standing in the market, over years.

In the field of consumer goods, price and quality are of prime consideration. Lot of competition in the market is experienced and brand names are very important. It is obviously expected, the brand name goes with years of experience in market and struggle in competition to withstand the market share. Sellers take years to stabilize, with good customer following. A certain uniqueness is maintained by quality seller. Several factors are obvious, when branded goods of repute are bought. Quality, price, life, utility, good service, dependability. Generally, the sellers will have reputed service and sales outlets. Continuity of product availability, in near about places of use, are incorporated with good organizations. Since these sellers deal, with large number of discriminating customers, with severe competition in the market, sellers maintain their reputation in various vital fields and certain customer confidence. It is difficult to change the concept of buyers, who always looks for uniqueness in the products they buy, as the markets are huge and turn over is very high. It is generally not necessary to bypass good brands and go for sub-standard goods.

In case of consumer non-durables, the top criteria are price and quality, the markets are huge. Demand for products is very high. Sellers are many to choose from, there is very severe competition as prices of individual items, are less but consumption is more. Here also brand names are very important. It is necessary to ensure continuity of supply at easy reach of customers with many sales outlets. Competitors vie with each other in maintaining the quality, reduced prices, with less profit margins, availability of stocks in plenty, at users reach, since market is assured and customers have to go in compulsory for these materials. Lot of advertisement, superiority of their brands are highlighted to attract more customers and at the same time maintain, their market share which they have maintained over years. In the process of sales, there are some commodities, where the buyer goes to a seller straight away, bargains the items to be bought, buys then and there, and comes back with the items, closing the deal. Here value or quantity of commodities does not pose, any restrictions on the transactions.

In case of purchases, where the items are used for long term service, used by many multiple agencies, more people, used in processes, factories, items, which give long useful life, sophisticated engineering equipment, equipment brought for setting up projects, major services which last long, major spares, repairs etc., multiple considerations, have to be given, by buyer and seller. Here, the markets are very choosy. In case of similar identical commodities, prices, payment, transportation, life of commodities, agencies selling commodities, pose many issues, which have to be considered. In one-time purchases, because the organizations or individuals have to live with them, great care is taken, in finalizing the purchases.

In case of discretion, where long detailed judgment is required, individuals, or mostly organizations, resort to getting offers, quotations, open or limited tenders, domestic or global tenders. Here thorough scrutiny, before deciding on purchase, is made by the buyer. They carefully weigh all the advantages and disadvantages, of the deal, before finalizing it. In such cases, sellers have to submit variety of offers, budgetary or firm for commodities, systems, products of very high value, services, projects, depending on the transaction to be dealt at that time.

In the tables shown in chapter 8, the various terms, details, which the seller has to give to help the buyer to decide on the deal, is given for general reference. In some cases, the terms may be more exhaustive and stringent, depending on the organizations, who go in for the transaction. The details shown are only suggestive and not mandatory and will change from seller to seller, as also from buyer to buyer, discretion of their management and their identified authorities that finalise the transactions/ contracts.

In case of individuals and organizations doing purchases, the activity goes on as follows :

The sales activity of each commodity takes place in a particular pattern. The seller knows, the particular type of buyers he has, for his commodities, except in some exceptional cases. The buyer also knows, who are the sellers of the commodities from whom he has to get them. Both sellers and buyers know the market, the type of commodities available, the way of selling or procuring them. The sellers know, their competitors, the various brands of goods available, prices and likely delivery.

In case of private individuals there is maximum flexibility as to from whom, they can buy goods. Slightly, there is more rigidity, in private sector organizations, as a certain degree of accountability sets in, as to what goods they have to buy, the quality and sellers. More rigidity in procedures and accountability comes in case of, co-operative sector and joint sector buyers. The accountability increases with public sector on its purchases. More set and laid out procedures have to be followed by them. Here procedures are very rigid. For relaxation of procedures or for purchasing goods from unscheduled sellers, special sanctions from concerned authorities are required, quality and price are strict, with lot of accountabilities. The ordering systems and procurement systems of all commodities are very rigid in government departments. The purchases are mostly from registered sellers and jobs are entrusted to sellers, after following strict procedure in quality, price and other terms of contract.

In case of commercial organizations, the terms and procedures will be relaxed depending on the situation, by the competent authorities after considering prices, terms of contract, delivery requirement and their commitments to their clients.

Established sellers who maintain quality of products generally stick to laid out procedures of sale, as they know they have a standing in the market and their goods are in demand.

In case of big reputed organizations, there will be competition in the sellers to woo their customers. They want to woo them to keep a good profile of reputed buyers in the market to enhance their turn over and credibility. Lot of efforts is put in to catch opportunities where big reputed customers are in the run for purchases.

2
Definition of Important Common Commercial Terms

Item/component/article

These have specific identity and characteristic with a size, shape and weight. These are relatively small.

Equipment

It is an assembly of items or components or sub assemblies, which make a compact integrated entity. This gives specified output, to known input, in terms of known parameters.

Project

It is a big assembly of various equipments & systems which makes a big costly venture, intended to give certain known outputs for known inputs. This is a very large, capital intensive, long gestation, well designed and planned activity.

Spare

It is an item or sub assembly, in good condition, used as a replacement for damaged part and gives on replacement, performance similar to the original part replaced, before it was damaged.

Recommended spares

These are of seller's choice. These spares are supposed to be compulsorily kept by the buyer and brought, along with the main equipment. These spares are often, the targets of likely trouble, in the experience of the seller and needs replacement to avoid major break downs of equipment and keeps idle time to minimum. These are also replacements required for parts, which wear out with lesser, operating time, compared to the life of the equipment in general.

Maintenance spares

These are optional for the buyer. These spares are needed as replacements during service in the operation of the equipment. Sellers, request the buyers to keep with them these spares as standby for easy replacement, when the equipment gives trouble in those areas, which are proven to have more wear and tear or give frequent trouble compared to the other parts of the equipment in the specified life of successful operation of the equipment.

Repair

It is a work or correction, made on any part of the equipment to make the equipment work normally when a trouble arises, with the equipment or when the equipment fails partly or totally during operation. The repair can be in the form of better operational advise, requiring re-engineering, technological improvement or other suitable attention. The compensation for repair is to be decided by seller and buyer or a connected third party, as the case may be.

Service

It is advice given to buyer on any matter regarding proper operation of the equipment. It could be free or on chargeable basis by supplier, his agent or a third party, as the situation demands. The compensation to be paid for service is decided by the seller, buyer or connected third party as the case may be.

Cash

It is the currency, which is payable for ready use. It can be in various forms, such as physical cash kept in various types of bank accounts and as amounts, which can be withdrawn, in the form of a draft, instruments of payment on demand in treasury, post office, at short notice.

Credit

It is the amount valued in currency, which a party owes to other party. It is not readily available for use and is the opposite of cash.

Price

It is the consideration to be paid by the buyer to the seller, in known currency for purchase of an article, item, equipment, project, etc. as the case may be.

Prices are specified as ex-show room, ex-railway siding, Port of dispatch, sea or airport, high seas, a godown, site of use etc. as indicated by seller and mutually agreed with the buyer.

Prices may be firm for a certain period say a week, month, 2 months, 6 months etc. as the case may be, at the option of the seller. The seller has the right of changing the price if he so desires after this period. The period is also called the validity period of the price.

Price can be subject to price variation during the period of delivery or contract period on the basis of an agreed formula. This is generally done for very high value and long delivery contracts. The formulas of price variation are well defined. Examples of some price variation formulas being applied to contracts are given in the chapter on price variation.

Payment

It is the consideration to be paid by the buyer for purchase, service or any such obligation to the seller. There are various currencies in which this can be made, which are specified in the contract.

In case of small jobs, which are of small duration and also in cases, where even bigger jobs get completed in short duration, 100 per cent payment will be payable with all applicable duties, taxes, etc. in one go by the seller.

In cases where the amount is high and duration of the contract is long, a percentage of the total contract value is insisted to be paid along with the order as advance. This advance varies from 10 to 90 per cent of the contract price. Balance is to be paid after completing the job/contract.

In case where contract duration is more, progressive payment is agreed. Some percentage of total amount is paid as advance. Some percentage as progressive payment linked with the duration of contract or completion of an activity and final payment is to be made after the completion of the activity. In some cases, 2 to 10 per cent of the contract value is to be paid by the buyer after completion of the contract, or after observing successful working of the equipment or project for a predetermined period. This is a sort of caution money, the buyer retains with him.

Some times, bank guarantees are taken by the buyer even though full amount is paid to the seller. This bank guarantee is for a certain percentage of the contract value, generally to a maximum of 10 per cent and is linked with good performance of equipment or product or for giving agreed technical performance as output with respect to known input parameters.

Taxes

These are levies on the amount of the sale of the product or contract price, which are to be paid by the buyer to seller. This amount ultimately goes to the levying authority, which may be a state government or central government. It is also called sales tax of state or central government. Some times special levies on these taxes, may also exist. In case of central sales tax, if the bought out equipment is for the buyer's use, and not for resale, a concession in CST is given, if documentary proof is given to that effect.

Duties

These are levies other than taxes to be paid by the buyer to the sellers. This amount ultimately goes to the authorities levying these duties such as local bodies, state or central government. Excise duty, customs duty, countervailing duties, come under this category, these are applicable only for certain sales and contracts as specified.

Octroi

This is a levy by a local body. It may be a panchayat, municipality or corporation. These are levied for certain transactions done in the geographical limits of those bodies.

Miscellaneous levies

These are in the form of cess, etc., which are levied for certain transactions by governments or local bodies. These are to be borne by the buyer.

Mode of payment

Payments are made by the buyer in various specified forms, such as by cash, cheque, draft, letter of credit, etc. Some times when outside financial organizations like IDBI, world bank, ADB, state or central government, etc. give loans, the seller can draw money for the transaction by satisfying the concerned authorities, about completing the agreed activity and agreed terms.

Discount

It is generally a percentage of the sale value given by seller to buyer as an incentive for various transactions made on the value of the job/contract. This discount is applicable for certain duration up to which the transaction is allowed.

Delivery

It is the time taken by the buyer to supply/complete a contract as agreed, between the buyer and seller. There will be some times, different deliveries for different quantities of equipment or completion of different activities of contract or project.

Freight

It is the charge paid by the buyer, for transportation of equipment by road, rail, sea, air as the case may be from certain place to another identified place or places as agreed in the contract.

Letter of credit

It is an amount earmarked in a bank, by a party by setting apart a certain amount lying in their banks. This amount will be paid to the seller on production of concerned documents or authority for which this amount is kept apart, for realization. This amount cannot be used by the buyer for any other contracts or transactions without the written agreement of the seller to whom it is earmarked.

Demurrage/wharfage

When equipment is transported or delivered at a point such as transporter's godown, Railways, etc. if there is delay in immediately taking delivery of the consigned equipment by the buyer, the transport authority, which keeps the equipment, levies charges which may be due to more storage time, more storage space occupied, handling etc. This is to be borne by the buyer or consignee.

Transit insurance

Generally in all high value jobs, the buyer insures with insurance companies, for the transit of the equipment for covering possible damages, which may occur during handling or storage during transit. A small portion of the contract value is paid as premium for taking up this insurance to the insurance company. The insurance companies make good, the damages by way of compensation after making satisfaction of the damage and the charges that are likely to be incurred by the insurer for rectifying the damage and making good the equipment. The buyer does this insurance generally. In some agreed cases, seller does the insurance on behalf of the buyer and claims are settled by the buyer or seller or both as the case may be with the insurance company.

This insurance is also done some times to cover safe storage for a period or for erection, handling during transit, testing, commissioning and commercial operation by the buyer. Where risks involved are more and the period of insurance is for varied periods.

Guarantee

It is the commitment of seller to the buyer for free replacement or repair of equipment or part of equipment when there is damage or failure due to defect in material, labour workmanship or design as specified for a particular period mutually agreed. It is also called warranty, with an emphasis, that it is to be executed by the seller under more forceful conditions.

Inspection

There are various types of inspections. Inspection by seller. Inspection by buyer or his agent. There can be inspection in stages. When various activities are completed or at the end, when the transaction is supposed to be over, as mutually agreed. If more similar items are in the contract then each item will not be inspected by the user or his representative. Only certain samples picked up at the discretion of the buyers representative will be inspected and suitable decision will be taken regarding acceptance.

Validity

When an offer is made by a seller to a buyer, the condition and clauses incorporated in the offer or tender, are subject to compliance for a certain duration of time and after that period, the clauses are not legally binding on the seller. This period is called the validity period of the offer. The seller has option to alter any terms including price or delivery, if he so desires after this period is over.

Income Tax

Central government, some times even state government from time to time levy taxes on income or earnings of individuals or commercial organization, when the income of the individuals or organizations cross certain slabs. For organizations, the tax is on the turnover by the organization in a year. This is payable annually, before 30th September of each year. For individuals it is 31st March of each year on taxable income.

Packing

It is the work done for safe handling, storage and transportation of the item or items, during the contract period. This is done generally free of cost by seller. Various types of packing are in vogue, such as all weather packing etc. as agreed depending on the items and the necessities for such packing.

Storage

After the equipment is ready to be dispatched to the site or sellers place, if for some reason, the seller keeps the equipment in customers premises, for longer periods, a charge is levied for the extra duration of storage. The storage charges depend on the value of the consignment or the space occupied by the items or its weight in the storage area.

Jurisdiction

Generally for settling disputes, arising out of a contract on certain clauses of contract or terms during the execution period of the contract, seller and buyer agree, for a jurisdiction of the geographical area for settling the disputes.

Arbitration

In all cases of disputes between the seller and the buyer on the contract, when both of them cannot settle the disputes, a third agency intervenes to settle the disputes. The decision then is final and binding on both the parties. This is called arbitration. The agency, which arbitrates, is predetermined.

Credit rating of an organization

The financial soundness of every major non banking, financial institutions and organizations, which are involved in production and financial growth and where public borrowing and financial participation by public is involved, a credit rating will be given by accredited institutions which work independently taking into consideration the assets, liabilities, turnover, physical and financial management, output goals and track record of the organizations. These are ratings given by organizations to help the public to know how any of the investments made by them either already or intended to be made by them in future, will progress. The rating given to an organization, indicates the degree of the safety of money deposited. Independent organizations giving this credit ratings are :

1. The credit rating information services of India briefly CRISIL.
2. Investment information and credit rating agency of India briefly ICRA.
3. Credit analysis and Research Ltd. Agency floated by the Industrial development bank of India, briefly CARE.

3

Interpretation of Tender and Contract Clauses

Offer

It is a simple document, which seller makes, spelling out the details of the item/product/equipment, being sold by him to the seller. It contains all-important clauses, like details of item, price, delivery, terms of payment, validity etc., which are minimum basic things required by the buyer, to buy the things without much paraphernalia.

Quotation

It is a more sophisticated document, given by a seller to buyer, detailing out as many relevant details of the sale, as may be required by the buyer and protect the seller also. Generally, it will be in response to a requirement or a written request by a buyer, which the seller also gives in detail in writing.

Tender

It is an offer called for by the buyer, for which the buyer gives a complete document, giving details of the item/projects/ products to be supplied or undertaken in full documentary form, with clarity for compliance by the seller and seller gives the offer, detailing his offer with deviations if any which buyer may like to know. It may have to be submitted by the seller within a time limit, if there is a tender due date, complying with the tender conditions.

Limited tender

The buyer calls limited sellers, who are qualified to sell or execute the job to participate in the tender. It is not open to all other participants.

Open tender

All sellers, who can execute the job, can participate in this job, after fulfilling the conditions stipulated by the buyer in the tender.

Tender fee

It is the amount to be paid for procuring copies of the tender documents.

Tender due date

It is the time within which the seller has to submit his tender proposal to the buyer.

Earnest money deposit

The buyer some times asks the seller to pay a certain amount, which will be a small percentage of the total tender/contract amount, to participate in the tender. The buyer returns this amount to the participant sellers after the tender is finalized on a seller or a group of sellers.

Tender negotiation

Where big jobs are involved, before giving the contract to a certain seller/contractor, the buyer negotiates with important tender participants, on various or select tender clauses, before finalizing on a supplier.

Domestic tender

It is a tender open to all domestic sellers or contractors within the country to participate in the tender.

World-wide or Global tender

It is a tender, open to all the likely sellers in the world, who qualify to participate in the tender.

Commercial offer

It is a part of the tender, submitted by the supplier which details out the commercial terms of the offer or any deviations from the tender called for by the buyer.

Technical offer

It is a part of the tender, submitted by the supplier which details out the technical proposal of the equipment or project, with the relevant technical data and giving details of the deviations if any from the tender called for by the buyer.

Tender drawings

These are preliminary drawings given by the participating seller, giving details of the equipment, project offered by him. Some times, buyer also gives drawings of the equipment he requires, at the time of tendering.

Contract drawings

These are final drawings of the product/project, which are made after the contract is finalized and final designs drawings are made for manufacture and submitted to buyer.

Preliminary data

These are generally, calculated design data given by buyer to seller for participating in the tender.

Contract data/Performance data

These are final design data, which seller gives to buyer after contract is given, when the final design of equipment to be supplied or project is completed.

Indent

The buyer issues, various documents after he gets the contract allotted to him. It may be, to carry out the design, technological work, testing, preparation, production, supply by subcontractors or other allied supplier/sellers of certain items, erection, commissioning, post commercial operation, as the case may be.

Stage inspection

It is the inspection carried out by the buyer on the purchasing equipment, during production or supply at a particular stage, before next activity is commenced by seller or authorized by buyer.

Customer hold points

These are stages, where after suitable satisfaction the buyer, authorizes the seller to go to the next activity, it is also a stage inspection by buyer.

Core material

It is the basic material used by seller in the equipment.

Consumables

These are items, which are certain common materials, which the seller uses in the production of equipment or in the construction of project, in addition to basic core material.

C.K.D.

It is a completely knocked down condition of equipment or project. Some times the seller supplies his equipment in this form, either from his works, or from his collaborator or principles, to the buyer. The equipment would have been totally manufactured, assembled, tested and will again be dismantled and packed for supply to the buyer.

Scrap

It is that part of material, which comes out extra during production, or other activities, as unusable small parts, in the area of the seller, during the manufacture of the equipment or materials used in the manufacture of total equipment.

Letter of indent

It is preliminary document given by buyer to the seller having accepted the seller's quotation. It does not give full contractual details.

Letter of acceptance

It is a document given by seller having accepted the sellers offer *in toto*.

Purchase order

It is final document given by buyer to seller, asking him to supply items, equipments etc. This has all conditions of supply, mutually agreed by seller and buyer.

Terms and conditions of offer/tender

The buyer and seller stipulate various terms, which are technical as well as commercial on the product or project under negotiation. If it is tender issued by buyer, it will be tender terms or offer terms by buyer. If seller puts terms in the offer or the tender given to buyer it will be seller's terms.

Contract terms/Purchase order terms

Once a tender is finalized by the buyer on a particular seller, the buyer and seller, mutually agree to certain terms, which are applicable to the purchase or contract. These are likely to be technical conditions or commercial conditions, which are binding on both parties.

Routine test

These are final tests, which the seller of equipment conducts before offering the equipment to the buyer. These are mandatory in nature.

Type tests

These give details of full tests, for the equipment done for a particular design by the buyer. These tests are optional and buyer may or may not insist on seeing them even sellers do not conduct these tests if such tests are carried out once for a similar design.

Tolerance

These are the acceptable limits, or parameters, within which, the buyer accepts the equipment from the supplier of the equipment. It may be physical dimensions or technical data.

Regular line of production

Some suppliers or sellers have certain products regularly manufactured by them, irrespective of which customer buys. These items or products are called regular line of production. These will be earmarked for these products always. These generally form a percentage of turn over each year.

Tailor-made

In certain situations the sellers manufacture or supply equipment or items or executes a project to the specific requirement of the buyer. This equipment is not likely to be the same supplied to other buyers. This type of deal, calls for doing a totally separate job to the requirement of the buyer, this equipment is called tailor made equipment.

Bought out item/Direct delivery

It is an item bought from outside source and supplied to the buyer directly for using in the sellers equipment. In case of direct delivery, bought out items generally go directly to the customer without doing any work on them by the seller.

Manufacturing item

It is an item, where manufacturing work is done by seller, at his work place or else where, before using it in the equipment supplied to the buyer.

Goods in transit

It is the goods, lying midway between, sellers dispatch port or buyers receiving port or other modes of transport.

Production capacity

It is the seller's capacity to make various equipments in physical numbers and financial figures in his organization/works.

Capital utilization

It is the extent to which the production capacity of seller is utilized by seller at a particular point of time.

Batch production

It is production made by the seller in a batch which is a multiple of similar items or products made at a time during manufacture.

Raw material

It is the material, which the seller uses, to make the buyers equipment in the finished form.

Finished product

It is the product made ready, by seller for dispatch or use, after making the necessary production of the material for the users consumption.

Cost of tools

It is the price, the seller incurs for tools, to make the buyers equipment.

Cost of fixtures

It is the price, the seller incurs for making fixtures required to make the equipment.

Product profile

The various equipment the seller can make for selling to a buyer, in his works or which are in the jurisdiction of supply of the seller.

Maintenance charges

These are the charges incurred by the seller during production for making or giving service, limited to the period for which these activities are carried out. These depend on the quantum of production or the period for which services are used.

Capital

It is the amount invested by the selling organization to equip itself to carry out the set activities of the organization.

Proprietary article

Only some sellers or a group of sellers can sell the items or goods as allowed by the government or make these items. Example coal, petroleum products, defence items/equipment etc.

Part consignment

When equipment is received or sent by a seller to a buyer in part or parts without making full load by road or railway wagon or sea it is part consignment.

Full consignment

When equipment is received by seller or sent by a seller or his agents to a buyer as a full truck, full wagon or ship it is full consignment of despatch.

As-is-where-is-basis

When equipment or any other goods are sold to a buyer in the condition in which they exist without doing any work by the seller it is said to be sold in As-is-where-is-basis.

Indigenous item/market

Items or products made in India. Indigenous market is Indian market.

Imported item/market

Items imported from outside our country are imported ones. Sellers are from other parts of the world beyond the Indian geographical area. These items of equipments are from imported market.

Protected market

Some sellers have a market where buyers invariably have to buy from the same sellers certain identified material or goods. Buyers cannot get these materials from any other source.

Open market

When things are available with several sellers freely, the buyer has open choice to buy from any seller of his choice.

Bill of lading

These are documents, which are proof of having dispatched goods by over seas by seller to the buyer, giving quantity, size, dimension, weight, price etc., with the contents. It may also include insurance and freight, if the same is paid by seller on behalf of the buyer or any other such expenditure during despatch.

C.I.F.

Cost, Insurance and freight. This is what the buyer pays to a seller, when equipment is taken at sea port, airport of dispatch of seller. This excludes the inland freight, insurance and handling changes before reaching the sellers destination. It excludes customs or other duties to be paid for the goods by the buyer after dispatches leave the port before reaching the buyers point of receipt.

Packing list

It is a document, which gives the title of the packed item, quantity, size, weight with dispatch details, no. of packed cases, free items supplied to the buyers.

Delivery note

It is the document which gives what goods are dispatched, mode of transport, consignor, consignee address, carriers name and carrier details, packing details, date of dispatch and whether any escort is there.

Proforma invoice

Some times, the seller sends the specimen copy of invoice or likely replica of the sample of the bill or invoice which will be made for payment in advance, for part payment, dispatch, services or any amount, which the seller proposes to collect from the buyer or which amount is likely to fall due from buyer. It is a specimen document detailing reason for payment to be made by buyer. Based on this, buyer makes payment to seller. After this when the amount actually becomes due regular invoice will be sent to buyer. This is a convenience extended to the buyer in advance for payment and payment how it helps to know has to be made to the seller by buyer as agreed in the contract.

Invoice

It is the same as above, but is a regular bill, against which the buyer has to make payment to seller mandatorily.

All details of work done, goods supplied, events completed, service rendered, or any other reason, why payment has to be made, will be given in the invoice, as a result of contract document of business. Several details will be clearly given in this document, say excise duty, sales tax, freight, insurance charges, handling charges, documentation charges, any discount allowable, time when payment became due, to whom it has to be paid. Details such as testing charges, inspection charges, special or extra work done, TA & DA for people or any work or service charges payable, at a particular period of time.

Penalty

If a contract is so agreed, that seller has to pay any amount, for delay in supplying goods, giving service, completing an activity, or contract in a stipulated time, as per the rate payable for the delayed period, the seller pays to buyer.

Straight penalty

This is a penalty levied by buyers on seller for the delayed period of fulfilling the contractual obligation, as agreed in the contract, based on the specific days of delay, but not linked with reasons for delay for which, no cognizance will be taken by the buyer.

Penalty subject to force majure conditions

In cases of delays made by supplier in fulfilling the contractual obligation, regarding completing the supply of goods or service, in a stipulated time, it will be so agreed in the contract by seller and buyer, that for genuine reasons, which are beyond the control of the seller, the buyer gives concession for that period of delay in collecting penalty. The common reasons could be strikes, shutdown of the plant due to war, natural calamity, failure of power supply, etc. The seller gives suitable proof for such events, which happens in the stipulated contract period.

Bonus

In case where the supplier supplies goods or renders services or completely agreed activity as per the contract, before the due date as per contract as would have been agreed between seller and buyer, that buyer gives extra amount, other than contractual price, for the period to complete the agreed job within the contractual delivery date mutually agreed.

Counter guarantee

In some very important contracts or special jobs, entrusted to a supplier, the buyer takes additional guarantee from the seller by a higher agency, may be a government department, collaborator or some such authority, who in the opinion of the buyer, has more stakes in the transaction and acts in the interest of the seller to supplement the guarantee given by the seller already. This is special security to buyer, to shield the seller, for slippages in contract terms.

Foreign exchange

These are currencies of countries, other than our country, which may be involved in the contract, the amount of the equivalent rates to be paid for other country's currency for our rupee. This is reckoned on a particular date, as these rates keep changing for various reasons from time to time.

Examples are American dollars, British pound, French francs, German Konars, Euro/European currency, Russian rouble, Japanese Yen.

Labour rate

It is the amount of compensation paid to a worker per hour of his work taken by seller in a particular currency, where work is done. If it is our country rupees per hour.

Borrowings

It is the amount taken from lending agencies by the seller or buyer as the case may be in a known currency for which certain agreed rate of interest will be paid by the party who takes the loan.

Liquid cash

It is the cash kept by a party for ready use in a withdrawable form, at any time; say in a bank, post office, etc. for day-to-day operational use of seller.

Profit

It is the extra earnings got by the seller, after paying for all the activities involved in the transaction and paying fully all expenditure which organization has incured.

Devaluation

At the discretion of the central government at a particular point of time for reasons, which are forced on the government, the rupee value is reduced compared to prominent world currencies on that day.

Debtors

It is the parties who owe money to the sellers at a particular date of reckoning. It may be from his buyers or other organizations.

Bad debts

These are amounts due to an organization, which in the normal course of transactions the organization should get, but with all its efforts is unable to get from the concerned parties. The organization decides that such payments are not recoverable by the organization from the concerned parties who owe the amount to it. In course of time the organization may take out these debts from its books.

Gross profit

It is the profit an organization makes in a particular transaction may be at the particular date of recurring without deducting taxes payable to the government.

Net profit

It is the amount, which the organization gains, in the overall transaction, at the date of recurring after deducting the tax payable to the government.

Overhead

It is the cumulative amount of expenses, involved in running an establishment. These expenses are distributed on all products manufactured or services rendered. These include, rental charges of building, other premises used. Salaries of staff, other than labour. Interest and depreciation charges of capital equipment used. Interest on capital employed. Fixed charges, such as for buying electricity, water, gas and other items used. Production facilities, communication equipment, such as telephones, computers, transportation facilities to staff and such other charges incurred by the seller, which are fixed in nature, irrespective of the turnover or actual sales.

Value added

It is the difference between the selling charges and manufacturing charges, expenses of goods produced.

- It is termed as value added per employee, when the total value added is distributed over the total number of persons employed by the organization.
- Value added is also assessed on the value added, per share, where total value added is accounted in respect to the share value held by the selling organization.

Order book

Every organization will have physical and financial details in figures of the orders on hand, to be executed and under execution, from various customers on a particular date. This is called the order book on that day.

Contribution to exchequer

The government organizations and public sector, which make profit after setting aside for all their expenses, give a portion of their earnings in the form of profit to the government. This payment made to the government is contribution to the exchequer.

This is other than indirect payments earned by the organizations of the government in the form of taxes, duties, etc.

Zero date

When all commercial and technical terms between the sellers and buyers are resolved, a date will be reckoned for the purposes of commencing the activities, between the two organizations. It may be for submitting drawings, releasing indents for all activities, including placement of purchase order for raw materials, bought out items, sub contract items, completing the contractual drawing and such type of activities. This date is also reckoned for making payments for completing the contract. This date of reckoning the activities is the zero date of the contract. This date is given lot of importance where high value products and projects are involved.

Collaborators

Organizations in public sector, private sector, cooperative sector or joint sector some times even government departments in states and center take the help of well established and reputed, production and engineering organizations to help them in setting up units. The type of collaboration is decided between the giver and taker. The terms and period is also decided mutually. This collaboration is made in various forms as, royalty, equity up to certain percentages, etc. The collaborators help in setting up and running projects, production units, setting up technical consultancy organizations and give all help with their know how and resources to mutual benefit.

Consultants/advisors

Generally, all organizations take the help of well qualified, well informed, well organized group of persons or organizations, who have specialized in their respective fields, to help them in planning and execution of projects. The normal consideration given to these advisers ranges from 2 to 10 per cent of the value of the total contract/project. Depending on the area help is taken, these specialists make not only the blue print of the project or product but also see to it that, they are commercially viable and help owners to run the organizations profitably and successfully.

- Consultancy is taken for making overall feasibility report of the product or projects. Making tenders both commercial and technical. They help in the resolution of the terms while accepting tenders and execution whether it is the seller or the buyer. They take care of scrutinizing, tender drawings, tender specifications, and various tender clauses. Later preparation and release of purchase orders and letters of indent. If required, they approve, the contract drawings, contract clauses, technical and commercial terms, its parameters, its standards, its limits, tolerances etc. production, stage inspection from starting to final testing, disassembly, packing, transportation, erection, trial running, commissioning and commercial operation and post commercial operation.
- They help in the site analysis, stage inspection of equipment, stage testing of projects and products, authorize the release of payment to sellers at various stages, prepare various contract agreements, documents and pre commissioning tests. Advise on the running of the project, in getting optimum results, such as output remuneration and profits from products and projects.
- These people help, in the proper selection of equipment, personal, source of funds, time of execution, agencies capable of executing various activities, identify agencies and individuals who do the inspection, acceptance and final settlement of deals etc. The consultants make a detailed study of the various permutations and combinations of financial and technical inputs and outputs and advise the buyers. They involve themselves at every stage, from concept to commissioning of products and projects and it is up to the buyer or organization going for the ownership of the projects to choose and appoint suitable and capable consultants and decide in which areas, these consultants are to be appointed.

Copyright, patents

Certain documents or literature is owned by some individuals or group of individuals or organizations. These people hold the rights for these documents. Anybody using these documents have to take the permission of the owners to use these data by them.

In case of patents, when standard items or products are made to a particular design and also to particular technological process, the owners of these particular patents, hold the patent right. The permission of the owners has to be taken for using the patent, by others.

4

General Terms used in Contracts and their Meaning

Management

It is the authority and its legal representatives who own the organization and make all the decisions on the activities of the organization.

Permanent staff

These are employees, who are on the permanent rolls of the establishment employed on specific terms of service.

Temporary staff

These are employees, working for the organization, who are on the rolls of an establishment for a particular period of time, but subject to the condition that, they cease to be on the rolls of the establishment, when the organization does not require them at any period of time for any reason.

Casual labour

These are people employed on daily wage basis for doing any particular piece of work for a consideration. They can be removed, whenever the management does not require them.

Government department

These are departments directly controlled by the central or state governments as the case may be.

Public sector

It is an organization managed and owned by state or central government. But having separate identity responsible to the concerned ministry for all major activities decided from time to time. The capital however is not necessarily from the concerned government, fully but not less than fifty per cent of the total capital invested. Other funds can be from nongovernmental agencies accepted by the government. Now the equity of government is also being reduced below 50 per cent in cases where government so decides.

Private sector

It is an organization owned by private individuals or group of individuals where the government does not invest in its capital.

Joint venture

It is a conceived venture of central or state government with private organization or by private organizations themselves.

Co-operative venture

It is an organization run by the representatives of people or organizations, who have taken shares in that cooperative venture.

Foreign exchange earnings

It is the foreign currency earned by an organization from a particular transaction.

Name plate

It is the details of the equipment or items, whose main details of performance are written or embedded and securely fixed on the item or product as an integral part in a prominent place with full name of the organizations.

Logo

It is the symbol of the organization mainly short-term representations of the name of the organization. This Logo goes in almost all activities of the organization outside, to identify itself, as a separate important entity. It is a mark of the organizations prominence and importance.

Swot analysis

It is the strength, weaknesses, opportunities and the threats with which the organization lives at any point of time. In other words it is the indirectly declared status of the organization of which it is made of, at that point of recurrence.

Balance sheet

It is the statement of an organization giving the assets and liabilities of the organization at a particular date, either yearly or half yearly say 30th September and 31st March of each year. It also gives an idea how the organization has roughly transacted in a particular period.

Profit and loss account

It gives in a simple statement, the profit and loss of the organizations for a period say a year or on 31st March.

Statement of Source of Funds and its applications

Some big organizations give details of the sources from which funds were received and utilized in a period and it is given for public consumption.

Share capital

It is the consideration, which the shareholders invest in an organization, with a particular share value of a particular period.

Preference shares

The holders of preference shares get the dividend from the company for a particular period, generally a year. But they are not to get the return of their share value invested in case the company goes to liquidation.

Equity shares

These shareholders get dividends from the company for a particular period, generally a year. But they are not to get the return of their share value invested in case the Company goes into liquidation.

General reserve

It is the accumulated balance of all the profits reckoned on a particular date. It can be used by the company in any manner it likes. Dividends on this may not be declared. However, if desired, bonus shares may be given to shareholders.

ABC analysis

It is the priority allotted for any work by segregating the issues in the order of importance/urgency. 'A' is for first priority, 'B' is for second priority, and 'C' is for third priority.

Prime cost

It is the total amount involved in buying raw material, wages paid, various overheads put together for a particular item or equipment.

Breakeven point

An organization invests a certain amount, when starting the organization. After a few years of operation the organization receives the invested capital. From that time onwards, if the organization makes profits then it is said, the organization has reached the breakeven point.

Goodwill

A good commercial organization gets profits for the transactions it makes in various areas. It is quantified in so many rupees. In the same way, the organization also gets from its customer another appreciation for doing service or sales, which is by the satisfaction derived by the buyer from the dealings of the organization. It is called goodwill which the organizations gets from its clients. Examples of how an organization gets goodwill are as follows : The organization supplies critical spares, which are necessary to put the equipment, which has failed, in record time. By using the spares supplied in time puts back his equipment or plant to use and starts getting his production without much gap and loss. There will be some fault, which has developed in a product or a system in a project. By sending experts immediately and rectifying the mistake, the user will be happy to use the equipment well. If a project is to be commissioned in a certain time, the supplier keeps up his commitment of delivery, erection and commissioning schedule, as agreed, the buyer will be happy, that he has been able to commission his plant in time and use it. Some panic situations arise, where a supplier can help attending to the troubles, which bring appreciation to the organizations.

By this earning of goodwill, the buyer gives good appreciation to the organization. This might result in supplier getting repeat orders for products or projects. If two suppliers are similarly placed in supplying an equipment and both of them satisfy the technical and commercial conditions of offer, still the buyer prefers the organization which has helped earlier in times of crisis and gives preference to it by giving business. The buyer recommends to his fellow customers the good work done by the organization, which enhances the market value and reputation of the organization. This in turn helps the organization to grow. If there is a contract under execution by a seller, the seller will be happy to make huge payments in advance, if he has resources, which helps the seller. These are examples where goodwill gained by an organization helps in doing good business and bring growth for the organization. Customer patronage is an asset to the selling organization.

Return on investment

An organization invests capital for producing goods, rendering services invests in expansion and other development activities. These activities fetch good business and profits in this way, the seller gets benefits from the customers and enjoys returns for his efforts in the form of investment to his plant, machinery, goods sold, services rendered. This is called return on investment after taking out the expenses incurred in the transaction by deriving additional returns.

Budgetary offer

Many times a buyer wants to know the value of equipment, which he wants to buy but he may do the transaction later. He would like to know the repair charges for rectifying his machinery or equipment. He may like to know the price for buying and keeping spares. If he is putting up a project, going for expansion or other activities, he would like to make a provision for the funds or make a budget for the work he wants to undertake. For this purpose from the market, from the suppliers of reputed products and services, he asks for an offer to know the likely provision he has to make for the funds likely to be incurred. The supplier gives a price for that equipment or service and time required to supply the same. This is called a budgetary offer. Here the seller increases the prices by keeping a margin on the higher side to take care of certain unspecified eventualities. This budgetary offer is used by organizations for estimating purposes, creating facilities in future, making plans for growth, etc.

Open order

In cases of big and reputed organizations, the user takes advance action to place order for procuring the goods or services. Here he will have confidence in the seller about the dealings. To save time without waiting for getting a regular quotation, the buyer gives a go ahead for his supplier to supply equipment, undertake a work such as repair, supply of spares, sending experts to help him for various works. This order is binding on the buyer. The supplier relies on the customer from his previous transactions with that customer/organization and carries out the job. Regular offer for the work will be given at the convenience of the supplier. The buyer in turn places a regular order and pays as per the offer given by the supplier for the goods supplied, services offered, repair work undertaken, spares supplied as the case may be. As reputed organizations the seller does not misuse the faith the buyer has in him and over charge the customer or take advantage of the anxiety of the buyer, in the time of special need. The open order placed is used by seller and buyer as authentic deal and required transaction will be done in the normal way.

- Some situations arise when the supplier is not able to assess how much expense will be incurred or he has to charge to the buyer, till the whole activity is completed in giving the service, say a repair as is required by the supplier. However, an authentic document is required for fulfilling the formalities such as spending from his side in advance for carrying out the work, preparing bills after the job is completed and regularize the contract by collecting payment. There may be procedural problems for supplier, to carry out a job for his customer without the customer placing an order. At the same time for the customer to pay for a job done by the supplier an authentic document has to be there for getting the job done to release funds to the customer. This gap is filled by placing an open order by customer on the supplier so that at a later stage the prices and other obligations will be supplemented by seller and buyer gets the required service or supply from the sellers. These open orders are accepted from organizations who have standing in the market and suppliers also take the risk of doing jobs for the customers out of confidence in the buyer and both parties honour the transaction.

Dess no.

Dess no. is design number. In big organizations where products and projects of high value are transacted when several different products are manufactured by the organization, the supplier makes detailed design of his products. Each product comprises of several types of items, assembles, subassemblies and assemblies are many. For purposes of correct identification, in the drawing stage, manufacturing stage, design stage, inspection and testing stage, disassembly, assembly, commissioning, post commissioning, operation, every item will have a design no., in that product, in that assembly, subassembly, system and so on depending on the part in question. This design number helps the seller and later the buyer, to make a reference for easy identity to replace, repair, purchase, make good whatever is the need that arises of that part. So in the design and drawing, the item can be physically identified with this number. The supplier always refers to this number, when manufacture is done, procurement or supply is done.

Project schedule

When a buyer orders a project or a big product after mutually agreeing to various formalities involved in the transaction, right from price, delivery, dispatch, storage, assembly, commissioning, etc. of the project. The supplier makes an exhaustive list of equipment being supplied to the buyer from his side for the project. Here all products are detailed, the assemblies and systems where these products come are identified. Several subassemblies assemblies coming up to the individual product as also the parts consisting the subassemblies, etc. are identified.

- From the project details, the product details, assembly details, systems details are made to micro level. In each product the parts are clearly identified, upto micro level, item drawings, physical description, composition, quantity where exactly a part comes will be made out. This schedule up to micro level which goes into the project is called project schedule. From this the seller and the buyer know what seller has to supply to buyer. The project schedule gives the following :

- Title of the project, Name of place where it comes
- Contract reference, purchase order reference, as placed by buyer and date.
- The system numbers
- Names of products, quantity of products, physical description of products.
- Name of assemblies, name of subassemblies
- Description of parts
- Physical dimensions

Next, this project schedule helps in generating a completion schedule. This completion schedule has the following details :

- Name and description of project
- Purchase order contract reference and date, place where project comes.
- Description of product
- Description of system
- Description of assemblies
- Description of subassemblies
- Physical number of parts, dimensions, how they will be dispatched?
- The mode of transport, name of transporter, consignee, name and address, consignor name and address.
- Delivery note number, giving the date of dispatch, place from which sent, the name and identification of carrier. The package number, how packed, as totally closed or loose item etc.
- Packing list, details giving dimension, size and number of packages.

Project status

After a contract is signed or placed by buyers authority on selling or manufacturing authority, selling authority gives project schedule to the buyer. From the project schedule, till all the items are supplied by the seller to buyer, periodic review of the project position is taken. This is called project status. It is on a particular date. The project status helps the buyer to know what items are there in the project, what items the seller might have supplied, what items the seller has to supply for each product or system or assembly or subassembly.

- This helps to monitor the progress of supply of material, its source of origin, the agreed date of supply, the actual supply date etc. the buyer can make an assessment as to whether the supplier has been keeping up his delivery schedules or completion of jobs, whether the jobs are getting completed before the agreed dates or going on as per the agreed dates or are there delays in the events getting completed and so on. This helps the project authorities that are the buyer or user; to plan his activities at the site or other connected places. The details which project status gives on a particular date are :
  - Project reference, purchase order reference, place of project or name.
  - Items against the project
  - If supplied already, details of project, assemblies, systems, sub deliveries, subassemblies supplied.
  - Place from which they have been supplied
  - Mode of transport
  - Delivery note number
  - Transporters name, identification
  - Whether it has reached site or desired place, if so details
  - In case items are still not supplied, the condition of those items.
  - Likely dates of readiness at various places

From this buyer and seller can plan so many activities from time to time. Payments to be made by buyer, facilities to be created by buyer or seller, at site or at other places. These will be done timely.

Project completion

Depending on project schedule and project status at various dates another document will be generated where jobs are completed. This document is called project completion report. From this the buyer or seller or their authorities can know the following :

- Jobs completed, details and dates
- Equipment supplied, details and dates
- Systems completed details and dates
- Any damaged items replaced, dates etc.
- Any tests done on assemblies at site, date?
- Any products, supplied, erected tested OK dates?
- In case of small items still to be supplied will be known by this document, as it is a record of project, its equipment, source, events, completions etc.
- This helps the buyer and seller to settle the contract obligations before closing the contract.

Opportunity cost

In certain situations the business organizations have to do jobs other than, what they would have normally planned to do. Even though, they have all the facilities to do, these jobs in a planned way, they will be obliged to do these other unscheduled jobs at once and in the process, they have to forgo their commitments to their clients. To compensate, for this loss of regular line of production and in this place to do unplanned jobs, these organizations load their prices on the customers, to whom they do out of way jobs. This is normally what, organizations cannot help doing, because of forced circumstances. This loading of the prices of the jobs done out of way is called opportunity costs. Examples are as follows :

(1) From a reputed customer, who would have placed several strategic orders, some emergency occurs. One of the running plants may stop, due to failure of some equipment. To continue to have the goodwill of such customer, the supplier obliges the customer, by attending to the failure of the equipment, which may have been supplied by this supplier or it may be allied equipment, in suppliers product profile which the organization is capable of repairing. This attending to some emergency out of way will result in stopping regular production, till the equipment is put back into normal operation. Here very obviously the supplier loads his prices, than what he would have normally charged in the normal situations.

(2) Some times, a project will have to be stopped and will result in loss of production in that project. The reason may be, some spares will be badly required for some equipment in that project. To oblige the project authorities, the seller makes the spares out of way in some important work center and puts back the project to normal operation. In this case, normal production work in the work center gets dislocated. Here to compensate the loss, the seller loads the spares, than what he would have charged in the normal circumstances.

(3) There will be certain service staff, who can attend certain services. To help some client these staff will be diverted to that customer, as against the normal scheduled work, which they would have otherwise done. Here the supplier loads for the services, extra amount than, what he would have normally collected in a special situation.

(4) Some contract will be accepted in special circumstances. The reason may be to get extra orders, after getting that job completed. To do this work, some prior commitments will have to be postponed. To work on the new situation, extra amounts will be collected for doing a non priority job. This may result in diverting material bought for some other order. Time will have to be set apart in a work center to do the new job. These are some examples where organizations go in for collecting more money, to compensate for not doing routine jobs, as per normal commitments.

Inflation

In certain times the prices of commodities suddenly rise, people will have to pay more for buying routine items or for services. This situation is created because the value of rupee in practice reduces or purchasing power of rupee reduces compared to the rates previous to this happening. This process is called inflation. Example : The price of rupee reduces in comparison to global dominant currency say US Dollar, UK Pound, Russian Rouble, etc. Here the government or authorities may try to do some fire fighting job, to contain inflation but will not be fully successful. This happens when demand is more than availability of the commodity.

- If the price for crude in the international marker increases suddenly to a higher value, which the market cannot absorb, the price of petroleum products increase, transportation charges increase, hence automatically the commodity prices increase. The purchasing power of rupee decreases.
- If there is less industrial production, as it happens for various reasons, imports increase, foreign exchange reserves decrease, resulting in having to pay more for the same commodities.
- Thus there are many reasons, where the prices of commodities and services go up for the same available funds and this results in inflation.

Recession

In certain situations, there will be more goods available in the country. Demand for the goods will not be in keeping, which the commodities available in the market. Demand for goods decreases, then the market is supposed to be undergoing recession. This recession may be comparable, to certain markets and commodities. It will not happen with every product or goods or services in the market. Such recession for the whole market is very marginal. Here money value goes up to a degree, commodities value remain stagnant. This situation occurs when major export of certain commodities stop or get reduced than normal conditions. The goods will have to be absorbed indigenously, which results in lessening of prices or less demand for these goods.

Surplus

Some commodities in the market, during certain situations will be more than demand or consumption or sale. This situation is where commodities are available more than what market buys. This is surplus situation. Example, prices of some agricultural goods may reduce, when there is good agricultural production. Consumption of steel or cement, some times may temporarily reduce. Here the commodities will be more. Since production cannot be reduced in the factories beyond certain limit, the prices go down due to excess availability of commodities.

Deficit

Commodity supply will be short compared to demand, this results in reduction of material in market, prices may go up. One example is electricity supply/generation being short of consumption. This results in several problems, say power shut down for long hours. Less production in factories, non availability for use in domestic and other priority sectors. Another example that is common is, scanty rainfall. This results in non availability of drinking water, less water for agricultural production. Less water for Hydro projects resulting in less water for generating power and also for agriculture.

Demand

This is a common situation, which comes for certain parts of business. If there is less commodity in the market then there will be more demand for that commodity. If there is more scarcity of money supply, this results in less business, the opposite occurs in that demand for money is more commodity available is less.

TYPE OF CONTRACTS

The commercial contracts/purchase order placed by the buyers on suppliers are classified on the following lines based on the work content of the contracts :

- Supply
- Erection contract
- Turnkey contract
- Commissioning contract
- BOT Build operate and Transfer contract

Supply contract

The contract between a seller and buyer is for the supply of commodities. It may be projects, products and spares and such commodities. Here the suppliers responsibility gets limited to only supplying material to a known point may be suppliers premises or buyers premises or any other agreed place. It does not cover other jobs, such as storage, erection, commissioning operation, post operation activities.

Erection contract

Except, if it is separately mentioned that the scope of work is supervision of erection of products or projects only, the contract includes, supply of material to a place identified and erecting the product/or project there, will be in the scope of supplier. All liabilities, such as transportation, making good the damages during storage, handling and transportation and further any damage or failure that occurs, during successful erection of product or products or project, comes under the preview of the supplier. The buyer takes charge, after the products or project is successfully erected to the satisfaction of customer or users.

Turnkey projects

The supplier designs the project, does civil work of the project and additionally in this, are the responsibility of the supplier, to supplying all material required for the project as the case may be, then the supplier has to successfully erect the products or project, test the operation of the products or project, successfully run the product or project on any system, in the contract. All the liabilities connected with damages in storage, transportation, handling erection, operation will be to the account of the supplier. Any replacement, re-work or repair required will have to be done by the supplier, to the full satisfaction of customer or user. The customer takes over the products or project, when it is successfully operating for a stipulated period.

Commissioning contract

Here a particular organization does the commissioning work for the customer. Supply erection and all liabilities, till commissioning stage is the liability of buyer. The commissioning agency only looks after trial run and successful operation till the desired results are obtained from the products or project. All facilities replacement, rework, repair is to the account of the buyer. The commissioning agency only supervises the commissioning operation and leaves it to the user, when the products or projects are working successfully under their supervision and leave them to buyer to take care of further operation.

Build operate and Transfer contract

In this concept, the design, purchase of material, erection, trial operation, commissioning, operating the plant successfully till commercial returns come, for a specified period is looked after by the seller. The buyer takes charge, when the plant is giving commercial output successfully for further running of the project.

EXPORT INCENTIVES AVAILABLE FOR SELLER INCLUDING MANUFACTURE

Where an organization produce goods and exports to customer outside our country, certain additional incentives are given to the suppliers, in the export trade, other than what the organizatiron gets for sales, within our country. The incentives and benefits are :

- The foreign exchange earned by the organization can be used for buying any other material from the country or countries, where that currency is valid. If in case of not buying the materials or using the currency there, the organization can use the currency by converting to rupees.
- Duty concession in the price will be given so that the suppliers can get the business for selling at lesser price than in India. To the extent the duty has been charged, the government gives compensation, by way of duty draw-back, when claims are made to pay to the seller by the government, covering, the difference in price, by calculating the prices at duties applicable normally to Indian buyers.
- There will be no excise duty chargeable and to be paid to the government for these exportable goods.
- The organizations who produce exportable goods and market them, get several incentives at the time of starting the undertaking by state governments and central government that are in force, at that particular period of starting the plant. The type of concessions will be, in the form of land for construction of plant at less price, infrastructure like roads and water and such other facilities. Tax rebates, concession in electricity charges. Rebates on capital taken as loan, both in repayment period and rate of interest, which they have to pay otherwise.

- ❖ Priority in allocation of critical raw material, shipment of finished goods, tax holidays.

MARKET RESEARCH

- ❖ Every organization, which has big product range, which caters to large markets, where the organizations turnover is high, the marketing of the products by such organizations and the necessity to keep a prominent place in the chosen field, is a big task. To assist the organization in getting feedback of the market, such as the various brands of goods, their prices, deliveries offered, by those organizations, the individual special features of the products, or other goods, buyers reactions to other goods, type of marketing done by various organizations, buyers reactions to other manufacturers products, reactions to products and services of the concerned organization, in the market, the demand pattern, the quality, customers various needs, how they are being fulfilled by the concerned organization and its competitor, and many more such issues will be evaluated and fed to the management of the organization. This work is called market research and this study is continuously being done by the market research wing of organization concerned.
- ❖ By this regular feedback of market, the organization does not remain isolated from the actual facts happening in the market. The market research department, helps the organization to keep abreast, with the happenings in the market and sees that the operations of the organization are in the direction of the growth and earning profits, by taking corrective actions and remain dynamic. The areas where organization needs to be knowing the market operations are the following :
- ❖ The demand for the products, in the immediate future and in the coming years.
- ❖ The number of the competitors in these fields, their strengths and weaknesses.
- ❖ The share of the market by concerned organization as a percentage of total turnovers. Proportional share of fellow competitors.

- What the customers are expecting about prices, delivery, quality performance, and life of equipment, how they are comparing with other competitors?
- What are the terms and incentives offered by the competitors? What are customers expectations?
- Which technology is getting more markets and how attractive is the technology of the products sold by this organization?
- How are services rated by the customers? How are the services of the competitors? If market is hankering for some other rating of products or features incorporated to those products, what the organization can do to counter this trend?
- Some sophisticated products need lot of gestation period for customer to use and accept them. The suppliers have to wait, till their products become popular and build up demand in phases.
- A study of financial condition of the market. How the organization should adopt its strategies to its benefit and stay competitively in the market?
- Raw material position of the market?
- Plans for increasing production capacity of the plant. Product mix of the plant. Changes likely to occur in the demands of various products. It is necessary for an organization to know, the performance of the equipment as well how the popularity of the organization is in the market and how the organization, should adopt in future and the strategy to be adopted by it, will all be advised by the market research department to its management.

5

Interpretation of General Terms used in International Business

Mode of pricing and incoterms

While finalizing the terms of import contract, the importer, should *inter alia*, be fully conversant with the imports. As regards mode of pricing, the overseas supplier should quay the terms presenting in the international trade.

The importer for his benefit, should know, the meaning of the technical terminology. To avoid ambiguity in interpretation of such terms, international terms, popularly known as 'INCOTERMS' are used. These terms have almost universal acceptance and are explained below.

Ex-works

Ex-works, means that the sellers responsibility is to make the goods available to the buyer at works, or at factory, the full cost and risk involved in bringing the goods from this place, to the desired destinations, will be borne by the buyer. This term thus represents the minimum obligation for the seller. It is mostly used for sale of plantation commodities, such as tea, coffee and cocoa.

Free on rail (FOR)

The terms are used when goods are to be carried by rail, but they are also used for road transport. The sellers obligations are fulfilled, when the goods are delivered to the carrier.

Free along ship (FAS)

Once the goods have been placed along side the ship, the sellers obligations are fulfilled and the buyer has to contract with the sea carrier, for the carriage of goods to the destination and pay the freight. The buyer has to bear all costs and risks of loss or damage of the goods thereafter.

Free on Board (FOB)

The seller's responsibility ends, the moment the contracted goods are placed in board the ship, free of cost to the buyer, at a port of shipment, named in the sales contract. 'On Board' means, that a received for shipment bill of lading is not sufficient. Such B/L if issued must be converted into 'shipped on Board' and must bear the signature of the carrier or his authorized representative, together with date on which the goods were 'boarded'.

Cost and freight (C & F)

The seller must on his own risk and agent of the buyer, contract for the carriage of the goods to the port of destination named in the sales contract and pay the freight. This being a shipment contract, the point of delivery is fixed to ship's rail and the risk of loss or of damage to the goods is transferred from the seller to the buyer at that very point. As will be seen through, the seller bears the cost of carriage to the named destination, the risk is always transferred to the buyer at the port of shipment itself.

Cost insurance freight (CIF)

The term is basically same as C&F, but with the addition that the seller has to obtain insurance, at his cost, against the risks of loss or damage, to the goods during the carriage.

Freight to carriage paid (FCP)

While C&F is used for goods which are to be carried by sea, the term "FCP" is used for land transport only, including national and international transport by road, rail, inland waterways.

The seller has to contract for the carriage of goods to the agreed destination named in the contract of the sale and pay freight. His obligations are fulfilled when the goods are delivered to the first carrier and not beyond.

In case the buyer desires the seller to insure the goods till destination, he would add 'including insurance' before the word paid in freight or carriage paid.

Ex/Ex-ship

This is an arrival contract and means that the sellers make the goods available to the buyer in the ship at the named port of destination, as per sales contract. The sellers have to bear the all cost, risk involved in bringing the goods there, the seller's obligation is fulfilled before the customer board of the foreign country and it is for the buyer to obtain necessary in part license at his own risk, expense.

Ex Q/Ex-Quay

Ex-Quay means, that the seller makes the goods available to the buyer, at a named quay. As in the term Ex-ship the points of dimension of costs and risk coincide, but they have been moved one step further, from the ship in to the quay or what *i.e.*, after crossing the customers border at destination. Therefore in addition to arranging for carriage and paying of freight and insurance, the seller has to bear the cost of unloading the goods from the ship.

Delivered at frontier (DAF)

The term is primarily intended to be used when the goods are to be carried by rail or road. The seller's obligations are fulfilled, when the goods have arrived at the frontier, but before the 'custom border' of the country named in the sales contract.

Delivered duty paid (DDP)

This term may be used irrespective of the type of transport involved and denotes the seller's maximum obligations as opposed to 'Ex works.' The seller has not fulfilled his obligation till such time that the goods are made available at his risk and cost to the buyer at his premises or any other named destination.

In the later case, necessary documents (*e.g.* transport document or warehouse warrant) will have to be made available to the buyer, to enable him to take delivery of the goods.

The term 'duty' includes taxes, fees and charges. Therefore, the obligation to pay VAT (Value added tax) levied upon importation will fall upon the seller. It is therefore, advisable to use 'exclusive VAT' after the word 'duty paid'.

FOA/FOB Airport

'FOB Airport' is based on the same main principles as the ordinary FOB term. The seller fulfils his obligation by delivering the goods to the air carrier at the airport of departure. Without the buyer's approval, delivery at a town terminal outside the airport is not sufficient. Seller's obligations with respect to costs and risk do not extend to the arrival of the goods at the destination.

Free carrier (Named point) FRC

The term has been designed particularly to meet the requirements of modern transport like 'multi-modal' transport as container or roll on root-off traffic by trailer and ferries. The principle on which the term is based is same as applicable to FOB except that the seller or the exporter fulfils his obligations when he delivers the goods into the custody of the carrier at the named point.

Freight carriage and insurance paid (CIP)

The term is similar to 'Freight or carriage paid' however, in case of CIP, the seller has additionally to procure transport insurance, against the risk of loss of damage to the goods during the carriage.

The seller contracts, with the insurer and pays the insurance premium

6

Diagrammatic Representations of a Typical Sales, Contracts and Projects Department and its Interaction with other Functional Departments in the Organization

Every commercial organization falling in any category whether public sector, co-operative sector, joint sector, private sector and if by chance central or state government or local bodies do have irrespective of the business personnel, a particular set for its functioning as decided by the concerned authorities of the organization. This set up is usually in line with the policies and procedures laid out by competent authorities. The set up has its main moto, a laid out procedure of working, which all the employees of the concerned organizations know and follow. This information is also kept posted/informed to associated agencies and organizations for easy interaction and smooth working of the establishments.

When the organizational set up is laid out, as an important feature because of high stakes and sophistication involved, how a sales, projects, spares, repairs and service organization in medium and large industry will generally be, is shown as a specimen example. Here even though main interaction is done by these departments in the organization with customers or users of products and projects, the interrelation of various internal departments which are equally important, are shown for information. It is not out of place to mention, that quantum of work and importance of work turned out by several departments

LAYOUT

CHART SHOWING SALES, CONTRACTS, PROJECTS & SERVICES DEPTS. WITH CONTACTS IN A MEDIUM & BIG PRODUCTION ORGANISATION

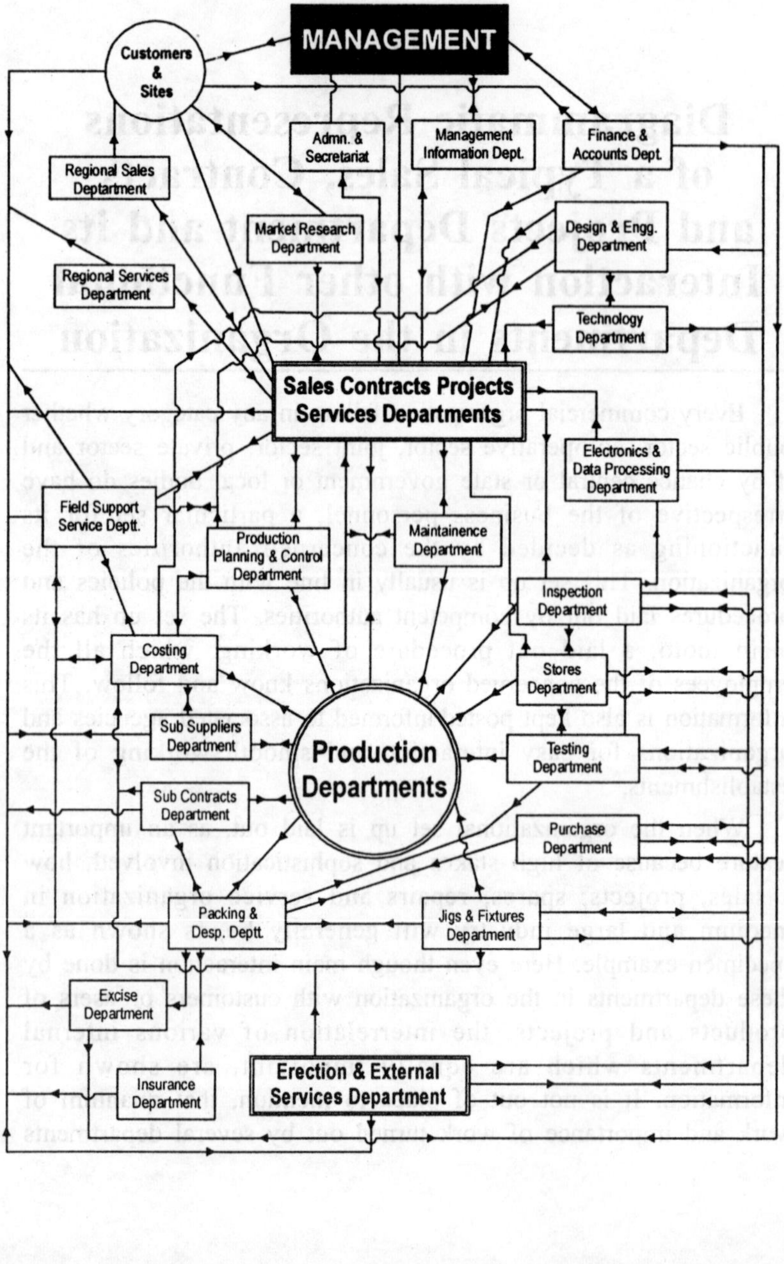

in the organization will be more important and vital as also indispensable. By knowing the working of each departments, its responsibilities and accountability, the managements give their best possible attention, time and importance to the survival and operation of the organization in day-to-day working. It helps out buyers to imagine and assess how things work in these organizations, systems adopted and how works entrusted to these organizations get executed. It also helps outsiders to know which department staff have to be contacted and screwed to get their jobs done effectively and what machineries they have to tune in their own set up for doing these jobs for interaction.

While the departments in big organizations will be handling diverse activities at a given time the customer or user can find out and ask the concerned supplier to cycle their jobs undergo and which departments will be getting involved from the starting of a transaction. It helps buyers specially while dealing with all commercial organisations with whom they may have to associate for large periods to know their working. Similar tactics will be followed by other wings of customers, at a given period of time with the suppliers. Knowing the working of a supplier's organization is an asset to buyer of equipment of large value or at important critical activity stages.

7

Flow Chart Depicting the Working of Sales, Contracts and Projects Department in Preparing Tenders and Execution of Contracts

Activity 1

A chart, showing the sequence of events in the working of sales, contracts, spares, repairs and projects department, from offer stage to getting a purchase order/contract is shown below. This applies to medium and heavy industry dealing with high value sophisticated products and projects. In case of small industries a few individuals take care of the operations there.

Activity 2

For a commercial manufacturing organization, getting orders to its full capacity for the products, it manufactures, including spares, tools, repairs and services, it can undertake, is an important job. For organizations, which have the capacity and infrastructure to conceive projects, supply the project material, erect them, commission them and operate and maintaining them, is a very major activity. Getting order for projects to the organization, is one part of the activity and the next important activity is to execute the order received, to the best satisfaction of customer, recovering good profits, in reasonable time, using optimum resources of the plant, including man power. After the equipment is supplied the organisation has to see that the customer is properly guided, to use the equipment. Well, get optimum profitable results out of it and enlarge the market. For the supplying organization, it is also an equally difficult and important activity.

ACTIVITY CHART-1

MODEL OF A TYPICAL SALES ACTIVITY IN MEDIUM AND LARGE MANUFACTURING ORGANISATION

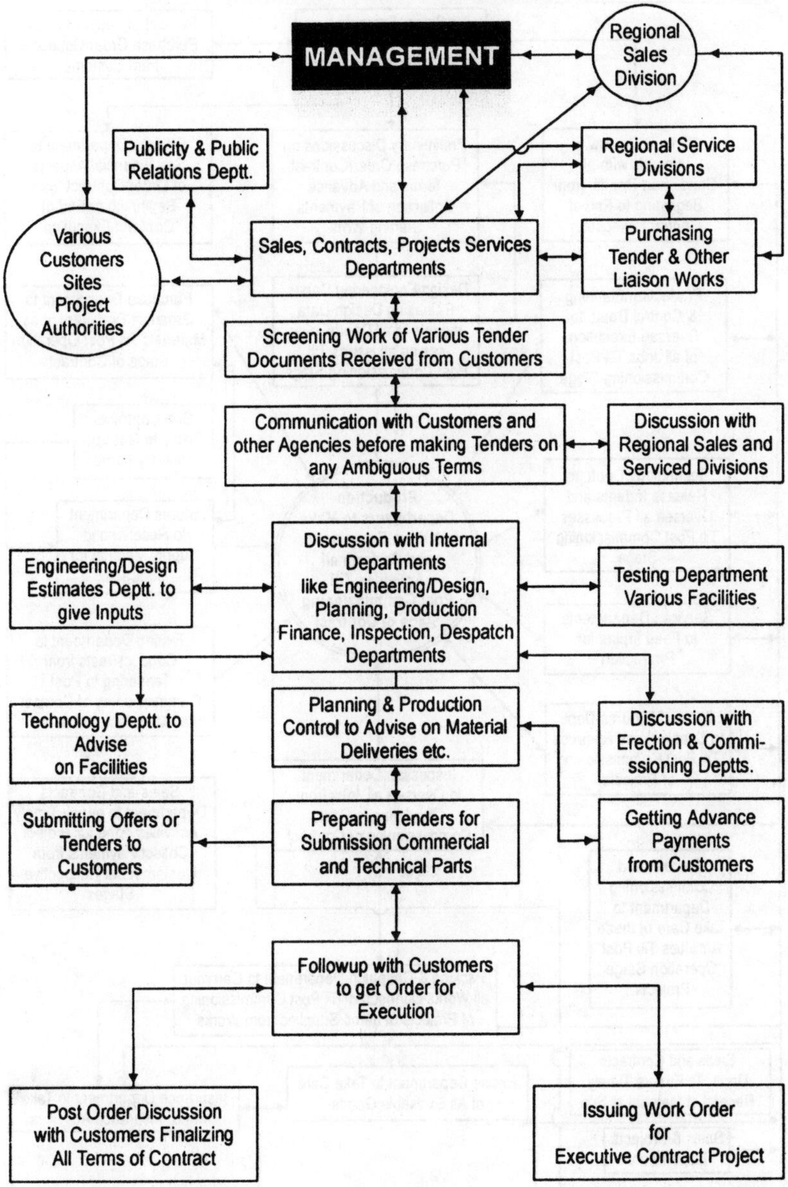

ACTIVITY CHART-2

EXECUTION OF CONTRACTS AND PROJECTS AFTER PLACEMENT OF ORDER A MODEL EXAMPLE FOR MEDIUM AND LARGE INDUSTRIES IN CHART REPRESENTATION

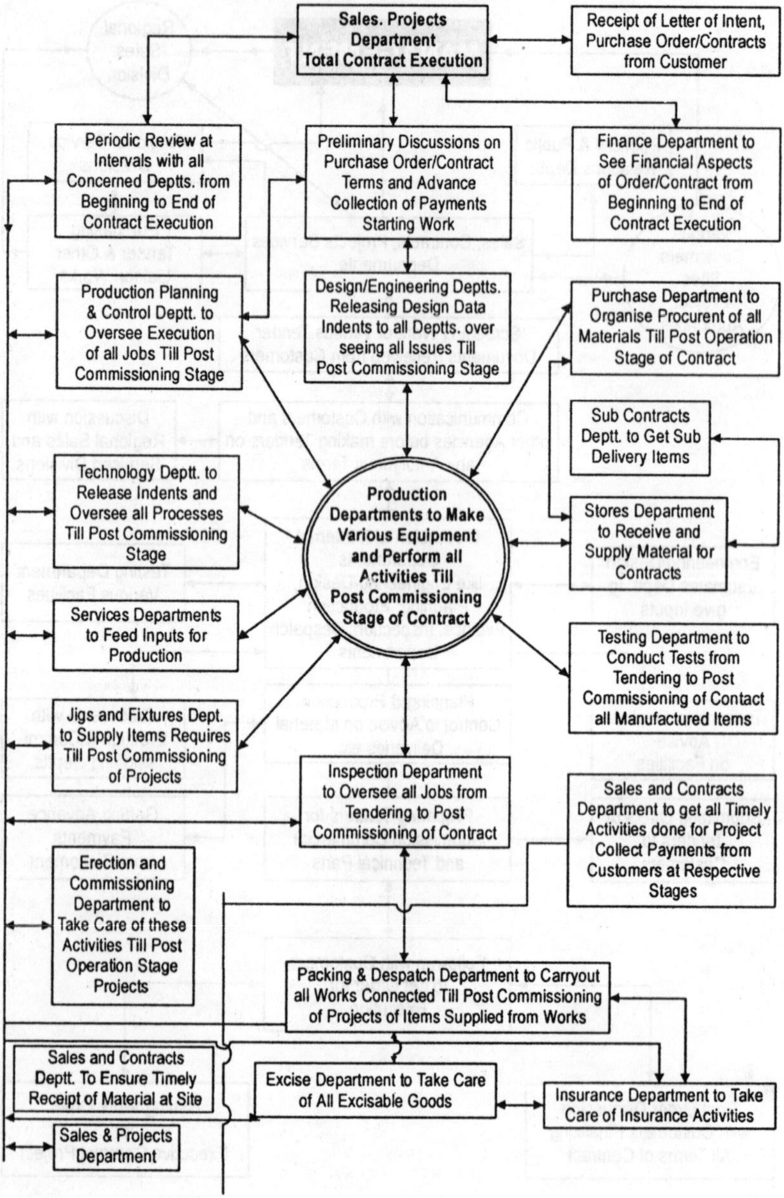

In the activity chart 1, how the orders are received and for that what work, an organization has to do, has been given in the term of activity chart or flow chart. In case of 2nd activity chart, after the organization gets, an order, be it for equipment, spares, repairs, services or projects, how to go through the various processes, to execute and complete the order, is shown as activity chart or flow chart.

To begin with, every organization that is, the supply organization, has a budget for the equipment it can supply, services it can render, in a year. To that extent, orders from customers will have to be booked. To be on the safer side, the organizations book orders, for more than a year or two of its production capacity, so that, there is no dearth of work for the organization and there are assured market returns, growth, profits for the organization and optimum use of man power and resources.

First, the sales department, looks for the tender floated, by various clients, for jobs, such as, supplying equipment say products, spares, repairs, services, projects, which fall in the conceived preview of the organizations. Tender documents are purchased by sales or projects department, and offers are prepared, for the equipment coming under the organizations scope, and submitted to the clients, within the stipulated tender date. Afterwards, when tenders are opened, depending on the condition how, the organization is placed, regarding the tender, with respect to its competitors, who have participated in the tender, looks forward to getting orders. The buyers go through the tenders received from various suppliers, in their own way, to derive maximum advantage to the organizations, which buy. The factors that are generally considered for selecting a tender are as follows :

1. Complying with the specification of equipment or spares, services, repairs or projects, which the bidders have offered in the tenders.
2. Prices of the jobs, asked for in the tender.
3. Compliance of delivery or very near the requirement of delivery by the buyer.

4. Terms of payment, offered by the seller.
5. The import content of material, indigenous content of material, used in the job, offered by the seller.
6. The dimensions of the equipment, offered by the seller.
7. Compliance to the specification, for which the various jobs are to be done or supplied.
8. The technical parameters, which are offered by the seller, in comparison to buyer's requirements. The deviations if any, and the extent of deviation from the proposals asked in the tender proposal by buyer.
9. The number of similar jobs, handled by the supplier, the credibility of the organization. Capacity of the organization to carry out the jobs satisfactorily to buyer.
10. How the organizations, have previously performed with the buying organization or to its other customers so far?
11. If the organization is new, and has collaborated with another organization, in doing the job, how the collaborators have performed? How the collaborator is helping the bidder, in the job is also a consideration?
12. Financial capability of the organization to do the job.
13. Technical competence of the organization. The type and number of technical specialists and skilled labour, the organization employs.
14. The facilities, the organizations have, in doing the job successfully to the satisfaction of the buyer.
15. Reliability to do the job, job competence, integrity of the organization, in keeping up to its commitments.
16. Quality compliance, of the products, services of the job which the seller is prepared to undertake.
17. Special achievement of the organization that has come forward to execute the contract.
18. R&D facilities, the organizations possess.
19. How much up-to-date technology, the organization has? The capacity to which it has geared up in this technology?
20. The load on the organization, already on hand.
21. Performance that can be expected, in comparison to other

bidders. The cost of products or jobs, the cost of services. The caliber of staff, who are going to execute the jobs.

These are some of the considerations for the buying organizations in entrusting the job or project to the bidder.

In case of small offers or tenders, the review is not so rigid. Some of the guiding factors are the following for entrusting the job :

1. Compliance with the technical parameters of the job as detailed in the tender proposal.
2. The price offered by the supplier.
3. Terms of payment offered by the supplier.
4. Quality of equipment, which the tenderer, wants to supply.
5. How the organization has performed, in the past and what is the confidence level now, in entrusting the job to the concerned supplier.
6. Time of completion of the job offered by the seller.
7. Compliance to other important conditions, which the buying organization feels is important in its interest.

REPAIR

First, the organization using the equipment at which the equipment has failed, has to deliberate on several issues, before calling the supplier or other agency to conduct the repair. In case the buyer proposes to get the repair done by another agency, other than original supplier, which normally happens, if the guarantee period of the equipment is over and user feels, that there are other organizations also which are capable of repairing the equipment equally well, and the job can be entrusted to them. In case of small repairs however, which are not of much consequence, many problems will not arise.

When an equipment fails, first thing the user does, is to investigate the nature of failure, if it can be identified and if repair can be done easily, he will get it done, by his own maintenance staff or takes the help of nearest source, to help in repair. However, if the failure is of a major nature, and it is not possible for the user to get to know what failure has occurred, he calls the seller to investigate, and tell, how the equipment can be repaired, and put back to use. In several cases even the seller may not be able to find out the reason for failure and do the repair, and put back the equipment to use. The equipment may have to go to supplier's works for investigation and repair. In cases, where supplier has to do major repairs, whether at site or at his works, it is not possible to give a firm offer to the buyer, to place an order for repair. He has to first authorize the seller to investigate and carry out the repair, by placing an open order, which gives authority for the seller to repair and get money for the work done. So, price will not be known in case of repairs which are not simple and where investigation has to be done, fault identified and remedial action taken. This process of investigating the fault will be laborious, and at times, trial and error methods, have to be used, to come to exact fault finding. If the faults have occurred, deep inside the equipment, at not easily accessible places, and if lot of dismantling work has to be done, even after repair is done, to bring back the equipment to good original shape, takes time. The repair charges have to be estimated, after completing the job, taking the material used for repair, the time taken for all activities, facilities used, etc. In such cases, generally the buyer has to pay advance, based on estimation to the seller and total repair charges, will have to be cleared at the end of the completion of job. The accounting and other formalities will be completed, at the last stage. In this way, the repair jobs are unique, compared to purchasing new equipment, spares or bringing new project.

In case, the organization has already supplied, products or spares, or done repairs, or given services, and has executed projects, for the buying organization, it then becomes easier, for the buyer to take quicker decision to entrust job again to that organization based on past experience.

SPARES AND SERVICES

Where spares are required for some products, or services or repairs, are to be conducted on the products, for the supplier from whom, an organization has purchased, invariably, the customers have to go to the some organization, for fear of experimenting with other suppliers, unless, it is an old project or old products, where other supplies in the field, are equally competent and the buyer has confidence that even others, can do the jobs, successfully to its satisfaction.

While giving orders to organizations buyers have so many, such factors to take into consideration to place orders. Generally it is the purchasers in the market who decide, the load on the selling organization. In case of proprietary goods or services, the buyer, invariably goes to same source of supply, as there is no alternative.

GENERAL SALES EXECUTION

Once the tender or enquiry comes to an organization, the sale or project department, scrutinizes all the aspects of tender, the commercial and technical side of the job to be undertaken. The sales department consults, with its engineering and design departments and gets their opinion on the technical part of the offer. It also gets, cost estimates, based on the preliminary design of the job, material used, latest sources of raw materials etc. Some time, if outside suppliers have to supply auxiliary equipment, these details will also be studied. The planning department, decides, when the job can be taken up and how much time, the plant needs, to complete the job fully. The purchase department, gives opinion of the market for bought out items, sub delivery items, sub-contract items, based on the market conditions. The technology department, given opinion on facilities available in the plant, how they are loaded, any new facilities to be rigged, etc. It also tells, when the jobs can be completed, processes involved, based on the quantum of present job and other jobs on hand, in various stages. The testing department, tells the opinion, on testing, at various stages, final testing and how these facilities are already loaded. Time required to complete the present job. Expenses if any, for doing extra tests, if called for by the customer.

In case of services, spares and repairs, the planning department, the production department, the auxiliary facilities departments, erection and commissioning departments, engineering department, technology department, give their views. It is for the sales department or project department, to make a suitable offer, with the inputs and opinions given by other associated departments, to decide on the technical side of offer and the commercial side of the offer as well. Further, the finance department will also be consulted in big jobs, for the cash outflow, at various times, in case job is executed and also how well, the organization can fund, the production or execution of the job. The finance department also, scrutinizes, the returns, after the job is completed, from the estimates, terms in the tender and final cash outflow on the job, from the organization *vis-à-vis* estimates.

After a job is ordered, the execution of the job, by the organization and how the sales department goes about it, is given in activity 2 flow chart already shown.

The contract is studied well. All clauses are reviewed, technical parameters are studied. The agencies, who are involved are taken into confidence. A work order to execute the job is issued by the sales or projects departments, asking the various wings of the organization, to go ahead, with the execution of the job.

In case of unresolved or ambiguous issues or clauses in the contract document is sued by the buyer, by series of discussions, correspondence, timely resolution of the job content, contract implications are resolved, to the satisfaction of buyer and seller. No ambiguity in the job content, terms, will be left open, except for unforeseen conditions, which may crop up, at a later date, on either side. Generally, finance is one aspect, which is important and seller ensures that, timely flow of funds, is ensured from the buyer as per the contract.

Both sides mutually, co-operate in giving their help, in resolving the issues, throughout the operational time of the contract, by concerned agencies, to their satisfaction. This way, the jobs get completed, well, successfully and in time, and both buyer and seller derive the benefits, planned in undertaking the jobs.

In case of repair jobs both the organizations, who are using the equipment which has failed and which needs repair and the organization which has supplied the equipment to the project, which has to carry out the repair, the procedures to be followed by the buyer and seller will be different, than in cases of purchase of main equipment, spares, tools, services or projects.

8

Illustrations of Specimen Offers and Tenders and use of Commercial Clauses Necessary

GENERAL INFORMATION TO BE GIVEN BY SELLERS TO CUSTOMERS ON VARIOUS KINDS OF OFFERS, QUOTATIONS, TENDERS, PROJECTS EXCLUDING VARIOUS SPECIAL TERMS OF BUYERS

1. Budgetery Offers

(✓) INDICATES SELLER HAS TO INCLUDE IN OFFER FOR CLARITY.

Sl. No.	Type of Job, Details of Equipment, Services offered etc.	Approximate Price in Rupees or as desired by customers currency	Delivery period offered by Seller	Place of Delivery	Terms of Payment	General Condition of Sale if applicable or quoted by buyer. Any special terms or Conditions included
(1)	(2)	(3)	(4)	(5)	(6)	(7)
✓	✓	✓	✓	✓	✓	✓

This type of offer is made at the request of the customers for all commodities including spares, repairs, services, projects.

II. Regular offers, Quotations, tenders

(✓) This indicates the connected information has to be furnished in the offer. (*) This information to be given is optional.

Sl. No. of the Job	Details of the Job offered	Qty.	Price given in desired currency	Place of delivery	Freight charges	Validity period of offer	Terms of payment	Guarantee period offered	Transit insurance	Comments on technical offer	Comments on commercial offer	Any special terms of offer	General terms of condition of offer
1	2	3	4	5	6	7	8	9	10	11	12	13	14
1	Main Equipment Products, Bought out items	✓	✓	✓	✓	✓	✓	*	*	*	✓	✓	✓
2	Total Project (Package) Systems	✓	✓	✓	✓	✓	✓	*	*	*	✓	✓	✓
3	Tools, Special Tools, Jigs and Fixtures	✓	✓	✓	✓	✓	✓	✓	*	*	✓	✓	✓
4	Recommended Spares	✓	✓	✓	✓	✓	✓	✓	*	*	✓	✓	✓
5	Maintenance Spares	✓	✓	✓	✓	✓	✓	✓	✓	✓	✓	✓	✓
6	Civil Works	✓	✓	✓	✓	✓	✓	✓	✓	✓	✓	✓	✓
6.1	Various Systems in case of Projects	✓	✓	✓	✓	✓	✓	✓	✓	✓	✓	✓	✓
6.2	Other spares and tools	✓	✓	✓	✓	✓	✓	✓	✓	✓	✓	✓	✓
6.3	Details of equipment in each System	✓	✓	✓	✓	✓	✓	✓	✓	✓	✓	✓	✓
6.4	Details in case of supply Contract	✓	✓	✓	✓	✓	✓	✓	✓	✓	✓	✓	✓
6.5	Details in case of supply and erection contract	✓	✓	✓	✓	✓	✓	✓	✓	✓	✓	✓	✓

6.6	Details in case of supply and erection and commissioning contract	✓	✓	✓	✓	✓	✓	✓	✓	✓	✓	✓	✓
6.7	Details in case of only erection and commissioning contract	✓	✓	✓	✓	✓	✓	✓	*	*	✓	✓	✓
6.8	Details in case of only erection contract	✓	✓	✓	✓	✓	✓	✓	*	*	✓	✓	✓
6.9	Details in case of only commissioning contract	✓	✓	✓	✓	✓	✓	✓	*	*	✓	✓	✓
6.10	Details in case of post commissioning and operation contract	✓	✓	✓	✓	✓	✓	✓	*	*	✓	✓	✓
6.11	Supply, erection, commissioning and operation contract	✓	✓	✓	✓	✓	✓	✓	✓	✓	✓	✓	✓
6.12	Any other Jobs such as consultancy, inspection etc.	✓	✓	✓	✓	✓	✓	✓	*	*	✓	✓	✓
7	Repair Jobs	✓	✓	✓	✓	✓	✓	✓	*	*	✓	✓	✓
8	Renovation Jobs	✓	✓	✓	✓	✓	✓	✓	✓	*	✓	✓	✓
9	Modernisation Jobs	✓	✓	✓	✓	✓	✓	✓	✓	✓	✓	✓	✓
10	Expansion Jobs	✓	✓	✓	✓	✓	✓	✓	✓	✓	✓	✓	✓
11	Diversification Jobs	✓	✓	✓	✓	✓	✓	✓	✓	✓	✓	✓	✓

9

Estimation and Costing

ESTIMATION

Money is the prime mover of any commercial organization, getting proper returns from the organization, make it grow more healthy, with sound planning is very important for which all their managements strive for. In this context proper resource planning is necessary. In a commercial organization, knowing fully what are the resources available to it, how these resources are put to optimum use while taking the external market environment into consideration is necessary. In business price of an equipment or article or a project is of prime consideration. This is important for seller to remain in business and for buyer to get the best from the market for what he spends. The pricing is influenced by various factors like market environment, internal facilities available with the seller in the organization resources that could be diverted for a particular activity. All these influence the pricing. The pricing has to be done very meticulously. It needs full knowledge of the organizational finance and external market to put the price tag. Estimate is the prime tool of pricing. It is the blue print with which prices are worked out and decided. The Price decides, the return on investment and the capacity to the sale of the product, project and services, in the market. The policies of the organization on prices are also of prime consideration, the estimates here tell what the prices have to be like, from economic viability point of view even though other considerations do influence the prices.

In effect for arriving at a price a thorough estimate has to be prepared first. The estimate consists of the following parameters/factors :

1. Cost of material both indigenous and imported used in the commodity.
2. Cost of labour including labour rate per hour and number of hours required to complete the job.
3. Engineering overheads
4. Technology overheads
5. Production overheads
6. Financial overheads
7. Commercial overheads
8. Administrative overheads
9. Cost of tools, jigs, fixtures, royalty, if any to be paid to collaborators cost of bought out items.
10. Packing, storage and dispatch costs.
11. Complaints reserve, for attending to warranty obligations
12. Cost involved for various communication facilities, which are today of much consequence.
13. Cost of transportation to known destinations if they are to be borne by seller.
14. Discount to various agencies, commission, provision for unforeseen expenses based on the experience of seller.
15. Interest on capital, repayment of capital main interest, on borrowings, bad debts, provisions for renovation, modernization, replacements of capital equipment, taking into consideration, life span of the equipment already installed.
16. Plans for modernization, use of latest technology, if any.
17. R & D expenditure.
18. Collaboration charge, if any.
19. Brief explanation of these parameters is given below :

1. Cost of material. Materials used in a product, for making the equipment spares, tools, repair, which consists of indigenous and imported material. It is not necessary, that imported materials are used compulsorily, if there are indigenous sources for getting equipment material, which meet the required specification and give output and service as imported material, it is easier to procure indigenous material, than get imported material, because of the procedures involved, such as identifying good and competitive sources. If common material used for other products in the organization are used then there will be bulk procurement of these material. The cost of such material will be distributed, with experience, for the job content, particularly, as an example, if material used is for making 10 units and materials for making only 2 units are used, then 1/5th of the material cost for procurement, storage, interest on capital, handling, miscellaneous charge, if any, will be charged. If on the other hand, material for making only 2 units are available, if the material is of non moving nature, then the cost of 2 units materials will be accounted for one unit itself.

2. Labour cost. Comprises of the charges in hours, multiplied by the labour rate for doing that job. Here all jobs, their making time and the cost per hour at the particular work center will be taken. Generally the labour charges vary depending on the number of jobs done by the staff in a year, in a work center and the labour average rate so calculated per hour. The number of hours utilized for each category of jobs and their charges are calculated depending on the work center involved and then charges will be summed. This charge will reduce, if more jobs are done in a work center and the price per job will therefore be less.

3. Engineering overheads. These go with the expenses of the total engineering department in a year, divided by the various jobs done in the year and the total hours of work put in by complete staff. Individually, for a particular job, how much charges will get incurred has to be assessed. Here also the various engineering departments that do the job will have various rates depending on the staff in each department and the total job undertaken by the group of people in each engineering department will be considered.

4. Technology overheads. These are calculated in the same way, as engineering overheads and these charges are applicable proportionately for the particular job and will be charged accordingly.

5. Production overheads, Financial overheads, commercial overheads and administrative overheads. These get charged on proportionate basis again as in the case of overhead charges discussed above and its total charges for the particular job will be estimated.

6. Cost of tools, Jigs, fixtures. If these are procured for one job and no other job is expected to come up in a reasonable period, then full charges will be levied. If 3-4 jobs are done in the life of the jigs, its proportional charges will be taken. The original cost will be spread over all the jobs, which can be done and interest on capital will also accordingly be charged.

7. Royalty. It is the amount of cash earned, excluding taxes and duties. It will be a percentage of the final estimated cost of the job. It is payable to the collaborators, if collaboration is live in the job period.

8. Bought out items. These will be charged on actuals. If the bought out items cater to more than one job, then proportionate charges for this job will be levied. It will also have handling charges.

9. Packing, storage and dispatch. If the cargo goes to a place, amount incurred for procuring the package material for a particular job, dispatch of cargo will be on actuals, depending on the charges incurred in dispatch to a known identified place. Some buyers ask for proof of charges, charged for the particular job to make payment where dispatch is involved.

10. A small percentage of sale price excluding taxes and duties, ranging from 1 to 2 per cent of the selling price will be identified for attending to the complaints, free of charge, till the guarantee period exists. After this guarantee obligations are over, customer will have to pay for actuals incurred by the seller.

11. Communication charges will be spread over all the jobs done in the year.

12. Transport charges to customers place of choice will be on actuals for a particular job incurred by seller.

13. If discounts are paid for jobs then these discounts will not be borne by the seller. For this purpose discount will be calculated in advance and included in the price charged to customer.

14. Interest on capital will be on actuals for that particular job, apportioned taking the total jobs done in a year and total amount incurred on the whole operation.

15. Modernization charges will be recovered over some years, on the actuals and spread over jobs done each year, based on the prices collected from the buyer.

16. R&D charges are distributed on all jobs done per year and charges incurred for each job depending on the work done.

17. Collaboration charges are collected as a proportion of the total amount billed for the job. The sales will be taken on yearly basis and total charges recovered will generally be paid yearly on actuals.

18. First actual cost of the item, component, product, spare, repair or spares, will be evaluated and the total cost of jobs done in a year, will be counted. Proportionate price of each job is taken into consideration depending on the prices recovered from customers in that period.

19. If it is sellers market, where there is good demand for goods, there will be more profit. If it is buyers market, where there are less takers and more competition, then the profit margin will be less. Various strict measures of economy such as cutting down unproductive expenditure to minimum will have to be taken by the organization to avoid making losses.

COSTING

1. When an equipment or item is sold and services are rendered an eye on the returns have to be kept. All the amounts recovered from each order or projects have to be totaled up. The returns obtained on each job gives actual profit of loss incurred in each transaction or sale. The assessment of the cost incurred by each job in the organization gives an idea as to whether the jobs done have been beneficial to the organization, whether working of the organization is giving profits or not.
2. From a study of the actual costs incurred, restructuring, corrections such as changing of product mix, improvements if any, in the products, can be done, within the

organization to suit the sales policy of the organization to improve profits and return on investments. This is more necessary, when several products are made from the same organization using common facilities. This helps in restructuring the policies both for short and long time depending on the market, for each product in the product mix.

3. In a particular product mix, costing helps as a guide for investment, data for expansion plans, choice for supplementing the already available facilities etc. It also helps in correcting and improving the agencies, which are functioning in the organization, to get the optimum benefits from the resources, both financial, as well as human. Future pricing also can be decided from these assessments.

Costing methods

A. First in first out method (FIFO)

The cost implication by the use of all first received material before using material received later.

B. Last in first out method (LIFO)

This is a matter of opinion and debate whether this results in profit or savings.

C. Weighted average method

Take costs of materials first purchased at different periods and take their costs for calculation. It is a laborious method, for arriving at costs. This reflects on prices and manipulation of balance sheet.

1. Prime cost

Direct material cost, direct wages for making finished products for labour and charges for making these products or facilities. This together is prime cost.

2. Production overheads

Cost involved other than material for facilities to make the particular product. Example factory, buildings, lighting, power, depreciation of plant and machinery, salaries of supervisors etc.

3. Works cost

This is prime cost of production plus overheads, Administrative overheads. Salaries and expenses for marketing and business activities from the time of production storage area to customers premises, commission for sales, advertising expenses, warehouse rentals, whole sales commission, retailers commission, cost of production, plus transportation storing and distribution expenditure gives cost of goods sold.

4. Variable cost

Some costs vary with the volume of production and sales, increases with production. Increase in sales, increases sales expenditure. This extra amount of variation in both production and sales is variable cost.

5. Fixed cost

These are not related to actual quantity of production or sales, but is fixed depending on plant capacity. Example are insurance of factory, building and machinery. Managing directors salary which generally belongs to administrative costs.

6. Semi variable cost or semi fixed cost

These belong to neither fixed costs nor variable. These costs are in between the two partly, these are fixed and partly variable costs. These are also called semi fixed costs.

7. Depreciation costs are under this category. The depreciation is spread over years of useful life of the equipment or machinery. It is also dependent on the use as wear and tear can decrease the life of the machinery when it is used more. Another category is equipment, which comes under two slab tariff, consisting of fixed cost and variable cost. Electricity, telephone bills, public water supply and sewage are some of the examples. These are based on the installed capacity charges and usage charges after certain limits of use.

8. Overhead or common costs

These are certain expenditures, which have to be spread over all the products made and also all the departments as no single product will be able to absorb these costs. Since the price of these individual products become part of production made in the organization and absorbed in the estimate, while making the price structure of the products. The prices of the cost list and the cheapest items have to take these costs proportionately and costing section has to absorb these charges judicially.

The expense, which come under the category of overheads are detailed below :

1. Building rents, which are paid from the common expenditure, electricity charges, water, depreciation of assets, publicity, advertisements, sales promotion, highlighting, certain common services, like steam, oxygen gas, acetylene gases from gas plant.
2. Head office expenses where common jobs are handled which are for the over all organization and not incurred for the production of one product. These are free of turn over and inevitable expenditure.
3. The overheads of the management includes the expenses in running the offices of the management, special pre-requisites and facilities including salaries of the staff, infrastructure and incidentals of common offices of the organizations like corporate office, finance, sales, personal, security, amounts given as subsidy for welfare of the employees.
4. Research and development expenses of the organization.

10

Pricing

PRICING

Price is based on market conditions, demand, for products number of competitors in the field, who sell similar equipment, the structure of the organization, which sells the material, the availability of the material to fulfil the market requirements. If demand for commodities is more and availability of material to cater to the requirements of the customer is less, then prices will rise, contrary will happen if, commodity availability is more and demand is less. Suppliers cannot keep stocks indefinitely, with passing of time, more supplies pour in and they have to sell with less margins. If old material has not been sold, in a particular period or demand. The prices are dependent on the commodities sold. Basic goods will be sold at lesser price than equipment, the intermediate commodities will have a pricing structure, which is more than basic material, precisely calculated, these prices are naturally less than finished equipment. Simple material, made by simpler processes, will cost less than, materials made by complicated and costly sophisticated processes, since the expenditure on processing get added to the cost.

In case of managements which deal with single products or commodities, market fluctuations, affect their pricing fast, since they have only one product at their disposal and their operations are restricted and they cannot afford to keep fancy prices. In addition to demand and supply, manufacturers have to satisfy what market warrants for their commodities. However, in multi-product manufacturing organizations, the organization, have the flexibility and can safely compensate in another product where the organizations gets more profit, even though in other products, the profit margin is less or there is no profit, organizations can make over all profits.

Raw material costs, their availability, labour charges, overheads of the organization, technology and other input charges, distribution costs, storage and transportation charges, type of material sold, all contribute to the pricing.

In case of certain commodities, due to various strategic reasons, state or central governments decide the selling price. Here the supplier will have no option in pricing and have to rework on their profits, production, distribution, availability of raw materials, their prices, cost of process as involved. Since the organization comes in the category of making items, whose markets are regulated, their profit margins are speculative.

Pricing of simple commodities will be simple. They will mostly consist of raw material price and in addition handling, storage, interest on capital, transportation charges, charges to replace damages, repairs etc. The overheads depend on the organizational structure. The process that are used after raw material is brought to usable or saleable condition add to the price, commissions for distribution if any, will have to be taken into account.

In case of sophisticated equipment material cost forms a part of the total price, the overheads costs of various processes, tests, inspections, rework, rejections, cost of storage, handling, transportation, inventory at various stages such as raw material, work in progress, completed goods, the structure of the organization, the competitors pricing, technology, special features of the equipment, auxiliaries, factors such as utility factor, efficiency, margin between input charges and output charges decide prices.

Price holds the key to the growth and progress of the organization. The order book is partly influenced by the price, in addition to various other factors. Lot of consideration and care is exercised, in pricing of items, products, projects or services rendered by the organization.

Pricing policies are different with the composition of different organizations, whether the organization is a public sector, joint sector, cooperative sector private sector, or individuals. Each of these sectors, so fix the price keeping the policies and objectives of their organizations. In public sector price is decided by the return or investment, plus some margin for growth, without incurring loss, this is intended to see that the organization in this sector sustains in the market on its own without exploiting the customers. It also sees to it that their is no drain on public exchequer by under selling as for as possible, except when government takes the initiative and so fixes the prices based on its policies of the day and compensates from its side for the difference in the selling price and production.

Joint sector keeps growth and profitability as its motto, decide on the pricing by considering the situation that exists on the ground and always ensures profit margins exists by altering the various strategies with time.

Cooperative sector operates on no loss, additional margin for growth and moderate profits. This sector also does not exploit markets to make money. Generally helping its members who have stake in the organization is always kept in view.

In private sector growth and profit are main considerations. There is no bar on profits, when different opportunities arise with time the organization cannot expect any support from government or other bodies. This sector always has to absorb the market competition and strive to exist on its own strength.

In the early fifties when major public sector organizations came up, the policy of these organizations was to help in building the infrastructure of the country. There was a bar in big profit margin, since most of them being monopoly organizations, the government was not allowing to make high profits. This situation slowly changed with development of infrastructure, growth of economy, with organizations in other sector and also supplying similar goods made by public sector organizations. The pricing has now become the choice of the managements depending on various considerations affecting them :

Pricing is of three main categories :

1. Full cost pricing
2. Marginal cost pricing
3. Pricing below marginal cost

1. Full cost pricing

In this case, full cost of material, labour, common costs or usually called overheads are recovered in full. In addition, there will be profit, which the market can absorb. It is generally decided by the policies persuaded by the management with above goal. This pricing is safe for the organization, as it ensures full return on investment and growth and good dividends for investments. This can operate, well in areas where there is good demand for products, less competition and there is no recession.

2. Marginal cost pricing

In this case, the full costs involving material, labour, common costs or overheads are recovered. In addition a small portion of the price is covered for the growth of the organization. So that there is no overall loss for the organization. This costing is resorted to where there is lot of competition and there is no assured demand for products. In case where order book of the organization is not full for products and marginally booked and demand falls. This pricing needs meticulous knowledge of the market position and good market intelligence and restraint in optimum use of resources.

3. Pricing below marginal cost

This is resorted to when there is recession to keep the organization going for better performance in future, where surplus stocks are in market. To keep production capacity booked, use of resources to optimum use, to keep work force intact. However this type of sales is not to be followed for long period. The organization will incur losses and is likely to fall sick, unless there is good product mix and losses can be made good in other products, and so on, to ensure that, in the long run the organization can withstand from falling sick or making recurring losses.

Sellers have to decide their prices considering the freedom they enjoy, market environment, government policies, organizations continuing their existence in the market withstanding the various pulls and pressures prices get influenced when new organization come into the market, market demands, organizations prevailing situation at a given time.

11

Price Variation Clauses : Interpretation and Usage

1. Generally in all long duration and high value contracts, the seller and buyer, prefers to incorporate in the contract, price variation clause, for the prices agreed in the contract, to cover, unforeseen fluctuations of market, which affect, the prices, in the execution period of the contract.

2. It generally takes, a few months, at least after a tender is floated and order is placed, on a prospective supplier, to supply, the materials and carryout, the contract. The seller in his price, will generally take, the prices of raw material used both indigenous and imported, then existing foreign exchange rates, and labour rates, at the tender time. It is difficult, to foresee, when the tender gets finalized and when the job has to be executed, what price the supplier has to pay for the raw material, what rates of foreign exchange will prevail, what labour charges, he has to pay, for getting the jobs done, in his organization. In all probability, all these rates would have changed. Changes generally take place, on the higher side and it is obvious in the process, by the time orders are finally placed on sub suppliers and jobs are completed, the supplies and services are billed, payments are received, the actual expenditure incurred, by the supplier will not be same, as what the seller would have offered, when tender is finalized. It is necessary, in these circumstances, in view of long duration of contracts, some times running into more than a year or two, that the supplier has to be compensated, by the buyer, for the extra expenses incurred in the contract, to counter the losses, which he may incur for reasons which are not predictable and beyond the control of suppliers.

3. To tide over such a situation, on pricing, trading organizations include price variation clauses on prices included in the contract. In this way the price variation clauses takes care of fluctuations, in prices of material, labour, foreign exchange, for materials used, labour and foreign exchange rates. It is generally not possible to absorb the increase in prices and still maintain the intended profits.

4. From the formulas, the actual prices as per the contract duration will be calculated; by the agreed price variation formulas and suppliers get paid extra amounts, for executing the contract, so that there are no loses in the contract due to these fluctuations. In exceptional cases, the material, labour and foreign exchange rates, might decrease, then the sellers pays back the buyer, the price difference as per the contract.

The payments towards price variation will be paid in the normal course, as other payments to the seller by the buyer, and billing will be done accordingly by seller.

5. Standard formulas, which are in operation to cover material rates, labour rates and foreign exchange are given in the example clauses used as given below. There are several such formulas in vogue, practiced by trade. Whatever formulas are agreed for particular contracts between buyer and seller will be adopted.

6. In some cases by mutual agreements between sellers and buyers prices will be kept firm till the execution of contract by taking cushion in the prices to avoid extra billing and associated issues.

Specimen formula applied for turbine covering various variations

$$P_1 = P_0\left[0.15 + 0.35\frac{L_1}{L_0} + 0.30\frac{M_1}{M_0} + \frac{(100+CD_1)}{(100+CD_o)}\left(\frac{E_1}{E_0} + \frac{I_1}{I_0}\right)\right]$$

Where P_0 = Contract price

P_I = Adjusted price

L_0 = All India consumer price index for industrial workers published by Reserve Bank of India.

M_0 = German index Iron, steel, malleable casting published by statistics Bundlesemt

CD = Customs duty

E_0 = Selling piece (Dutch Mark or Yen as the case may be) published by RBI

I_0 . = Whole sale price index iron, steel and ferro alloy published by RBI

All the above indices will be as last published before one month prior to month of dispatch.

M_1 = Shall be respective indices as last published before the end of 2/3rd period from the month of order to the month of dispatch of material.

CD_1 = Custom duty similar to the period as M_1

I_1 = Same as I_0 for the period as for L,

E_1 = Same as E_0 for the period as for L.

Price variation formula for variation in foreign exchange rates and custom duty rates

$$\Delta P = 0.5P\left(\frac{Y_1}{Y_0}+\frac{D_1}{D_0}\right)\left(\frac{100+C_1}{100}\right)P\left(\frac{100+C_0}{100}\right)$$

ΔP = Variation in price on account of variation in foreign exchange rates and custom duty rates.

P = CIF content of the sale price.

Y_0 = Yen/Rs. exchange rate expressed as Rs. per Yen prevailing the day after twelve months from the date of order.

D_0 = DM/Rs. exchange rate expressed as Rs. per DM prevailing on base date.

D_1 = DM/Rs. exchange rate expressed as Rs. per DM prevailing on the day after twelve months from the date of order.

C_0 = Percentage of customs duty rate prevailing on base date.

C_1 = Percentage of custom duty rate prevailing on the day after twelve months from the date of order.

12

Work Order/Manufacturing Order

Of all the commercial organizations, organizations which are involved in production, have a uniqueness in several ways. Here responsibilities accountability, variety in working and tensions are certainly more and are of different nature, when compared to organizations, which work in other areas, than production or when activities do not involve production. In simple language, it is a physical activity and intellectual activity blended together. This will certainly be more appreciated by people who are involved in organizations, where they work in their other fields, which have tandem relation to production. The organizations, which are commercial oriented, which do very responsible, sensitive, critical, monetarily and strategically, very important jobs are named below in detail for information. These do not involve production in their activities.

1. Organizations dealing only with sales activity
2. Organizations doing consultancy in various areas, such as planning, construction, erection, testing, commissioning, inspection, post, commercial operations. Problem solving in various fields.
3. Banking
4. Shares, stocks and brokerage
5. Financial organizations other than banking, including consultancy, audit, accounting real estate.
6. Insurance, both personnel as well as those covering other risks.
7. Service organizations, say communication, transportation, information technology, medicine, etc.
8. Art, culture, crafts, etc.

Because of the special nature of work, in a commercial organization, where production is involved, very naturally many agencies come into operation, which are not there, in non production and non commercial production organizations. Production organization, being a commercial organization gets involved in more accountability, such as profit and loss to name a few, where its activities are linked. Every activity, in a commercial organization, is valued against money transacted, more so in a production organization. In fact, every hour spent, by every employee of a production oriented commercial organization, and is accounted to calculate the money spent on the jobs done in the organization. There is another uniqueness, in a production organization. No activity will be undertaken, which involves time and resources, unless there is an identified job, against which the time, resources used, money spent are accounted. So, in order to do any work, related to design, technology, planning, purchase, accounts, production, packing, despatch, testing, inspection, erection and commissioning, site offices, under the control of the organizations, R&D activities, Electronic data processing department, management information department, service departments, for that matter, except perhaps administration, security, hospital are exceptions and they are delinked from production and go to administrative overheads. When once an organization gets a contract or purchase order to the management gives a go ahead, to the organization, to execute the job. The jobs can be say :

1. Engineering/Design of products, projects, spares, services.
2. Planning, purchase, inspection, technology, testing of jobs.
3. Procurement of raw material, main matching equipment, machinery, sub-suppliers equipment, sub-contract work.
4. Various services which can be supervisory in nature, by engineering/design, production, outside agencies, collaborators, erection and commissioning departments, finance, packing, dispatch, transport, communication departments.
5. Auxiliary supply or support to services departments such as, steam supply, oxygen plant, acetylene, carbon

monoxide, Nitrogen, Hydrogen, compressed air, coal, coke, internal and external transport services, etc.

This document issued for carrying out, any job of significance, in the organization, is called manufacturing order or work order. This is a very sacrosanct document. It has lot of significance, in every sphere of working of an organization. Till this document is issued, no outflow of funds, use of resources, such as plant, machinery, human resources, will take place in the organization.

There are three types of work orders in vogue in a commercial organization :

1. Advance work order
2. Main work order
3. Stock order

The work order has a unique coding and numbering system. This coding carries with it a lot of information, which it conveys through its coding. In addition to, the work order numbering references of the purchase order or contract, with a customer, is also identified by a number. This number is called sale order number and refers to a particular contract, and to a particular customer. All the departments of the organization, refers to this number, in correspondence, internally and outside, including customer and all agencies where any action is taken to identify their job. The important features of the numbering of a work order are, detailed below :

1. It indicates the customer, whether, the customer is a private individual, private sector, joint sector, cooperative sector, public sector, state or central government departments.
2. It indicates, the serial number of similar contracts, received from an organization till that date.
3. It indicates, the site or location, where the product will be used or the project comes up. The spares or tools to be supplied, repairs which have to be carried out. Services that have to be rendered are also known.
4. It indicates, the serial number of the project from that customer, in a particular field and the serial number of order, in the total orders received from the customer.

5. It indicates, the rating of the equipment being supplied.
6. It gives, the details of the work in that job, whether, it is supply of equipment, testing of the equipment, erection of equipment, commissioning of the equipment, commercial operation and trial operation of equipment or project.
7. Whether, the job is limited to supply only, or service only, supervision of service only or any such extra details, such as repair, at site or at works.
8. Whether the customer pays for the job or the organization has to absorb, the expenses, incurred on the job.
9. Whether, it is a guarantee obligation, free of charge to customer.
10. Whether it is a replacement to damage, defect, in design, manufacture, testing, erection or any activity, where, such a contingency, has come up at a later date.
11. Whether, the payment is to be decided later between parties and at the time of taking up of the job, agency who bears the cost is known clearly.
12. Whether it is an extended guarantee supply or service being done to customer.
13. Whether it is for miscellaneous reasons, say goodwill, etc., that this job is being done.
14. The number indicates, whether it is an advance work order or a regular work order will be issued at a later date, to regularise the job.
15. Whether, the work order is intended to do work, including production or for stocking purposes, so that it can be diverted to a customer, when a firm order is received, from a particular customer.
16. In addition to numbering of the work order, work order contains, the following additional details.

The customers purchase order reference and date. Alternatively, competent authorities approval reference and date within the organization where manufacturing order/work order is being executed.

The billing address of the customer, including order placing authorities designation.

1. The quantity of products and details of project with full job description.
2. The project details, including name of the project and place.
3. Value of the contract.
4. The contractual delivery agreed, with the customer.
5. The specification to which the equipments are to be manufactured.
6. The name of the consultants, of the customer if any, for products or projects.
7. Whether in addition to equipment, spares are involved, details of cross reference to those jobs.
8. If it is service, details of service to be rendered and where.
9. If it is a sub supplier's supply, the name and address of supplier and details of equipment.
10. Any inspection agency is appointed by customer, with his name and address, internal inspections, if any, if inspecting, agency, is appointed by the supplier his details.
11. Stage inspections, if any and by whom, exact details of stages of inspection.
12. Special features of equipment to be supplied, if any.
13. Special work to be done on the equipment or at project site, with details.
14. Special tests with details to be conducted.
15. In case of stage inspection, tests to be conducted at the time of final manufacture, routine tests, any type tests or any extra special tests are to be done with details.
16. Any special packing to be made for items to be dispatched to customer.
17. Whether it is a penalty contract or bonus contract or export contract will be mentioned.
18. Special instructions, during dispatch, handling and storage if any, with details.
19. Special finish for products, special parts etc. if required.

In other words, all work to macro level, will be given in the work order. It is an unambiguous clear document for carrying out work. The work order is always referred as a check list by concerned agencies to refer and follow in case of any doubt. Information of issuing this work order, will be sent to all concerned departments, for example :

1. Concerned engineering and design departments
2. Estimates department
3. Purchase department
4. Planning department
5. Management information/department
6. Finance department, specially sales accounts and costing departments.
7. Inspection department
8. Technology department
9. Stores department
10. Testing department
11. Erection and commission department
12. Tool, jigs and fixtures department
13. Dispatch department
14. Packing department
15. Electronic data processing department
16. Concerned site office
17. Sub-contracts department
18. Excise department

This procedure is adopted for advanced work orders and stock orders also.

(1) After the work order copies are received by each department, they register the work orders, in the departments and each of the departments, take action as is required by them. The broad details are given below.

(2) The engineering and design department, studies the work order thoroughly, it takes note of the contents, to macro level. The detailed design of the job is done, by the department. Drawings required are prepared by the department, for use of customer, site office, production department and other concerned departments, who have to do special work on the jobs.

(3) The technical parameters of the products will be prepared in detail. These details will be compared, to the parameters given to customer, at the time of tender. Testing parameters, inspection parameters, will be clearly prepared and checked.

(4) Indents will be sent to purchase department, for taking action for purchase of all required material quantity, specification of material special source if any will be spelt out.

(5) The dates, when each activity will have to be completed, will be indicated to the concerned departments. Any special facilities required at works, or site or from outside sources, will be spelt out. Details of checks, by various agencies will be spelt out.

(6) The document will indicate the routine activity and special action to be taken by all other departments. The design department takes, every responsibility of design, manufacture, performance, testing, assembly, packing, dismantling, erection commissioning, and post commissioning activities. Any new trials to be made on the products or at site will be indicated for the information of the departments. It could be even, improvements in the product technology, processes newly introduced, etc.

(7) The estimates department, would have made an estimate of the material, indigenous and imported, the numbers of hours required for each department to complete the jobs, the rates of material and labour, as also foreign exchange rates of connected material on that date.

(8) Subsequent to receipt of the purchase order and execution of work, actual prices incurred or paid, number of hours spent on the total jobs, department wise recorded for purposes of comparison, as also to make total expenditure review, on the contract, *vis a vis*, estimated or purchase price received from customer. To make jobs competitive, in future, exchange rates estimated, exchange rates, when material was bought, will have to be taken at actuals, so that the estimates made for incoming jobs, will be more and more realistic profit and losses on the jobs will be evaluated as guidance.

(9) Purchase department gets indents from engineering or design departments, technology departments and other departments,

for various materials, required for executing the contract. Purchase order will be processed and procured for producing the products, or other faculties to execute the contract, to the convenience of ordering agencies. It ensures raw material, sub assemblies, bought out finished products, to be used in the contract, sub-contract material, help of agencies at specified areas, will be provided, by organizing them, as required. Periodic interaction, with outside supplier, concerned internal agencies, will be co-ordinated, for proper execution of the work order/manufacturing order.

(10) Planning department has the responsibility to see that all the activities, networks of activities and helps the sales department, in monitoring, timely completion of supplies, activities, in various places. It monitors, the working of all departments involved in the work order, keeping in view the commitment and work orders received from other buyers, or other contracts of the same buyer. Any latest position on the contract, at a particular point of time will be known to this department. Project schedules will be monitored, and necessary inputs arranged, to the concerned wings of the organization, to complete the commitments to customer

(11) Management information department keeps details of the work order from customer. Reviews its progress on behalf of management, to ensure completion of jobs. Every data, from enquiry or tendering stage, to post commercial operation of projects and products, supplied by the organization, will be kept with them, as data bank and also to help and assist, the departments to resolve, unforeseen problems, that crop up in the execution of jobs, fulfilling the obligations of the organization to customer.

(12) Finance department acts as a watchdog, on the execution of work order, as also regulating and controlling proper final utilization and realization, of money, from customers. It participates, to macro level in all organizational involvement, of finance, and in the execution of jobs and keeping accounts of all transactions. It is a key department, in the execution of contracts, with customer and alerts, the concerned departments, on the obligations of terms of contracts, and their implications on the resources of the organization.

(13) The sales finance department does timely billing, for goods supplied to customer, services rendered, and also keeps clear account of total receipts from customer. Full commercial implications on the job, with customer will be taken care of, by sales finance department. The costing department, periodically keeps, details of estimated cost, executing cost of the work order, *vis a vis*, the actuals, till the contract is completed with customer, and post warranty obligations are over.

(14) Inspection department, takes care of detailing and checking technical data, performance, quality of raw material received, from suppliers to organization, flow of proper material at various stages in the organizations, checks on physical dimensions, quality of the material used, the output check, as per laid out specification, at various work centers, during various stages of production, technology, engineering, testing, erection, commissioning, packing, dispatch, tools and fixtures used, processes used, quality of work carried out. It is the responsibility of the inspection department, to see that the concerned wings of the organizations, use proper material, resources and man power, to bring out, best quality product, cut down rejections, rework wastage in the operation. It keeps, a record of the whole process, of production of products, spares, services, repairs, project execution. It takes care to see that the organization at every stage from start to finish does the job correctly and see that the agreed output from products and projects are made available. There is no movement of any job at any stage, in the contract, to the customer without inspection department's clearance.

(15) The technology department advises the various wings of the organization of the methods and processes to be followed in the production of a product, spares, repairs, testing, erection and commissioning. It advises, on the tools and fixtures to be used, the moulds to be made, how to use the various machinery, and the plant in making the item, the sub-assembly and the total product. From the starting of work, in a work center, the sequence of operations to be done, and how, will be advised by the technology department. The various work centers, in production and allied areas, have to follow, these processes and procedures, to get the required parameters, from the completed product.

Whether it is a small item, or a big product, the several intricacies of processes, involved will be detailed and the concerned work centers, have to follow, these before passing on to next set of activity. In very costly jobs, neither, the equipment and processes, will be reused or replaced many times due to the importance of a particular processes, to be adopted, and the total job should not get affected. Hence, clear instructions will be given to every job, as it progresses. The technology and engineering/design representative, has to see the processes properly, and rectify the difficulties, or defects, before the next process is started, in the fixed time of production.

(16) Stores department, releases the material for the jobs, by identifying them to the concerned authorities, to perform the jobs. Storage, preservation, reporting on the condition of material, periodically ensuring timely availability of items, which come to the works, will be done by the stores department.

(17) Testing department at all specified stages, conducts the tests, at the time of production, and ensures, the product or particular equipment, or commodity, passes the requirements of tests and laid out parameters are obtained and the jobs are suitable enough to go to next stage of operation, or in case it is final tests, goes to customer, having fulfilled, the technical requirements, of the commodity as agreed in the contract, between customer and buyer/user. A perfect record of what are the results obtained, and when the testing was done, with duration and results, will be preserved, and made available to concerned authorities for review.

(18) Erection and commissioning departments, do the concerned erection and commissioning activities as stipulated in the work order, to the satisfaction of the buyer ultimately.

(19) Tools, jigs and fixtures department, provide the necessary tools, for making the equipment or product, as the case may be, the jigs and fixtures used in the manufacture, will be provided and made ready, at appropriate time, to match the production schedules.

(20) Despatch department, plans the despatch of finished goods or required equipment, or other necessary test equipment/ material needed by the buyer along with the products, at his

works, or site, as required in the contract. Proper and safe despatch by agreed mode of transport, will be ensured by the despatch department. In case, the delivery of product or commodity is contractually ex-works, the items, will be handed over to concerned representative of the buyer. Necessary facilities, for transportation, such as loading will be arranged, by the dispatch department. It ensures, safe handing over of materials to transporters, in good condition. If it is handing over at buyer's premises additional responsibility of safe transportation, unloading at site, and safe handing over, to authorities at the destination, will be responsibility of the despatch department. Many major payments, as per contracts will be linked, to safe despatch of material, to the specified destinations and their acknowledgements at sites.

1. Packing department, receives the material from various concerned departments, as per the schedule in the contracts, packs them stores and delivers, to the despatch department, for onward shipment to customer, to his required place of usage.
2. Electronic data processing department helps in entering the work order document and sufficient copies of the document will be made available to the sales or projects department for distribution to the concerned executing departments. Since computers have become an important tool in present day operations. All data concerning various departments and their activities will be stored with them and the user departments get details by retrieving the data, whichever is required. It is a service department, to all the wings of the organization. It helps the organization, by providing the facilities for proper use, at the desired time.
3. The site offices, take help of the work order to store the material, which comes to them at a particular time, as specified. Make these items available for the erection authorities, to undertake erection as desired. The site offices, report the condition in which the material is received and keeps a record of the time of receipt of the materials and agency which has delivered. In case of materials, which are not in proper condition site repair or

rectification or replacement activity, will be initiated by them. The scope of work at site, by site, authorities and other agencies, will be available in the work order.

4. Sub contracts departments; The job of the sub contract department, is to get the particular piece of work done, by an outside agency, identified by the organization, the raw materials, facilities like tools, fixtures, loading and unloading will be provided to the sub contractors. Sub contractors being registered as authorized ancillary, to the production organization, get a continuous feed of the jobs, which the sub contractors have capability to do, sub contractors help in reducing a part of the activity of main production at works. The organization, which has the facility, will be loaded to its capacity and jobs, which are expected to be delayed will be delivered to sub contractors resulting in off loading to a sub-contractor the extra work. The sub contract department identifies that particular, sub contractor, who will be assisting in that part of the job of the total production of the main organization. The help in the form of raw materials, process drawings, etc. will be given to the sub-contractor, to help them in doing that part of the work, which forms a part of a total production activity. Sub contractors assist in completing pieces of job, which the main organization off loads enabling the organization to concentrate on more complicated and big activities, relating to production of goods.

5. Excise department, keeps track of the goods made in an organization, and before it is packed and dispatched assesses, the value of excise duty being charged to the customer and ensures, that the organizations bills that value and pays to the excise department, excise duty at the rates applicable before the equipment leaves the organization. The excise department gives excise certificate for the value of the goods billed and duty collected from the organization. The vehicle/agency transporting the equipment can show the certificate for duty paid and pass through the excise check posts. The excise department, ensures whatever are excisable goods, against a work order, go out

of the department/organization, after they have paid the applicable duty.

6. In case of repair jobs, which were originally manufactured by the organization and have come back to the factory for repair, excise duty would have already been paid in the first instance when once the equipment left the works. If after repair, some material has been used, fresh excise duty will be collected, only for that part of extra raw material used and not for total repair charges incurred by the buyer. Buyer in subsequent transaction, when equipment goes to seller works, pays duty only on material newly used and not for any other work done on that equipment. No duty for tests conducted at the works, or other repairs, will be collected from the buyer for sending the equipment after first sale by the same organization.

Advance work order

(1) Certain situations arises, when buyer would have decided to procure equipment, get the project executed, by a supplier, get some repairs done. However, he will be organizing the procedures, for placing purchase order or make advance payments. These activities take time by the buyer to complete them. The seller will know this situation. Hence he will go ahead, with activities, concerned with manufacture or repair or whatever job that will come in the normal course at a later date.

(2) Organizing and earmarking funds, is necessary for seller to do any work to any customer without an authentic order from him. He also requires advance payments if the cost of contractor is high and calls for deployment of huge funds from his other resources. For this he needs authentic documents, to do so. This formality, he will fulfil, by issuing an advance work order. Advance work has all the impact of a regular work orders, only in exceptional cases in big jobs, the orders do not materialize for unforeseen reasons as expected. In normal circumstances, orders will be placed on the supplier as decided by seller, based on tender evaluation and necessity to procure the equipment, or get other jobs done by a particular seller for getting various advantages.

Stock orders

(1) Every commercial organization, will have regular orders for certain products manufactured by it, even though, there may be some other competitors in the field, to supply these equipment or give services to do repairs. It is a practice to assume these orders are there, in a year and will be placed by the clients in the usual course of events. So a manufacturer safely earmarks a percentage of his production capacity, for manufacturing those products of specific ratings. Further, in an extreme case of orders not forth coming fully, to the extent as it should be, there will be others, who place orders and buy the equipment. In effect the materials manufactured against stock orders, do not go waste. Based on this experience, the organization procures raw materials and manufactures these products, and keeps them ready, for delivery when regular orders come, by diverting the products to those customers, who place firm orders, clearing the stocks. This also happens for certain quantity of spares of certain types and capacities.

(2) The advantages of issuing stock orders are :

The products can be made ready by using the resources of the organization keeping manpower busy, in doing those jobs, later diverting to customers, who place regular orders. Customers will be happy some times, to get material at short intervals, after placing orders. Customers may not be paying, exorbitant prices since these equipment will be normally used by others and sellers do not over charge, for these equipment as they may do, in case of certain odd capacity equipment, which are slow moving in nature.

(3) The seller gets returns on sales, which he can use for important, urgent, financial commitments easily. Suppliers get, users goodwill for giving the products early, without his having to resort to chasing, waiting for the equipment or replacements, and get returns on capital invested by using the equipment early.

(4) Sellers some times can make more profits, if there is demand for these stock items, if market value is more with other suppliers and the seller would normally have made the equipment at competitive prices, leisurely. There may be cases, when in the

event of customers having failure of major equipment, they can put back their plant to use by getting replacement quickly, from stock items. Otherwise he would lose money, by idle plant and machinery because a part of which has failed and became unusable.

In certain organizations depending on its size, type of operations the various departments named above may not exist as individual entities. One department might be doing the work of several departments for the sake of compactness and quantum of work turned out. The structure of the organization decides how the activities that get allotted to each department.

13

Despatch, Billing, Cash Transactions and Funding by Different Sources

In the business of all commodities one issue of importance to the buyer for buying the various commodities, he is requires is to straight away go to the seller and purchase across the table by settling all terms of the deal, take delivery of the goods then and there, so that there are no further transactions from the deal unless it is warranted, specially and unavoidably. However, all transactions are not that simple and many issues crop up either at the negotiation stage of the deal or subsequent to that, which have to be settled before settling a deal with the seller. There are two factors which weigh heavily on a seller, which are vital to him before he actually parts with his goods to any buyer.

DESPATCH

(1) When goods are sold seller has to collect the money fully from the buyer. He has also to collect from buyer if so applicable other amounts payable to government, quasi government or other agencies such as sales tax. C Form, excise duty, freight charges, depending on where goods are being handed over to the buyer and any other documents of relevance to the sale. All these need to be settled meticulously, if in particular, goods are of high value and of sophisticated nature involving more than one agency in the transaction. The sellers would not like to part with the goods without getting full value of money and settle all terms unambiguously, before they part with the goods. This reduces chasing the buyer and be at his mercy, unless the market is so bad that the seller wants to push his business. He always likes

to see the liabilities with the buyer are minimum, when goods go out of his premises. Some times, the seller stands answerable to various agencies including his banker or financiers of the business, though indirectly in some cases.

The seller will only be safe, if there are no dues from customers and the transaction goes without strings, such as supply of auxiliaries giving services, executing other jobs, parallely and buyer keeps payment pending and the buyer looks upon the seller to fulfil his obligations. The seller is anxious to do the billing fully when a transaction is over. Some times in business, deals, will not be closed after sale is completed. Certain minimum time and risk will always be associated in business. In case documents of dispatch are routed through bank or if payment is to be made by a third party after he is satisfied, that all the formalities are completed as per the contract, the seller is at the mercy of the customer. In case there is competition, other suppliers may offer liberal terms for the sale and this makes things more difficult and complicated. Issues like custom duty, duty drawback, insurance claims, damages or defects that occur at various stages in handling, storage, transportations, erection, commissioning, operation, always continue to pose problems which have to be resolved with care and caution.

(2) In the second case, where equipment has to reach a different destination, invariably other than ex-works contracts, safe receipt of material at customers point of receipt or site is not easy and turns out to be an anxious issue. The liability of the seller will not cease if goods are not received in good condition and certified so by the customers authorized receiving agency. Correspondence keeps going on till all these issues are resolved and they generally take time.

In order to lessen the liabilities of the seller, he tries to convenience the customer to take delivery of goods at the show room at his risk by clearing all payments. As next best to delivery ex-works, ex-railway siding, export of dispatch. Maximum liability occurs, when things are to be given at customer's premises or site at the responsibility of seller. These terms are always insisted in projects, supply of high value products or long duration jobs, involving many products, auxiliaries, spares tools, tackles etc.

(3) In case of certain commodities, the buyer straight away buys, the equipment off the shelf and settles the terms, then and there and starts using the commodities.

(4) However, in certain cases, the items may not be available immediately, with the supplier there are several processes, to be followed, before a commodity leaves the seller, and goes to the buyer for use. The buyer has to give these details, clearly to the seller. The seller has to know, how he gets money, for the goods sold, services rendered by the seller. The many details that are required by the seller, to send the material to the buyer, when goods are ready to be supplied are given below :

(a) The purchase/contract number and date of placement of the order.
(b) The product details, such as description and quantity.
(c) The price of products, auxiliaries, spares, services, received by the seller with details.
(d) The paying authority for goods.
(e) Mode of dispatch.
(f) Place of dispatch and customers receiving place with details.
(g) The address of the consignee.
(h) Whether the goods should go in good packed condition, or whether the goods can go unpacked or with minimum packing, for handling and transport.
(i) Whether any transhipment is allowed?
(j) Freight charges.
(k) The authorities, who have to be kept informed of the dispatches.
(l) Packing list details.
(m) Delivery note details.
(n) Price with split up, connecting the number of items.
(o) Storage, transport and handling details.
(p) Storage, instructions.
(q) No. of packages, size and weight.
(r) Any instruction for storage, handling and transport.
(s) Guarantee certificates.

(t) Performance or other certificates, proofs of various payments made.

(u) In case of items supplied, from sub-supplier, the place where, they have to be sent by buyer.

(v) Any packing markings.

(w) Any other instructions.

Definition of Terms

Consignment

An entity being dispatched from a supplier's point of sale or works or identified place of shipment, the dispatch be through a person, road, rail, seaport, airport etc.

Open consignment

It is a consignment, which goes by any mode of transport unpacked but fastened to the vehicle of transportation. This consignment is open for exposure to outside climate and other conditions. There can be access to a third party to meddle with the goods.

Closed consignment

The contents of dispatch will be closed and not open to atmosphere. It can be waterproof, weatherproof and safely kept secured in strong closed enclosed packing case. It may be even a container, which is closed, or a closed truck, closed wagon or ship where items are not exposed to meddling by a third party/ unauthorized agency.

Part consignment

It is a consignment where the goods go in incomplete shape. If several packages are there, all packages may not go in the same truck or wagon or ship as the case may be. Sometimes the goods are transported differently from the total lot. There may be still some place left in the truck or wagon or ship to take additional goods.

Full consignment

The goods go as a complete truck load or complete wagon load or complete ship load as the case may be. There will be no place to put some other unconcerned goods in the same vehicle. Even if place is available, the transporter is not allowed to carry a third party's material with this consignment, from starting point to destination even if there is transhipment on the way. Transported will collect full truck charges whether the sender loads goods fully or partly to ensure quick and safe receipt of material at desired destination on the instructions of the buyer.

Transhipment

Here the goods directly do not go from seller's point of dispatch to buyer's point of receipt in the same vehicle. It will be changed in transit at least once by the transporter depending on his convenience mid-way. The sender or receiver have no control over the transporting company.

Warehouse

Place where equipment is stored.

Bonded warehouse

Where goods are excisable, the goods will be in the custody of the excise authorities before despatch from that premises, which generally belongs to seller, but controlled by excise authorities, the excise duty will have to be paid by the buyer or seller on buyer's behalf, before it leaves the warehouse, where it is kept.

Many formalities, as agreed between, seller and buyer and government or quasi government authorities, have to be observed and complied by the seller and buyer for taking the goods from seller's premises to buyer's premises. All these payments concerned to outside authorities, are to be prepaid as a must, before seller gives charge of goods to transporter. General details for dispatch of goods have already been detailed for information earlier for the benefit of the readers for reference, to facilitate easy and smooth movement of goods from seller's custody to buyer's custody.

BILLING

Billing is a transaction, which forms the essence of executing the contract, for the seller. It is by billing that the customer starts, his process of claiming payments due to him, from the buyer. Billing is done during the following stages in a contract :

(1) When an order is finalized, between the buyer and seller and if the terms of payment, involve payment of particular amount as advance, then to claim that advance, billing will be done. Some customers wait, for the bills to be sent by seller, to make this advance and some others pay, along with the placing of contract, without waiting for the bills, to come to them. In both circumstances, the formality of billing has to be done by the seller. To make this advance and some other payments, after placing of contract, some customers do not wait for bills from seller, but seller has the obligation to raise the bills on customer or respective of when payments actually come to the seller, whenever the date of payment due approaches in a contract without waiting for the bill, to come to them. In all circumstances, the formality of billing, has to be done by the seller. This will regularize, the contracted obligation also. Here, the amount billed will cover, the details of the advance, that would have become due, the date, when it is done, the contractual obligation for which this advance has to be paid, by the customer. It will be addressed to the paying authority, as agreed in the contract.

(2) Progressive payment. Here, when contracts are of longer duration and the completion of supply, or service, or any reason, for which customer makes payment, becomes due by the buyer, a bill will be made, giving the reason why that amount becomes payable by customer. If it is at a time after the placement of order, then it is payment due for elapse of that time. If payment becomes due, for completing an activity, the bill will highlight, completion of that activity, giving proof of that activity.

(3) If several commodities are to be supplied to a customer, at each time, when an item is dispatched, bill will be made, for supplying that commodity. As other commodities get supplied, bill will be made, and sent to customer after those supplies are completed.

(4) If customer has to pay for a service, when service is done, bill will be made, giving proof as having completed that activity.

(5) If some payments are for erection, commissioning, post commissioning operation, when these activities are completed, bills will be raised.

(6) If some payment is linked with total completions of contract, then, final bill will be raised, indicating proof of its completions.

Thus, bills will be raised, as per the terms of contract, depending on the activity, for which a customer has to make payment.

(7) Payment, if payable, towards price variation, bill will be raised, giving details of price variation calculation, as per the formula agreed.

(8) Some times, customers are bound to pay, for extra copies of drawings, instruction manuals, special extra tests conducted, for each category of such extra work done, bills will be raised. Bill is thus, an important document, claiming payment, and if customer pays, all the bills, for which the supplier in his turn, has fulfilled the contractual obligations, then from money angle, the contract will be closed. Other obligations such as guarantee, insurance, performance, if agreed, will remain before closing the contracts. Collecting money from customers is the ultimate goal of sellers billing is the instrument for getting this money.

Billing Instructions

To get payment from the buyer, for supplying equipment, spares, repairs, done or such services, the buyer shall give the seller, billing instructions to get payment for the work done by the buyer. These are as follows :

(a) Reference of purchase order or contract and date

(b) Paying authority and address

(c) Price details giving break up of prices of individual items auxiliaries.

(d) Prices of equipment, products, spares services

(e) To whom to pay and his address?

(f) Where the despatch documents such as packing list delivery notes, excise duty, sales tax certificates, etc., are to be sent?

(g) Mode of payment : Whether through a bank or directly by some authority in the organization.

(h) Payment terms when the payment becomes due and how it is connected in the purchase order.

(i) Excise duty or sales tax applicable

(j) Whether the prices are fixed or any price variation formula is applicable. Price after applying price variation formula, detail of calculations.

(k) Certificates enclosed such as test certificates, performance certificates, guarantee certificate, drawings, operating instructions etc.

(l) Any rebate or incentives

(m) Any inspection certificate or completion of events certificates. Any bank guarantee for contractual obligations like proper performance of equipment, input/output technical parameters included in the technical contractor offer.

(n) Any special instructions to be complied

(o) Any payments adjusted in the bills

(p) Transit insurance premium, if any

(q) Any charges for special tests, special services

(r) Extra charges for supervision of commissioning

(s) Commissioning, supervision charges

(t) Repair charges

(u) Penalty if applicable

(v) Bonus if applicable.

The customer checks fully the proforma invoice, or invoice before making the payment claimed. Activities are checked as stipulated in the contract, with proof of activities completed, description of activity. In case of progressive payments also, the proforma invoice will be checked, to see that the time for payment is correct and events leading to the claim are completed.

There are cases, when several bills will be raised, once dispatches against a contract starts. For each consignment, a bill will be raised and the bills will be accumulated, as supplies increase and activities get completed. Before final bill is paid, the buyer ensures the contract is completed and all the contractual obligations have been completed. The payment will be released, continuously at the later stage. In big projects, periodic reconciliation of billing is necessary, with supplier, buyer and consultant. At the final payment stage, more rigorous checking will be done, on the contract completion. This involves time. All agencies have to certify to have completed the supplies or activities, with documentary proof.

In case of big projects and where big products are involved, in the contract, lot of periodic deliberation, takes place with the representatives of seller and buyer, to ensure the supplier and services are completed. All parts to be supplied are discussed in detail and deliberated and checked for receipt at customer's premises, in good condition. In case completion reports have to be given, for completing the supply, lot of delay takes place in getting various completion certificates, from all concerned agencies. Completion certificates or stores receipt voucher, as additional documentary proof, with clear proof of receipt of all equipment in good condition. In some cases if customer has employed inspection agencies or consultants, these agencies also have to given written acceptance for customers to make payments. Customers in many big contracts keep prolonging payments after all conditions are fulfilled by suppliers for paucity of funds or for priority for making particular payments. Customers withhold part of full payment against bills if complete supplies are not made. Critical material has not been supplied. Supplier has not made sequential supplies and some important items have not been made or delayed. Some major damages have taken place to consignments needing major repairs, non utility by user etc.

CASH AND FUNDING

Paying money to the seller for the obligation, which the buyer undertakes, relieves the customer, the binding to pay, for the services, he takes from the seller. Payments, will be made by buyer, as agreed mutually, between buyer and seller. It may come as, payment before supplies are taken delivery, services are started or completed. Obligations, such as insurance, being completed.

The funds are organized, by the buyer. !t may come from his own resources, or from loans taken from government organizations, banks, World bank, Asian bank, or other aids for purchasing or executing the contract or bringing up a project or doing any other work on the project. Cash availability with suppliers in big transactions makes lot of effect for sellers to get money due to them from their customers.

In case of big contracts releasing of payments is a complicated affair. Many agencies are involved who have to issue several completion certificates and contract documents. Generally buyers give perference to old bills for various reasons for making payments. Recent bills have to wait though they may be in order for old bills to be passed and paid. This is a complicated activity. Even with best of relations customers take time to make payments against bills as they always feel, once payments are made sellers have a tendency either to delay or wash off this responsibilities to complete all the contractual obligations. The older the bills and older the payments delays in completing contractual obligations get dragged on.

Priority of payments for different customers and different supplies made by same customer all contribute to clearing payments. When both selling and buying or formations are big problems get compounded by priorities of various contracts with same organization and formalities to be completed by seller before he is eligible to get money against a particular bill.

14

Budgeting and Inventory

BUDGET

Every organization doing business, central or state government departments, local self-governments, civil bodies, cooperative societies and for that matter any organization which works with set objectives, works within a broad planned outline or a blue print, as we can call. This blue print elaborates, the objective for which the particular agency is working, its source of income and likely expenditure over a period which is generally a year. This outline which elaborates the policies, objectives, goals, income and expenditure with clear sources of income and likely expenditure channels is called 'Budget'. Budget in short is like a magnetic compass in a ship in mid seas. The captain of the ship will know the whereabouts of the ship with respect to the shores, so that he can take the ship in the direction he wants. In the absence of this compass the ship's position cannot be located and it is difficult to assess how to steer the ship as it is like groping in darkness. In the same way, if the set objectives and achievements are not easily identifiable, the working of the organization becomes haphazard. This budget is like a guiding light for the organization and shows the frameworks within which the organization can operate broadly.

This budget is formulated by every organization from another guide. This guide is called broad objectives of the organizations. Every organization worth its name will have broad objectives before it, worked out for periods ranging from say 5 to 20 years. Keeping this broad objectives in view, the organization prepares the yearly budget. These budgets are prepared in advance before the ensuring year to which the budget is made applicable for working.

All managements keep responsible agencies to work, on the budget. First the organization involves every functional wing of the organization to participate and take an active role to make the organization to get logical and scientific results detailed in the budget. The individual functional departments are first asked to make, the budgets for the respective departments. After the individual departmental budgets are made, considerable deliberations involving all these departments are made and a practical, workable and agreed budget for the organization will be decided. Again when the organizations budget is made and frozen, the budget document or budget manual as it is generally called becomes a sacrosanct entity. All the departments of the organizations will start working on the guidelines given in the budget all through the budgeted year by giving full credence to the budget in achieving the set targets. In government, local bodies, and corporations financial aspects of the budget are very rigid. Hardly any deviation in the budgeted expenditure side is allowed for making re-allocation in the budgeted figures fixed under various expenditure heads, except with the explicit sanction of the competent authority. Generally these changes occur rarely, as initiatives are not taken in going beyond the budgeted expenditure of these departments. The case is however different in a commercial organization, where, the working is flexible. Results and profits are more important and revision in budget is not a surprise and a well thought of revision will be made it helps the organization to get better results.

There are many uses in having a budget in an organization or department.

(1) The concerned staff of the organization know in advance what are the clear objective for which they have to channel their working.

(2) Unless it is a major deviation, people try and work in the framework of the budget smoothly and easily without recourse to going to higher management for approvals and concurrence, which may result in difficulties later.

(3) The funds that will flow, the channels from which they come, with all details and procedures will be available for

taking timely action for making free availability of money for working.

(4) Expenditure and payments which are spelt out to various departments also will flow smoothly, making operations easy and smooth.

(5) When difficulties arise any mid time orientation can be done for achieving the objectives for getting the required timely funds required for spending.

(6) Comparison of all parameters fixed for achievement in the budget for all the concerned departments in particular, can be easily made, with respect to previous years performance and experiences. Future years budget can be so oriented keeping these achievements, the strengths, shortcomings and organizations capabilities in mind.

(7) When budget is formulated, advance information is available about the advantages and disadvantages to which the organization will be put in achieving the results, and generally surprises will not come in a big way in the working of the organization.

(8) It is easy to give remuneration to the staff, shareholders and other connected agencies when results, are achieved and targets are exceeded. At the same time concerned agencies can be hauled up, when results are not forthcoming, when things are not going as planned normally, except for extraordinary reasons.

(9) Monitoring the budget is a very important activity. It is only when proper monitoring system is existing and a thorough monitoring is done, the full utility as also the energy spent in this exercise will give the desired satisfactory results.

(10) Monitoring is essential for various reasons and whatever is planned. What is going on, and what is likely outcome will be known at the right time. This facilitates the authorities with the tool to reorient and re-deploy the organizations, resources, make good use of them, where the achievements fall short of planned budgeted figures. With this in view an amount of flexibility has to be in built into the budget, so that the changes can be appropriately made.

(11) Monitoring has to be split period-wise say as half yearly, quarterly, monthly and weekly time frames as is necessary. This will result in less surprise creeping in and very little chances of regret for not taking corrective actions, which would not be otherwise possible, if things go on in their own way without taking stock at regular intervals. Though monitoring looks like policing, it is actually a way of inculcating dynamism in the working.

(12) For example, when sales budget is not likely to be realised in the area of planned order booking, the production can be rescheduled, to fill the vacuum, by preponing the priorities from later years plans and customers can at times be kept happy, if they are in need of equipments, and they welcome their products coming out early. If planned funds are not forthcoming in time, other venues of getting money can be thought of without sacrificing the output or turn over. In case of planned projects, where there are difficulties in pushing them through, other projects, can be substituted if possible, by shifting priorities properly to suit the production.

(13) In case both indigenous and imported materials are involved in the production of equipment other activities can be taken up to fill the gap as suitable alternative when imports are not forthcoming as planned. The purchase cycle can be re-oriented. Production can be suitably phased.

(14) Where inputs like power become a constraint at a particular period, equipment which need less power input can be substituted in its place and other work where power consumption is less can be done.

(15) In case of manpower, their optimum utility can be worked out, at all stages, wherever operations get affected. Same can be the case, with engineering, technology, development, expansion, capital investment activities.

(16) When for unforeseen, reasons, certain contracts are cancelled or put off, the possible inventory and other work done can be utilized, if possible to the best extent by taking all possible action to make optimum use of the locked up capital by diverting to other jobs.

(17) In case of delays in transporting input material from both in land and foreign sources, emergency action can be taken like air lifting, even if additional expenditure is involved to keep production schedules. Same thing applies, when supply of completed goods are to be sent out from works. Similar procedure can be applied to customer to get funds in time, which otherwise may affect the operations.

(18) These are some of the few issues, which generally come up in operations where timely monitoring helps to correct, the likely adverse effects in the operations. Many more corrective actions wherever necessary can be taken to get best results.

In all fields in general, it is the finance and accounts wing of the organization which does the monitoring and control in addition to other operating staff and wings of the establishment. Since all activities are valued against money natural importance has to be given to financial monitoring, which in essence is the biggest budgetary control. Budget heads are mainly on these lines. It can be slightly different if more departments are there which also have to be accommodated. It will reduce the budget heads if some of these wings do not exist or are merged with other departments.

1. Marketing, publicity and advertising departments
2. Production departments
3. Finance and account department
4. Planning department
5. Engineering, development and research departments
6. Purchase and stores departments
7. Administrative department
8. Packing and dispatch department
9. Various service and maintenance departments
10. Testing, erection, commissioning departments
11. Field service departments
12. Regional sales and service departments in case of big organizations.
13. Township administration departments in case of big organizations.

14. Human resources and training departments
15. Transport and communications departments
16. Construction department
17. Miscellaneous expenditure

INVENTORY

Inventory is a very special subject and very scientific and needs elaborate study of the product, production process, market for the products, cycle of procurement or production, source of material, the commodity sold, useful life of the commodity.

(1) Every organization tries to keep low inventories of raw material, work in progress, finished materials as it is profitable and economical to operate at optimum levels of inventory. More inventory than what is consumed in the process for raw material locks the capital. In addition to capital that is lost, there will be interest paid on borrowings which have to be added to the capital cost, the life of raw material, its preservation, space occupied are also factors which add to material cost for the buyer. Preservation of raw material is also an important factor. Inventory of work in progress, costs for the material, cost of work done on it, locked capital, interest on the material which is not moving, storage area determination of the material, on which work has to be done also are an important factor to be considered.

(2) In case of finished product inventory, cash gets locked up as inventory of finished products not sold block cash inputs. Cost of material, production capacity, interest on investment, cause burden on the supplier. If the material is manufactured on firm orders, till the material is taken by customer and converted into cash, finished inventory, gives negative returns, as interest lost on commodity, has to be subtracted from what customer ultimately gets from the buyer. Rotation of capital, is temporarily stopped, to the extent the inventory is with supplier, for which efforts are necessary to dispose off inventory and convert it into cash. If some equipments are manufactured in non sequential order, and if the buyer does not need the material immediately this capital and interest lost on that is loss to the supplier. Generally, customers do not take equipment, which are required at a later stage in their project. In exceptional cases, where seller wants to

manufacture non-sequential items ahead of its delivery due to loading of work centers, which are otherwise idle, he won't take-up manufacture of equipment, earlier than delivery schedule, unless he knows that buyer is prepared to receive the equipment in advance and pay for it.

Sometimes, improper planning results in inventory being created, by WIP or finished products. Cases are not lacking where material for equipment, whose delivery falls earlier is not available. If raw material supplier delays material dispatch or delay in transportation or paucity of funds, to get material released from transporters results in a chain of events, causing loss of returns on locked up inventory.

It is necessary to plan operations, to see that right material is available, at the right time, at right place, so that the supplier does not face delays, in making equipment, due to non-availability of other connected supplier. This can happen at the plant, at works center, during dispatch, timely receipt of finished products by buyers at sites.

Inventory carrying costs are categorized under various heads :

Financial cost. Interest paid on bank loans to maintain minimum inventory level if it is from bank loan. If it is from organization funds interest lost not for disposing off. This loss of interest is opportunity cost.

Insurance charges. Premium charges for protecting the inventory from theft, fire, etc.

Storage expenses. Space and wages for staff of go down and such expenses and for transportation back.

Handling charges. Movement charges from storage to production and such places and back.

Deterioration. Loss due to not using in the specified useful life, storage, shelf life, material like grease, medicines, chemicals, finished food products, consumables, insulation, resins, paints.

Cost of obsolescence. If the items are not quickly used the technology may become obsolete calling for throwing away the items when new items have to be used.

Ordering cost. Delays in ordering or not using the ordered material, which requires rework. Processing paper work. Formalities to be gone through again, revaluation of tenders where new procurement is necessitated.

Stock out cost. If enough stock of required material is not there, there will be short fall or loss of production or use of men and machinery, idle time, delay in supplies, delay in getting planned earnings, loss of profits, etc.

Economic ordering quantity. Taking into account the opening stock, the closing stock checks are made. This is a management decision to keep the stock level. The required material is ordered taking into consideration, the benefits of bulk ordering discounts, inventory cost, saving in money by not ordering in time. A stock of orders on hand and likely to mature in future is considered. Minimum ordering is done so that men and resources are put to optimum use and there is no hold back in inputs.

15

Inspection and Audit

INSPECTION

Every organization has as one of its important and major activities inspection of all its operations thoroughly during the running of the organization. For commercial organizations in particular the sellers and buyers have reason to give much importance to inspection. Inspection as the word implies acts as a practical control. Identified authorities of organizations, work hard to see that the supplies made by it and services rendered by the organization, satisfy certain predefined conditions, before the goods are used or the equipment are run, after the necessary activities are completed at the manufacturing or erection/ commissioning stage. For this purpose, a well-qualified and trained set up will exist in the organization that can look after every activity.

Inspection is done to ensure the following, by the seller and buyer, as a routine activity :

(1) The goods comply with, the desired physical dimensions, subject, to tolerances, as per an agreed standard specification.

(2) Material used for making the goods, comply with the composition as per the agreed specifications.

(3) The equipment or goods, give rated output to rated input, as per the agreed specifications.

(4) The goods during the manufacture go through the required processes and adhere to the stipulations of the specification, before and after the process is executed.

(5) Care is taken to see that goods can be assembled, stored and used, to a particular specification that is stipulated.

(6) The life of the goods are stipulated in the contract and hence the goods shall give this operational life, successfully.

SPECIFICATIONS AND STANDARDS

Every standard item which has market recognition and the manufacturers, designers, technologists, consultants, financial, organizations, Governments, users of products, projects services, scientific and research organizations, higher educational organizations, funding and executing agencies, inspection agencies, planning and all recognised organizations want whatever items are bought, sold or used in bulk quantities and repeatedly over a period of years to follow what is called a specification and pass set standards which are a type of graduations. These specifications and standards might have been conceived by individuals and organizations of repute. Generally when more than one seller and buyer are there, there will be common laid out producers/ specifications/standards.

When the buyer and seller/supplier/manufacturer/producers increase with the spectrum of activities and many things are at stake in addition to money specific organizations in countries and reputed bulk users set out these specifications and standards to which items and services should comply. In India we have Indian Standards Institution, popularly known as ISI. In Britain we have British standard organization abbreviated BS. Germans, Russians, Americans and for that matter almost all countries follow standards set out by specific organizations of their countries or follow the specifications and standards of other major and popular country. In addition we have international organizations which set out these parameters which are followed universally. These are in all areas such as say electrical branch, mechanical branch, communication and information technology. Chemical and metallurgy, Aeronautics and space for that matter all branches of science are covered.

With increased demand for better products and services all over the world and in order to have uniformity in terminology and rationalisation, international organization for standardisation has issued quality management systems in 1987, popularly known as ISO 9000 series.

These consist of five standards :

ISO 9000 : Quality Management and Quality assurance standards "guidelines for selection and use".

ISO 9001 : Quality systems — "Models for quality assurance in design, development, production, installation and service."

ISO 9002 : Quality systems — "Models for quality assurance in production and installation."

ISO 9003 : Quality systems — "Model for quality assurance in final inspections and tests."

ISO 9004 : "Quality management, quality systems and its guidelines."

Now for major projects, where the environment in which the project comes up, the location, inputs and outputs to the projects, their effects on the surrounding flora and fauna is of major consideration. In order to have good environment around the projects and to see that the project it self, production processes, wastes etc. do not have damaging effects, environment specification in 14001 series is considered, at the time of conceiving projects, approvals and operation.

The seller and buyer, take initiatives from their sides to ensure compliance of inspection checks, at the time of procurement and during important stages of intermediate activity and in the end of the process the goods give good and trouble free service life.

- Being a key activity of an organization, every organization of good standing, will generally have its own separate inspection department. If for some reasons, the organization does not have a separate inspection department, then there will be a set up which is affordable by the organization that will take care of the inspection activities in the organization, in a suitable, orderly manner, to ensure quality of products, projects and services, smoothly.
- The word inspection is very popular in every area of activity, whether it is administration, sales, production, engineering, technology, testing, erection, commissioning post-commissioning operations. In every area, a sense of high priority and sanctity is given to this activity, as the credence of the concerned organization, will be at stake.

Inspection is carried out in all organizations irrespective of what structure the organization is made up of and whether it is a government, quasi government, private or even philanthropic organization. This inspection is compulsorily resorted to as huge funds will be involved and laxity at any stage may do untold damage, if some activity, in the total chain or activities, goes wrong. Generally, in every set up, importance to this function starts at the top. The top management makes a thorough inspection of its own offices and operations, then it starts percolating down to the lowest strata in the set up. At lest one authority, higher in the hierarchy, takes the responsibility, for proper working of establishment below it and this process goes on. There is a built in procedure in every organization, to ensure accountability. Misuse of resources and avoiding any kind of losses, creeping in or quality being diluted, has to be arrested.

- In commercial organizations, which work on the principle of growth and profitability, inspection department, works more authoritatively and on decisive lines, without giving room to ambiguity to laxity in approach towards operations, by the staff. The production and service wings, always try to up hold, the name of the organization and its popularity, leadership among competitors, by sticking to supplying quality products and offer quality service.
- As more and more organizations, are getting into sophisticated technologies, buyers are always looking forward, to get best equipment and services, for what they pay. They expect quality and trouble free service from the products and in the running of projects, throughout the stipulated useful life. They avoid failures, resulting in down time by either faulty maintenance, or operation. They take care to see, sub-standard equipment is not bought and put in their operation.
- The area of inspection of late has widened. In this direction, the working of the inspection wing of the organization, has been split into two phases or departments, one which deals with quality assurance, that lays down

guidelines, in the organization and the second department, the quality control department, which sees to it, that the outline given by quality assurance department is strictly followed by putting them into practice from beginning till the end of a job. Quality standards are maintained, in the chain, from beginning to the end, so that by alertness in following the procedures, restricts, rejections and rework, resulting in reducing wastage of time, material and human resources, including machinery and operation time. The procedures laid down, by quality assurance department, are available at every work center, starting with design, indenting, procuring raw material, sub suppliers material, sub contract work, work at each work center, in production, technology, feeder departments, testing, erection, storage, transportation, commissioning, post commercial operation stage. The activities of checking staff and operating staff are clearly defined. Inputs and outputs are demarcated, at every stage, so that macro level accountability, before taking up the job, after the job is completed and when the job goes on, are recorded clearly for future reference and investigation.

- The inspection department works independently. It reports directly, to the head of the organization, so that other work centers, cannot influence its working and favours sought, which may result, in diluting the quality. All agencies, including purchase, stores, finance, are accountable for every phase of activity, in the organization, so that the system, not the individuals, take care of the quality of output, of the physical product and services rendered. There is a change in the outlook of the quality assurance and quality control department. They have changed from age-old fault finding agencies, to productivity agencies. They do both advisory and inspection clearance, role in the organization.
- One more development that has come in quality is total quality management concept. In this new concept, every wing of the organization, keeps its own self-correcting, quality ensuring system, built in it.

The specific benefits, which a good inspection department or good inspection procedure, brings to an organization by this total quality concept are :

1. It gives a good brand name to the product.
2. It reduces the loses due to rejections and rework.
3. The defects in the equipment or service rendered do not become cumulative, till the final stage and do not result in losses to the organization, in making the organization undertake, total rework, resulting in losses financially, spending, manufacturing and other time of the organization and make good use of resources for a particular job.
4. Losses due to hold up of jobs in manufacture get reduced, resulting in avoiding delay of jobs, which will not continue to occur. There will be no inconvenience to customer. Selling bad products or services, doing repeated inspections, result in delay in commissioning of products or projects do not generally exist now.
5. Time schedule of jobs, will be maintained by the inspection departments, starting from raw material procurement, starting production, assembly, testing, dismantling packing, storage, transportation, erection, commissioning and operation. This also involves direct ready made bought out equipment, which do not need generally additional work before using them on products or in projects.
6. The caliber of the inspecting staff, have to be high, as they have to look after the jobs, from concept to commissioning and post operation of products and projects and interact with personal of agencies inside and outside the organization and buyers at all stages.
7. Stage inspection and batch inspection will have to be quite up right. Any special features or complying with any additional specification clauses, have to be done correctly and meticulously. Duration of the job, beyond certain stipulated limits of tolerances, cannot be accepted and jobs cannot be allowed to go to next stage unless previous activity is O.K. This ensures, trouble free operation through

out the period of service life. There will be a record of jobs at every stage, from design to final post commercial operation, so that when jobs give trouble or in case of accepting any deviations, in the quality standards, these details will be available for cross checking. These records will be preserved for a long time, even after the projects operate well, for considerable periods, ranging to several years as product/project history.

The following flow charts, of inspection are for all jobs such as the sub contract items, outside procurement items, small mechanical and electrical items, big mechanical equipment, big electrical equipment, used in products and projects. These are given as models, which are used generally in practical application, in the manufacture of equipment, for the information of readers.

Model flow of chart of quality assurance tests, for small & medium, mechanical equipment and assembly, such as bearings, and covers, plate, couplings, sub-contract items, rings, hub ring units, etc.

CHART 1

1	2	3	4
Quality control at works/Material suppliers premises	Quality control checks at production center users premises on receipt	Quality control tests, during production process, users premises	Tests before dispatch for use of works, or at site, as finished material
Chemical analysis of melt, mechanical properties, Heat treatment charts, physical dimensions, non destructive tests, calibration tests, Packing worthiness radiographic examination, electromagnetic checks if used for electrical equipment	Material attestation, verification of test certificates, dimensions checks, visual inspection, calibration tests.	Verification of weld fit ups, LP on welds, verification of stress reliving test cycles, pressure/leakage tests, visual inspection. Mechanical surface finish, deburring, degreasing, liquid penetration, ultrasonic tests, kerosene leak tests, profile test if gear is involved. Gauge finish check.	Visual checks, oil cleaning dimensional checks, alignment tests, axial and radial clearances in case of assemblies. IR tests if for electrical equipment use.

Model flow chart of quality assurance tests, on big mechanical equipment

CHART 2

1	2	3	4
Quality control at at works/Material suppliers premises	Quality control at production center, users premises on receipt	Quality control tests, during production process, users premises	Tests before dispatch for use of works, or at site, as finished material
Chemical, mechanical properties. If for use in electrical equipment, magnetic properties, metallographic tests. Heat treatment cycles, Boroscopic tests, bore concentricity and dimensional checks.	Material attestation, verification of certificates, ultrasonic tests, visual inspection.	Dimensional checks surface finish requirements specific tests if any based on use of the material.	Physical examination, inspection of fixtures if any. Presentation of mechanical surfaces, identification marks for site use, checks.

Model flow chart of quality assurance tests on major electrical equipment

CHART 3

1	2	3	4
Quality control at works/Material suppliers premises	Quality control checks at production center, users premises on receipt	Quality control tests, during production process, users premises	Tests before dispatch for use of works, or at site, as finished material
Chemical analysis of melt, magnetic properties of plate material, if fabrication is used. Heat treatment charts dimensional checks, ageing, iron loss, packing worthiness, tensile, hardness, bend tests, electrical conductivity.	Material attestation verification of test certificates, critical and special alloy tests, dimensional checks, calibration checks, random mechanical and electrical tests. Dynamic Balancing tests for rotating equipment like stator or motor rotors, over speed and HV tests.	Dimension checks, weld fit up, visual inspection, machining check, liquid penetration tests, cleanliness tests, special tests like varnish, viscosity, temperature. Insulation resistance if required. HV tests liquid penetration tests.	Weld fitments dimensions tests physical examinations preservation of mechanical surfaces identification mark test for site use radial and axial cleanness balancing and over speed if required. Test parameters check.

Model flow chart of quality assurance tests, on minor and bought out items like metres, etc.

CHART 4

1	2	3	4
Quality control at works/Material suppliers premises	**Quality control checks at production center, users premises on receipt**	**Quality control tests, during production process, users premises**	**Tests before dispatch for use of works, or at site, as finished material**
Mechanical and electrical properties, chemical analysis, heat treatment charts, magnetic properties, bend test, packing worthiness, hardness tests. Electrical conductivity dimensional checks, calibration tests.	**Material identification test, certificates verification, random electrical and mechanical tests, dimensions, visualizing inspection for fans and ring assemblies, verification of shrink fit, dimensions, deburring operations, locking of ring nut and arrestments hubs and fans, visual inspection after all shrink fitting operations.**	**Dimensions checks, blanking, notching viscosity, temperature insulation, resistor hardness, HV tests, magnetic particle tests, profile checks to guage liquid penetration, brazing, annealing, punching tests.**	**Dimensional checks, physical verification, balancing tests, preservation of mechanical surface, identification marks, resistance tests, IR value phase sequence tests.**

Quality control checks, in the production of equipment (Specimen examples)

(I) Inspection of 10 HP Electric Motors. Batch inspection in batch production. (×) Inspection by the concerned agency. (*) Agency not doing inspection.

Sl. No.	Type of Inspection/ Tests	Inspecting Agencies			
		Factory quality control staff	Sellers appointed inspectors	Customers inspectors	Customers represen-tatives
1.	Raw material at works before starting production physical inspection, dimension check	×	×	*	*
2.	Production check during assembly	×	×	×	*
3.	Routine tests, dimension check	×	×	×	×
4.	Tests before packing and dispatch	×	×	×	*
5.	Checking consignment at site	*	*	×	×
	Customers premises	*	*	×	×

Quality control, inspection checks, on auxiliaries of equipment (specimen examples)

(II) Inspection of foundation frame, bearing pedestals for 100 HP motor, at sellers works,

Supplied by sub-contractor to seller.

Sl. No.	Type of Inspection/ Tests conducted	Inspecting Agencies			
		Supplier quality control staff	Supplier appointed inspector	Customers inspector	Customers represen-tatives
1.	Physical inspection, dimensional check as per drawings, alignment	×	×	×	*
2.	Inspection of consignment at site or customers premises	*	*	*	×

Quality control checks, in the production of equipment (Specimen examples)

(III) Circuit breakers and control panels, used in high voltage applications. (×) inspecting agency concerned. (*) inspecting agency not concerned.

Sl. No.	Factory inspection by quality control staff appointed	Inspecting Authorities		
		Factory management inspectors inspectors	Customers appointed	Customers representatives
1.	×	×	*	*
2.	×	×	×	*
3.	×	×	×	*
4.	×	×	×	*
5.	×	×	×	×
6.	×	×	×	×
7.	×	×	×	*
8.	*	*	×	×

Quality control checks, in the production of equipment (Specimen examples)

(IV) Boiler feed pumps, used in projects up to 70 MW Turbo generator sets. (×) Inspecting agency concerned. (*) Inspecting agency not concerned.

Sl. No.	Stages of inspection	Inspecting Authorities			
		Factory Inspection by quality control staff	Factory management appointed inspectors	Inspection by Customers appointed inspectors	Inspection by Customers representatives
1.	Supply of raw material, measuring gauges, meters etc. at sellers/suppliers premises	×	×	*	*
2.	Raw material, bought out items like meters gauges, sub-suppliers major items before assembling pump	×	×	×	*
3.	Assembly of pump with all accessories at works of supplier	×	×	×	*
4.	Physical inspection, dimension checks routine tests or pumps	×	×	×	×
5.	Type tests and other special tests if any or its documents at works	×	×	×	×
6.	Disassembly, physical inspection before packing/after packing	×	×	×	*
7.	Receipt of material at site physical inspection of consignments	*	*	×	×

Quality Audit/Technical Audit

- Just as an audit department, in a commercial organization, or a government department, in state or central government, takes an audit, of finance and procedural compliance, in these offices, in reputed big organizations is quality and adherence to technical standards of jobs, is checked by quality audit and technical audit.
- The inspection or quality department, will have with it, a small wing to check and supervise the overall adherence of the quality in the organization, by all the departments. This is a self check, conducted in the organization, by its own wing of technical staff. These people do periodic checks, in the working of the organization, from the point of adherence to quality. These are independent of quality assurance, quality control, customers inspection or the inspection of the particular job, by a third inspecting agency, appointed by the supplier, or customer. This helps the organization, to imbibe quality consciousness, keep records of quality followed by other producers, who supply equipment to it and keep a record of quality inspection of every job done in the organization. This is a wing, which checks and controls periodically, how the inspection departments are enforcing the checks, on quality and on individual jobs.

AUDIT

The function of audit is a stock taking of various activities of an organization by an agency. The things taken stock are, financial dealings, technical adherence to standards of various activities, such as production, engineering, testing, purchase, stores, finance, operations, dealings in sales transactions, purchase transactions, execution of customers orders etc. While finance, is the main factor, checked, its inflow and optimum useful outflow, the past and present performance, future plans and objectives of any given organization, a detailed review is taken at periodical intervals and remedial actions.

Any improprieties in the financial dealings lapses in following laid out procedures, skipping chain of sanctions, by passing authorities who have also to scrutinise and agree that the transactions are in order will all be investigated as they are necessary.

(1) There is what .is called, internal audit. This is done by the internal finance department of the organization. Another audit, called statutory audit, is done by organizations, appointed, and notified group of auditors, who do the audit of the organization, half yearly or once in a year, and prepare profit and loss accounts, as well as the balance sheet of the organization. The third type of audit, is done by the government through its financial departments, either of the state or central Government as the case may be, periodically, looking into the activities of the organization, of its choice, of any internal department, or particular transaction, as desired by it, on the goings on, in the working of the organization. Lot of importance and weightage is given to the findings by this audit and some times they have deep repercussions, on the organization and its authorities.

(2) In addition to such above financial audits, every reputed organization, has a unique audit carried out called "Quality Audit" in all fields and departments of the organization, such as engineering, technology, production, erection and commissioning, commercial operations, as also feedback, on the performance, where the equipments are in use, from customers on its products and services. Quality months, quality weeks etc. are observed by the organizations, every year, involving all its functional groups, within the organization, as an internal exercise, to know the technical and commercial standing of the organization, to make proper human involvement, of their staff, of all the departments of the organization, in the quality. This is to maintain and improve, the physical performance of the standards, products and services of the organization, in the long run.

(3) Every department can be audited at the will of the audit authorities. This could be limited to specific jobs or specific transaction of a department of the organization as a whole at the will or discretion of the concerned auditing authority.

(4) This inculcate a sense of care in dealing jobs by the staff or the management.

16

Monitoring Performance, by Flow Charts, Graphs, Bar Charts, Networks, Blocks and Pie-diagrams

For commercial organizations, certain values are very important about the working of the organizations. In this context, management's take exceptional care to see that the broad objectives, for which they have conceived the organizations, are always realized. They spare no effort, in the day to day working of the organizations, to promote these objectives, motivate their employees, in that direction, channelize the resources, at their command and strive hard, to achieve these goals continuously, by ceaseless effort. They only feel satisfied, when periodic reviews of jobs are taken, that efforts are not lacking by the concerned agencies. Each time, they improve in their approach, plug the loop-holes, make best use of the prevailing situations and derive maximum advantage, to benefit in their endeavours, without laxity in their efforts. It is this progressive approach that keeps the organizations grow, to their optimum capabilities and get utmost profits.

In order to get, the desired results, periodic reviews with the concerned agencies, about the condition or status of the jobs is monitoring. Monitoring is done on the jobs, be it the sales activities, purchase activities, planning, engineering/design, production, other manufacturing functions, inputs, billing, cash realization, satisfactory movement of inventory and timely action to achieve various goals.

1. The following are the main parameters, where the managements work hard, to see that efforts and

opportunities are not lost and difficulties encountered, in their progress, are resolved to the best of their abilities.

1.1 Maximum use of human resources, capital, time, plant, machinery and markets.

1.2 Identify, the efforts to be put in by all agencies by taking periodic review, of the jobs and take suitable action, as the situation demands, then, to get best benefits.

1.3 Avoid meeting with surprises, by failures, delays, extra investments, lessening productivity.

1.4 See that, things are moving in the fight direction, so that budgeted performances are realized.

1.5 While, monitoring the progress of jobs, from concept to completion are done, at various levels, there are various techniques, adapted in monitoring the jobs.

2. Monitoring of various jobs, big or small, even where there is no commercial objective, is done extensively in most of the organizations, central and state government departments, social and cultural organizations for that matter even, philanthropic organizations monitor, their activities for assessing, various progresses made and what further needs to be done.

3. The monitoring in commercial organizations is, for other basic reasons, such as the existence of the organization in the market, by proper performance. Return on investments properly, so that the investors continue to get returns, on their investments as per commitments and improve on their earlier performance. Organizations compete with each other, to capture market leadership. How monitoring at various stages is done, are detailed below, on various activities of commercial organizations.

4. At the tendering stage, preparing an excellent technical and commercial offer, helps in getting orders from clients, by establishing, an edge over competitors. Here, getting tender inputs, evaluations of inputs, before submitting offer, such as price, delivery, technical parameters, by highlighting the advantages of products, projects, services offered to the buyer, helps in getting the order. All these issues have to

be evaluated and brought forward properly, to catch the appreciation of buyer. Jobs already successfully completed, customer profile, giving various jobs done to them successfully, is a good point in view.

If special incentives are given, they attract buyers. Special features of jobs, have an edge in the evaluation. To do this lot of effort and track record are necessary.

4.1 When a tender is about to be allotted. And contract is to be settled, in the favour of the organization, settling as many terms, as are relevant to the execution of job, helps in completing the jobs easily. Much, after purchase order discussions, and negotiations will be avoided, except those that have to be done at various stages, mandatorily, when contract is being executed.

4.2 When repeat orders are received, from customers, it helps to keep a record of earlier experiences, where difficulties had cropped up. These difficulties should be avoided, in current jobs to complete jobs easily and effectively at the earliest duration.

4.3 Where customer stage inspection, is involved, or where customer his inspecting agencies, hold points are there, avoiding rework, rejections, by doing jobs properly, for the first time, in one go, helps in timely completion of jobs, and avoids delays, resulting in locking of capital, by way of raw material, inventory, work-in-progress, etc. otherwise interest on borrowed capital, will increase, reducing profits. There will be less money, for operations in such situations.

4.4 Material processes, men, should be geared up, at the appropriate time, for smooth completion of jobs, where, inter phasing of jobs are there, it is necessary, to ensure, connected jobs at other work centers, are also completed, in time, as per schedule, so that, next activity can proceed, without wasting time, for some activities to be completed, in the chain of events.

4.5 What time has elapsed to start that activity?

4.6 How much time the balance activities will take?

4.7 What corrective actions can be taken for the balance activities to be completed earlier, than scheduled time, for each activity, so that by progressively reducing the time of each, balance activities, as much likely delay in completing, the job can be reduced as is practicable. To this extent, the seller himself can take necessary action or the buyer can pressurize the seller to do the expediting.

4.8 Some activities, can be accelerated by allotting special priorities, such as changing the schedule of work, loaded to a work center. If materials are a constraint, if possible, their procurement can be speeded, they can be brought and taken by personal escort reducing the transportation time if possible.

4.9 These are some of the areas, where a job can be carried out in a specified time. There will be several unidentified job situations, where several alternatives, can be thought of, and implemented, to do the work effectively, in a particular span of time. Some times, deploying more men, doing jobs at more than one place, are all examples to help in certain difficult situations, to obviate the difficulties, to speed up completion of jobs.

The various activities which are cumulative in nature and which give final result after several activities are done need monitoring. A detailed plan how and where activities start where the next set of activities have to wait for completing the proceeding activities need a blue print to be made. This blue print gives the following information :

1. The final aim to be achieved in terms of activity or the output.
2. The various inputs available and from where.
3. The time available for total activity starting from the first activity.
4. The composition of such sub-activities which make the final activity.

This monitoring is compulsorily done where huge money is invested and money is not allowed to get locked up as also resources and manpower. More care is taken when any input is scare and particular activities are important in getting output on time from many angles, including return on investment and if certain facilities lapse if not used in time.

Examples where important activities are interlinked and which need to be closely followed from start to finish are :

(a) Construction of a building.

(b) Selection of staff for a particular organization at a particular time.

(c) Manufacture of a project.

(d) Execution of a project.

(e) Performing certain processes say in manufacturing drugs, paper, cement, chemical, steel, electricity generation, transmission distribution, irrigation projects, financial organization launching of space craft, water supply or drainage project in a town or city. The examples are too many wherever a planned schedule is involved and optimum results of quality are expected.

As bigger and bigger projects came up all over the world in the last many decades, all developed countries began adopting project-monitoring techniques. These in effect gave rise to several types of monitoring systems. The most popular being network analysis, which is a productivity technique involving analyzing and controlling all activities. The whole energy involved in the project in various forms as money, material, manpower and time is used very systematically.

The flow charts are generally raised for big, sophisticated, costly, jobs where number of processes are involved, in production, time taken for completing the total jobs, runs into several months, each particular activity taking some weeks. Many work centers, will be involved. Production facilities involved are more. Each work if delayed costs lot of money as waiting jobs cannot be loaded, due to pre occupation of the plant and machinery some times only one job, can be done at a time, in a work center, because of the size and area occupied by the jobs.

Flow charts — Explanation

1. The whole activity is broken into small important landmarks; they are depicted in the form of a chain right from the finish. In this flow chart, there are several things, which a user can find out.

1.1 What are the various activities involved?

1.2 What is the significance of each activity?

1.3 What are the advantages and disadvantages of that activity?

1.4 What is the likely duration of that activity?

1.5 What are the facilities required for doing that activity?

1.6 If that activity is delayed or there is a snag, what effect it will have on the total job?

Example below is of the manufacture of a turbo generator rotor and stator, where the flow chart gives the sequence of activities to be done for the manufacture.

FLOW CHART

Main manufacturing cycle

Big turbo rotor of generator

Rotor machining : D.P. Test → Slot milling → dimension check

Rotor wedges : Machining → suiting on rotor

Rotor coils Coil looping → vent hole punching → forming → dimension check

Excitation leads : Manufacture of components → Dimensional check → Use assembly in rotor → leakage test → H.V. test.

Rotor winding : Core assembly → Inter turn and H.V. Test → Baking → Dimensional check → Wedging → H.V. Test → Bracers suiting → Ring → Slip ring mounting → Fan Monitoring → Final machining → balancing → Over speeding → H.V. Test

Big turbo generator stator manufacture

Stator frame : Fabrication → weld tests → sand blasting painting → Final machining → hydraulic test → painting

Stator core : Lamination manufacture → Core assembly → Ring flux test → Core cleaning

Stator bar : Conductor cutting → Rebel transposition → inter slip test → slack consolidation → inter slip test → Main insulation → Final curing → Coating → H.V. and tan delta tests.

Stator winding : Bracket fixing → Bottom bar laying → H.V. Test → Top bar laying temp wedging → H.V. Test → Eye brazing → Wedging H.V. Test.

End covers : Machining → Dimension check

Bearings : Shell machining → Babitting → Bond test → Final machining.

GRAPHS

1. Graphs are a very common tool of depicting easily, various activities, either on paper or a board, for more viewers to see. It is a two dimensional depiction, of a work, quantifying work, comparing, work done in a particular time, at different points of time, say a month, quarter, half yearly, yearly over years, etc. it tells, the amount spent, profit or loss.

Plant capacity used at different periods, outputs from plants at different periods, comparison of time or money incurred versus actual. Man power utilization over a period or output from them as comparison. Return on investment, behaviour of a machine over a period in terms of input and output, how resources are used. How much time jobs have taken to complete, performance of a plant or organizations over a period of time in years. Almost all activities can be put on graph and depicted clearly in a sketch. This is simple to understand and operate and generally the work centers, advertising tools make use of these graphs to highlight the various performances and achievements in terms of money, time, manpower etc.

At a glance one can understand and appreciate the performance illustrated in a graph very distinctly. Graphs do not require such skill to demonstrate the performance or other objectives to the users.

Some of the graphs drawn below show the performance of an organization as illustrated to highlight them as examples of use of graphs to monitor performance.

Performance of organizations for the year 1998 in the areas of sales, production, investment and profit. (Fig. 1)

Performance of an organization relatively for three years 1997-1998, 1998-1999 and 1999-2000 in the areas of sales, investment, production in lakhs of rupees and monthly in the above three years.

SPECIMEN OF SALES, PRODUCTION & PROFIT

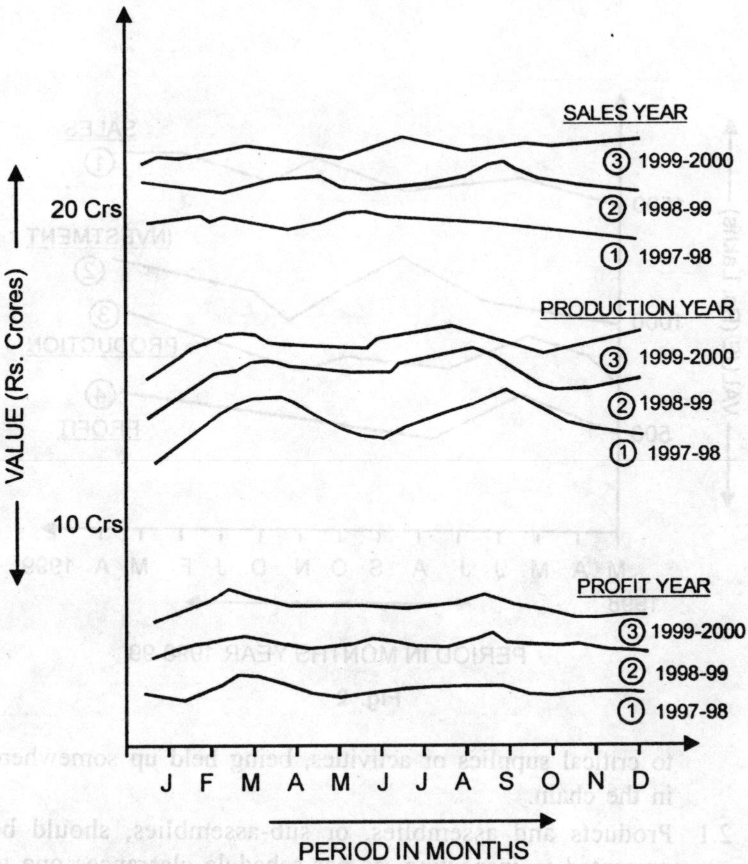

Fig. 1

The graphs tell the figures in rupees, the sales made by the organizations in three years and in those three years, the investment of capital on the plant, production. (Fig. 2)

2. In case of products, sequential dispatches should be maintained, to site, from various supply sources. The activities, which have a time frame, will have to go on, in the order of preferences, so that final erection and commissioning will take place, in time, without delays, due

SPECIMEN OF SALES, PRODUCTION & PROFIT

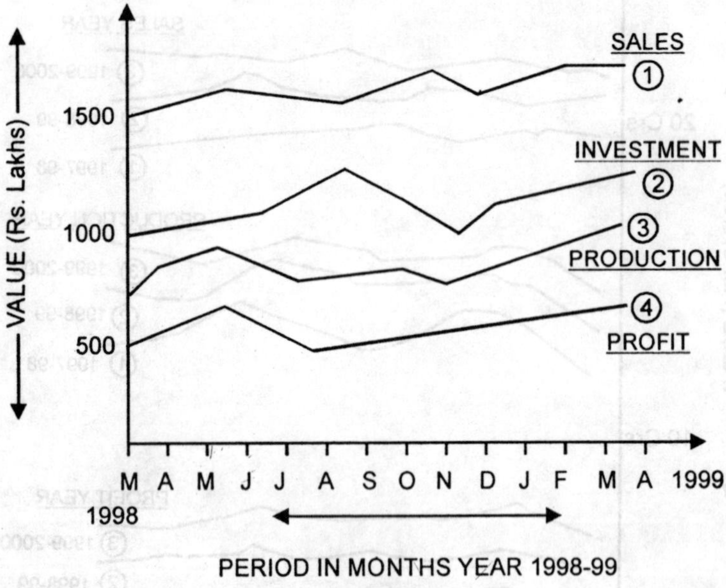

Fig. 2

to critical supplies or activities, being held up somewhere in the chain.

2.1 Products and assemblies, or sub-assemblies, should be presented to inspecting, as per schedule clearances one to be obtained, without delays, or resorting to rejections, rework etc.

2.2 The schedule of activities, drawn up, should be practicable, and should not create, unnecessary difficulties, in completing the jobs. The more, the work centers, the more will be the products, going into a project. The more, the supply and servicing agencies, the co-ordination, becomes more difficult and complex. It is very problematic, to co-ordinate, sequence of activities, which have to be completed, in the required order, when more agencies are involved.

3. When several systems are involved, in a project the sequence of completing, the particular system, in the order of precedence, should be followed. While, systems get ready one after another, for future jobs, more attention has to be paid. Much work done till a pint of time in a project, will remain unproductive, for small jobs left unfinished, at later stages. Huge capital and manpower resources will become idle, because the completions of activities are the only criteria, in commissioning projects and making payments to the suppliers. If the plants operation gets delayed, the project authorities, will hold up making huge payments and are likely to revoke penalties, for losses suffered by them, by the plant, not giving the output, in time. This results in huge interest loss, on returns to share-holders and also to the suppliers, due to delays in getting, rewards for the work done.
4. The activities to be performed on a contract in particular, and the progress of all the activities, in general, in all the wings of an organization are illustrated, by readily available and easily understandable techniques, depicting the activities in the form of illustrations such as flow charts, graphs, blocks, pie-diagrams, bar charts and networks. These illustrations at a glance, clearly help the readers to know the activities, status of various parameters say time, quantity of work turned out, relative amounts spent, relative profits, and losses, resources used, comparison of the input, output details, the hold ups in the jobs, how relatively the activities have gone on over a period, how comparatively various wings of the organizations have performed in respect to their expectations, advantages drawbacks or hurdles in executing jobs. The above parameters are displayed and can be judged by the various yardsticks used to monitor jobs. The organizations will be able to know, how they are placed now, how they expect to perform in future comparative results. This monitoring helps several agencies concerned who participate in the various activities. The buyer and seller will know the situation prevailing and can either feel satisfied or put in more efforts to achieve

their objectives in specified areas by monitoring jobs progress from the beginning at small intervals corrective actions will be simple. On the other hand if things are left to themselves over a period, it may not be possible to undo the past and with left out time it may become practically impossible to achieve planned targets.

PIE DIAGRAMS

There are simple ways of depicting performance in relation to other factors. This is used in depicting the material consumption, how the outputs were in a particular periods of time, how an organization uses its capacity in future. These several parameters can be illustrated as a part of a segment of a circle the total performance. Here the diagram is very simple to draw and very easy for the concerned people to understand what is highlighted there. Full circle represents the size of each segment of the full circle gives the size of that activity in comparison to the total activity.

The examples given below are 3 pie diagrams. These three diagrams illustrate the following :

1. How the resources of the organizations were used in the year for various activities.
2. The condition of the plant at the end of the year giving details of material used in the plants and how they were?
3. The utility of a special automatic digital milling machine for making various products.

Diagram 1

PERFORMANCE YEAR 1998-99

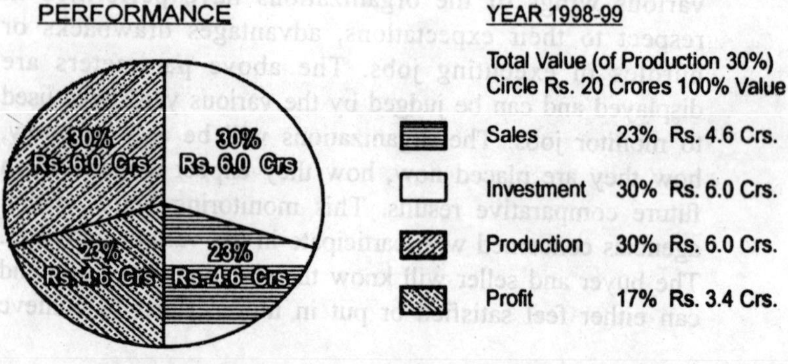

Diagram 2

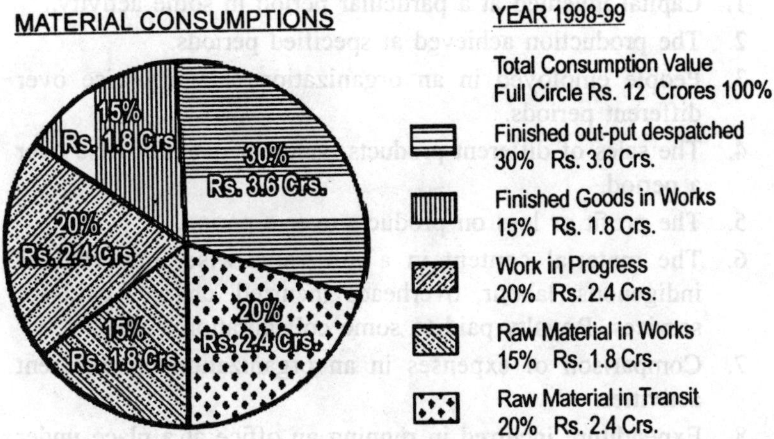

Diagram 3

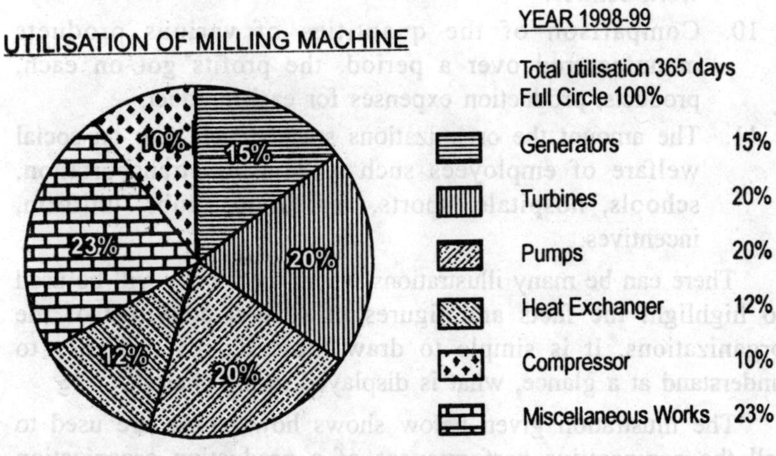

BLOCKS

These are simple isometric blocks, the height of the block indicates the value as per the co-ordinates which have been graduated from the figures used in the Y-axis. The blocks are prominently written with respect to X and Y-axis. The blocks indicate the relative values. These blocks are used for various purposes.

1. Capital invented at a particular period in some activity.
2. The production achieved at specified periods.
3. People employed in an organization category-wise over different periods.
4. The sales of different products, value or quantity-wise over a period.
5. The profit or loss on products over a period.
6. The material content in a job value-wise, imported or indigenous, labour, overheads incurred, charges paid for services. Royalty paid to some collaboration.
7. Comparison of expenses in an organization on different activities.
8. Expenditure incurred in running an office at a place under various heads.
9. The work center hours for doing a total job at various work centres.
10. Comparison of the quantities of various products manufactured over a period, the profits got on each, products, production expenses for each product.
11. The amount the organizations spends each year on social welfare of employees such as housing, transportation, schools, hospitals, sports, recreation, clubs, uniform, incentives.

There can be many illustrations where the blocks will be used to highlight the facts and figures of several activities of the organizations. It is simple to draw these blocks and easy to understand at a glance, what is displayed in the charts.

The illustration given below shows how blocks are used to tell the comparative performances of a production organization over 3 years for reference.

The chart (Fig. 3) shows the price elements of an automatic computerized, multipurpose, digital, lathe. Each cost element which goes into the price of the complete lathe is indicated element-wise by blocks which are drawn with prices indicated by proportional length of the block along the Y-axis and activity which makes up the price shown on the horizontal X-axis. As an example the

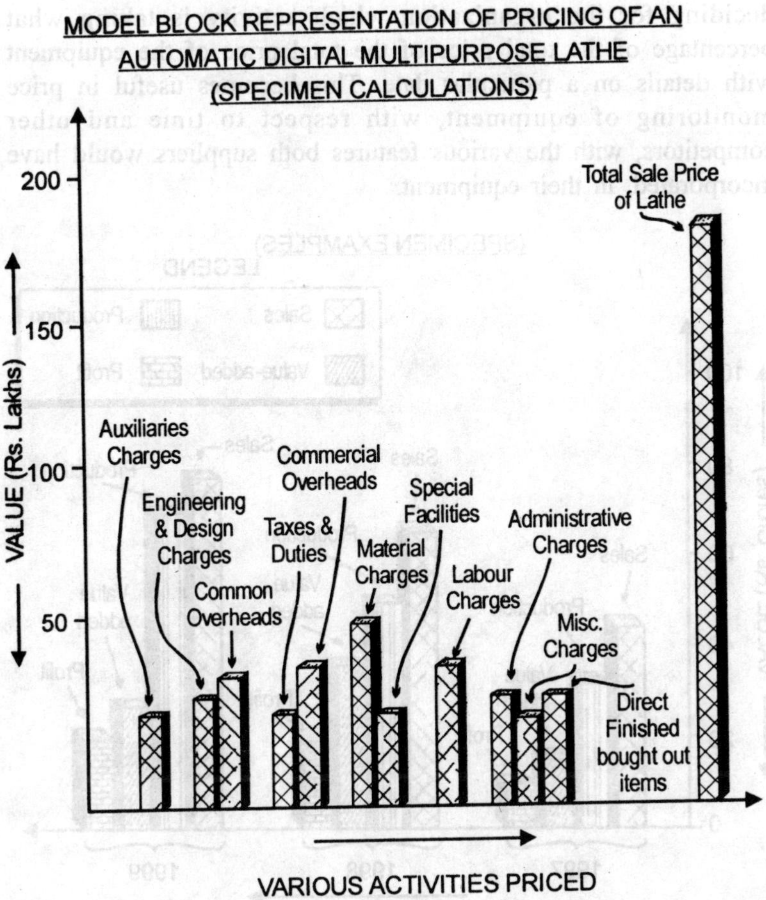

Fig. 3

changes for major groups for Engineering/Design departments, special facilities required for manufacturing the lathe, taxes and duties applicable. Charges for auxiliaries used in the equipment, commercial overhead charges, administrative overhead charges, miscellaneous charges, labour charges, material charge which include indigenous content as well as imported content, charges for items which are bought from outside sources and directly fitted on the equipment. Thus the use of blocks in illustrating the cost structure is shown for reference. If for some estimation at a later date a comparison is to be made this can be used. It helps in deciding for the organization which activity is taking what percentage of the total price of the total price of the equipment with details on a particular date. This becomes useful in price monitoring of equipment, with respect to time and other competitors, with the various features both suppliers would have incorporated, in their equipment.

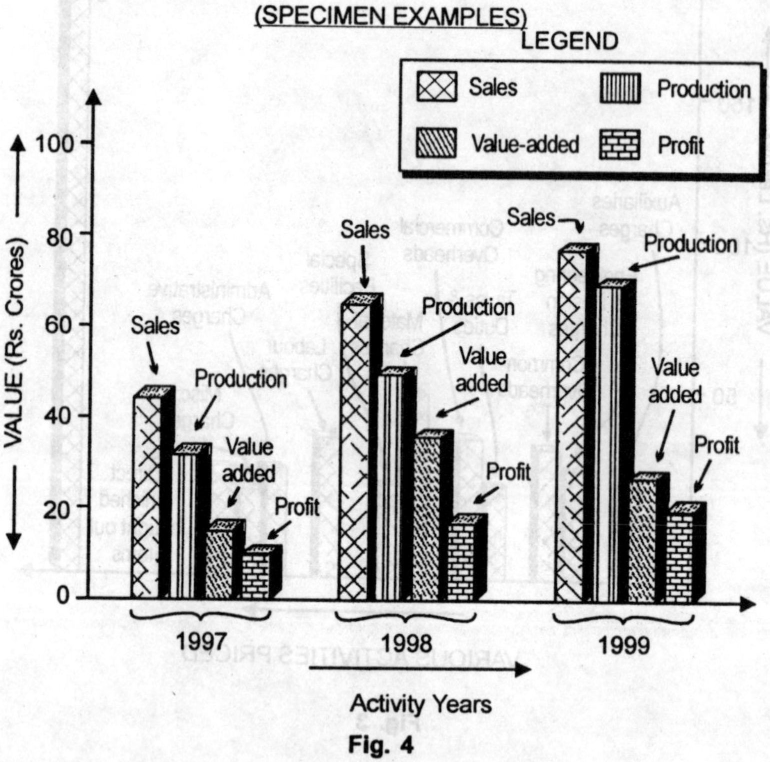

Fig. 4

BAR CHARTS

These are commonly used monitoring tools for all high value, multi-process, long delivery items. Here generally, many activities are done in the making of a product or projects.

Since it is very easy to represent even a very complicated project or systems or products on the bar chart, the bar charts are drawn in several cases. Examples are :

A project where many systems are involved, and each system will have many products in it which have to be procured, transported, unloaded, stored, assembled, tested, commissioned and then operated as trial and for commercial use. All projects irrespective of whether they are civil, electrical, transport, space, mining, information, and technology, for that matter all projects can be fitted into this bar chart representation of activity. These are used by manufacturers, consultants, financiers, inspecting agencies, users, management's of projects, site offices etc. specific timings of events, processes can be put on the charts to enable every kind of agency to know how their activity is going on, where they come into picture and who are others who are involved and whose work is going on, at which point of time which activity has got delayed, which activity is moving fast, which activity has stopped, etc. Every kind of correction, preparations, organizing facilities, finances manpower can be done by close monitoring of jobs by these charts.

Bar charts tell the sellers how they are placed in the project, where they have to exert more, where they are comfortably placed, where they have gained time, where they have to accelerate their activities, which system will become critical etc. They can plan their resources and men to suit the commitments.

Users can organize funds as to how activities are going on, they have to pull up agencies who are slow, which may cost them dearly at a later stage. They can prepone or postpone deployment of staff, allotting priorities, organize the inputs as the jobs go on in comparison to original schedules when project or products were conceived or ordered.

Consultants can keep watch on progress; see how their plans are keeping pace with time and how they have to gear up their clients, cautioning them in advance where necessary. Inspection agencies can plan the inspection as the jobs progress.

Fund deployment by management of project and also supplier can be properly taken care of.

Figure 5 is a bar chart where several products are ordered on a supplier and how the activities on each product is planned by supplier.

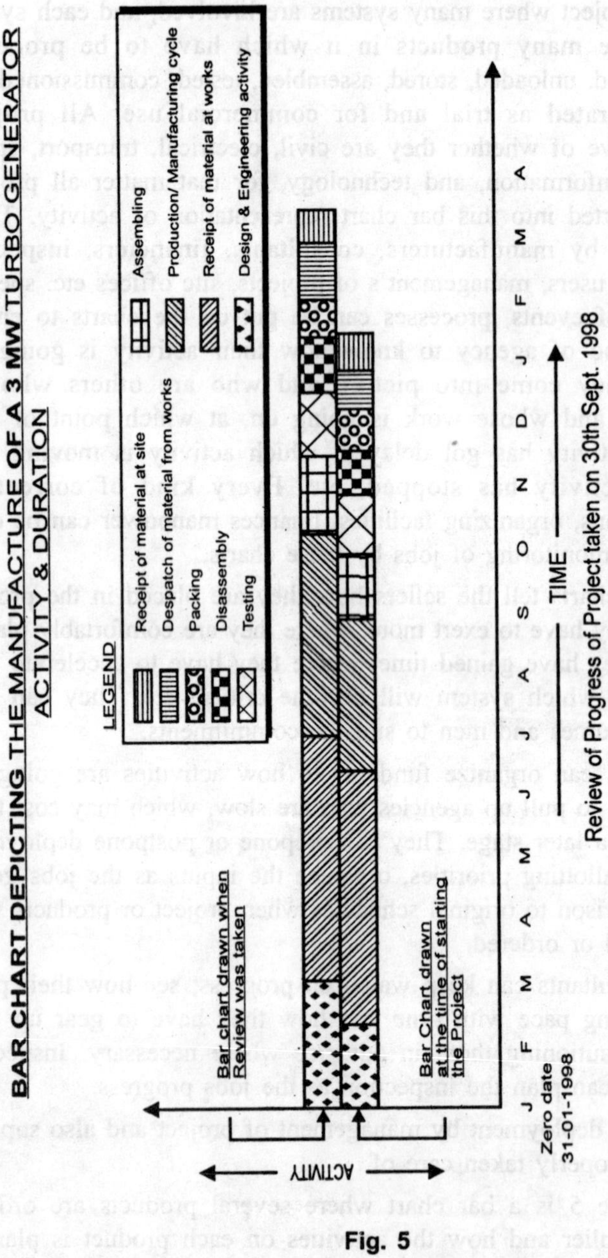
BAR CHART DEPICTING THE MANUFACTURE OF A 3 MW TURBO GENERATOR
ACTIVITY & DURATION
LEGEND
Receipt of material at site
Despatch of material from works
Packing
Disassembly
Testing
Assembling
Production/ Manufacturing cycle
Receipt of material at works
Design & Engineering activity
Bar chart drawn when Review was taken
Bar Chart drawn at the time of starting the Project
ACTIVITY
Zero date 31-01-1998
J F M A M J J A S O N D J F M A
TIME
Review of Progress of Project taken on 30th Sept. 1998

Fig. 5

BAR CHART DEPICTING VARIOUS ACTIVITIES
SUPPLY, ERECTION, COMMISSIONING AND COMMERCIAL OPERATION
OF A TURBO GENERATOR STATION

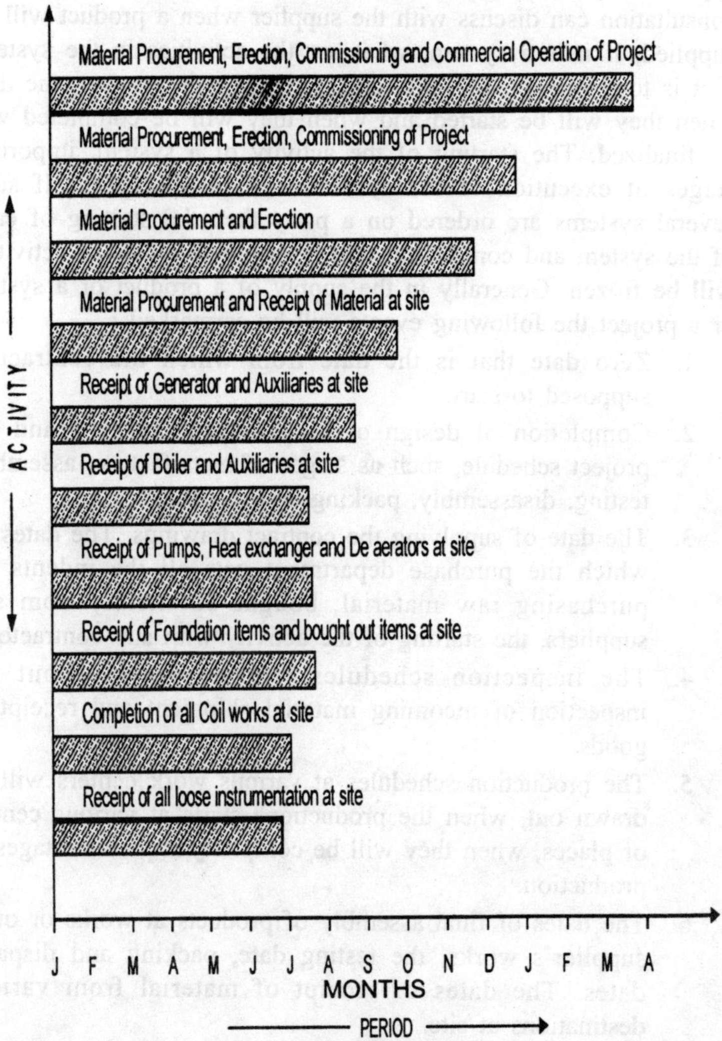

(ACTIVITIES VS. PERIOD)

Fig. 6

When a contract is finalized by a buyer with a supplier, in addition to important terms, like price, delivery, terms of payment, mode is inspection etc. If there is a consultant for the project, appointed by the purchaser to purchase, his consultant, by mutual consultation can discuss with the supplier when a product will be supplied, if it is a system, what are the activities in the system, if it is total project, the different systems in the project, the date when they will be started and when they will be completed will be finalized. The starting of the activity of a system, important stages of execution of the system, will be discussed. If such several systems are ordered on a party then the starting of each of the system and completion will be decided. Dates of activities will be frozen. Generally in the supply of a product or a system or a project the following events will be earmarked :

1. Zero date that is the date from which the contract is supposed to start.
2. Completion of design of the products, systems and the project schedule, such as stages of manufacture, assembly, testing, disassembly, packing and dispatch.
3. The date of supplying the contract drawings. The dates by which the purchase department gets all the indents for purchasing raw material, bought out items, from sub suppliers, the starting of the activity with sub contractors.
4. The inspection schedules will be drawn about the inspection of incoming material shipment and receipt of goods.
5. The production schedules at various work centers will be drawn out, when the productions starts at various centers or places, when they will be complete, important stages of production.
6. The dates of final assembly of products at works or other supplier's works, the testing date, packing and dispatch dates. The dates of receipt of material from various destinations at site.
7. Site activities, if it is a turnkey job, starting of civil works, completion of civil works. Fixing foundation at site, completing the assembly activity of various systems as site.

8. Testing, trial operation of each system and related products. Trial testing of overall plant.
9. Pre-commissioning test of the plant, commissioning of the plants. The dates of various activities will be frozen from start to finish.

Project schedule with details of system schedule product schedules will be prepared and frozen, new bar chart of each activity at works, as well as a site will be drawn. After the activities start, the buyer or his consultant goes on monitoring the events in each bar chart. If things are going as per the preliminary bar chart, then each event complied will be noted. If there are changes in the completion of events, either preponement or postponement, revised bar charts will be prepared as on the date of review. This review goes on till the jobs as per contract are completed. Preparing revised bar charts with new dates happens if events change from planned schedule.

Thus the bar charts help in telling at a glance, what was the date when an activity was planned to start and date when it was supposed to be completed. How things have been going on as per this schedule, what is the area where delays have happened? Simultaneously review of balance activities will be done. In the discussions with concerned agencies reviews will be taking place often. This helps in knowing the progress of jobs. Suppliers have certain terms of payments in the contract they watch the events before relating, the payments connected with time. The supplier will be interested to see the schedules are kept up so that he gets money for the work done otherwise it will pose severe strain on the resources of the organization.

Each event will have other repercussions, the agencies have to gear up to receive the material, provide services and see step-by-step event is completed.

In case of supply of major projects, the major events of the manufacture of the products will be identified. For each major product, the duration of the activity the starting and ending dates will be known. Which event comes first which event comes later will also be identified. In this way all processes will be identified with starting and ending dates. With the knowing of the duration of each process the commencement of the activity from the zero date to the total despatch of the product to site or even its receipt at site can be linked in the form of a big bar, the dates of event will be shown on the X-axis and Y-axis tells the major activity. When the visual bar chart is drawn as time progress review of the various activities will be taken by supplier/buyer and their agents. Actual events as they occur will be written over the original bar chart the events completed up to the date of review will be drawn, the time planned for completing other events as they occur will be written over the original bar chart the events completed up to the date of review will be drawn, the time planned for completing other events will be drawn as extension to that chart. The total chart tells the date when relevant events take place, when final dispatch of product takes place. Then and there by comparing the original bar chart with the chart, which gives the activity dates as the events have progressed, tell how the scheduled dates are adhered to. How, in case of delays each event is getting postponed which gives the cumulative effect of extra time needed for that product by drawing bar charts for each product or system at a particular review date the occurrence of events, shifting of schedules will be known. This helps in pooling up the activities to be done to revised dates at supplier end and customers end.

Bar charts are very useful in this way for monitoring the activities connecting the manufacture of products and execution of projects their related activities such as deploying funds, deploying man power, deploying facilities, deploying agencies who do the various jobs in the chain of events taking actual position of the jobs going on.

But charts are not only used for reviewing production of products and related activities in the execution of projects, they are also used for illustrating fund position, material position, resources position. Loading of work centers, deployment of staff, return on investments, and comparative performance of similar jobs over a period for evaluation, these charts help how to speed up jobs with past experience. How to conserve resources, make more profits, higher productivity reducing rework, rejections, repair, avoiding failures, reducing customer complaints, plan events, obtain better results with given resources. It also helps in strengthening, weaker areas, and use excess manpower at a work place *i.e.* other deficit areas.

It helps to foresee the profits, losses, analyze interest payments, wastages, idle machine hours, reduce the outflow of capital, avoid accumulation of inventory, work in progress, these are indicative, informative tools to get right signals before activities are going out of control of executing authorities.

NETWORKS

Networks are ideal representation of events for big projects, Projects where huge money is involved, huge resources of material, manpower, machinery, plant and multiple executing agencies are involved. Generally the period of completion of major jobs in projects is more because of the enormous quantum of work involved, obviously money, resources manpower and other facilities required for executing the projects will be more.

To have a control over multiple activities, which take place at different places by different agencies, it is necessary to have a plan from major activity level to macro activity level. These are done by networks.

When a project is to be undertaken, the agency, who are going to own the project make an analysis of the following :

1. Location of the project
2. The output expected from project
3. The consultants who do the planning and execution
4. The input material sources
5. Technical and other manpower requirements
6. The major systems in the project
7. The major and small equipment
8. The probable suppliers of equipment, systems or project executing authorities.
9. Source of funds
10. Likely date of starting the project
11. Project completion date

Monitoring the project form concept to commissions ensuring the procurement of right products and material and executing the various job sequences in right time and optimum use of time and money.

- After the first stage, when the execution of project comes, when the executing agencies are decided to the major and small contractors a network of major activities of the project is made. The activities are identified with respect to time generally weeks or days.
- The first network of the entire project in its full shape is called L_1 network. This network tells what other sub major activities are involved in the project and how their timings are synchronized. From this the project authorities know the starting date of the project, when contracts are given to various contractors, after their terms are settled, the starting date of project, the zero date is decided.
- From zero date, as reference the L_1 network is drawn it shows the dates and events of all major activities from start to finish. This network is drawn with the help of consultants, representatives of major suppliers/contractors. All major contractors, the project authorities will have this network.

Next the sub major activities of the project will be drawn. The next set of major activities to the main project represented by L_1 network is L_2 network. An L_1 network will have several L_2 networks originating from the zero date as reference and with individual completion dates. Each L_2 network gives elaborately all the activities in that system whatever activities are done in the system and by whom will be shown.

The dates of major events in each L_2 network will be drawn with dates of starting the events completing the events duration of events and title of events. The several L_2 networks put together all are synchronized in L_1 network. The suppliers in each L_2 network know which is in their scope of work right from supply to dispatch, erection, commissioning. The customer keeps all these networks. These networks will be available with consultants and those who monitor the jobs.

Now in a L_2 network, jobs of different duration with the details of jobs will be pooled up. The supplier of L_2 system will make further split of activities for convenience in knowing other jobs to macro level. These L_2 networks are split into smaller networks. The smaller networks are called L_3 networks.

L_3 networks tell days to work in that set of activity; several such set of L_3 networks make an L_2 activity. In L_3 the date of start and date of completion of activity will be drawn in weeks or days. This helps the executing authority to ensure the activities of L_3 network are done as indicated in the L_3 network, whatever facilities, material, men, machinery, plant, will all be geared up and the processes shown in L_3 network will be monitored by the supplier or contractor who has taken the job.

These networks give all the details of projects, the activities from major to macro level. It is for the agencies involved to see to it that all the activities go on as shown in the network.

With the passage of time, the activities with respect to time will be monitored depending on whether the jobs are going on as per the network or getting delayed in some areas and getting completed in advance in some other areas, help in making amendments to the networks periodically, whenever services are taken by the concerned authorities. Depending on changes in L_3, L_2 gets modified, depending on how each system in L_2 is going on overall L_1 will get amendments. These amendments are done only when major shifts take place in activities and not otherwise on daily basis.

This is the best tool for execution of products because of the multiple agencies involved and multiple activities take place at multiple locations. The networks help in not only knowing how activities are progressing, it also helps in planning properly for execution, by taking appropriate actions at different levels and stages by concerned authorities.

L_1 NETWORK GIVING PROPOSED COMMISSIONING OF 25 MW TG SET FROM DATE OF CONCEPTION

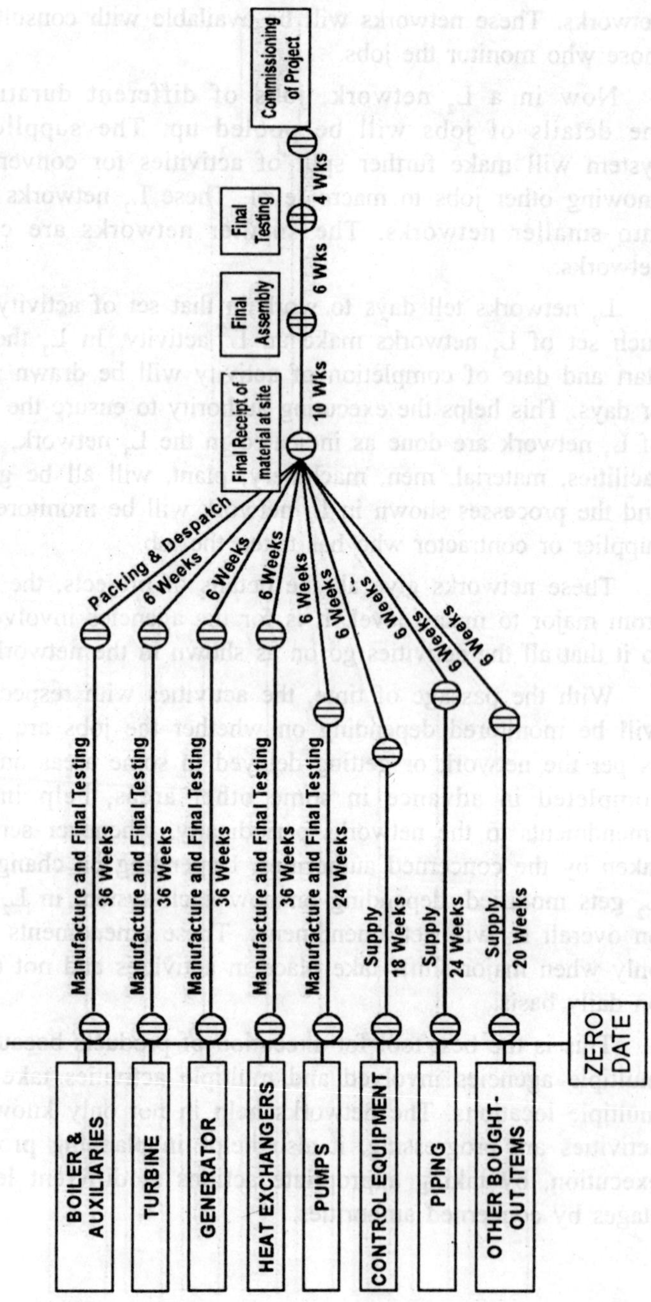

L_2 NETWORK GIVING MANUFACTURE OF GENERATORS

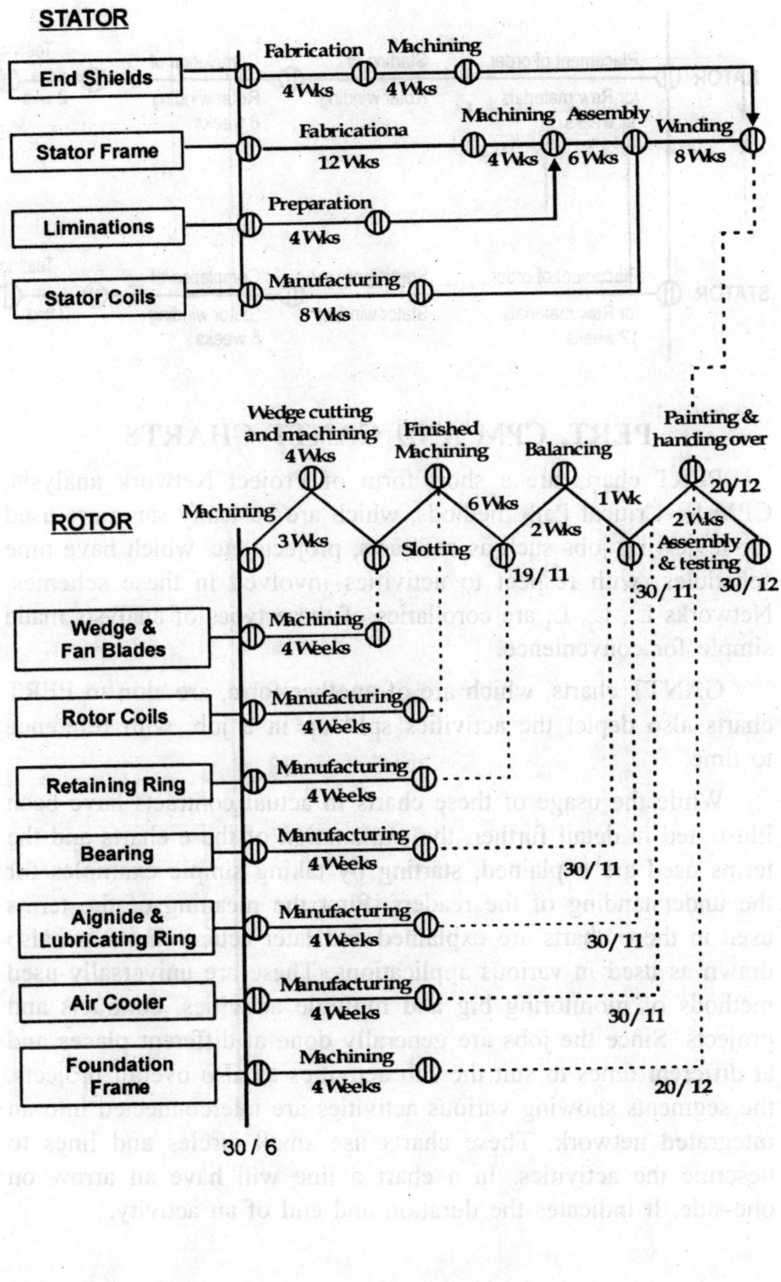

L_3 Net Work Rotor & Stator Winding of Generator

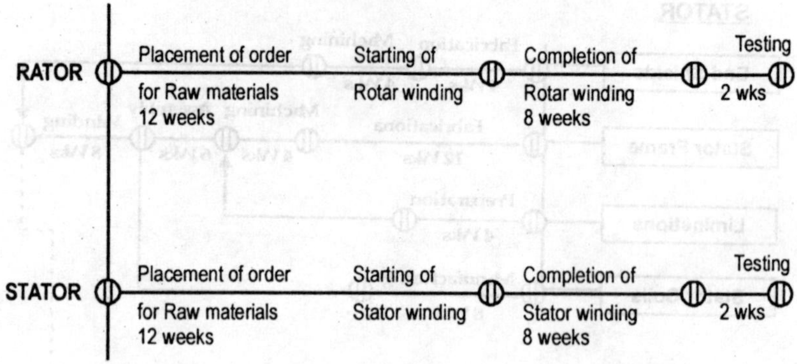

PERT, CPM AND GANTT CHARTS

PERT charts are a short form of Project Network analysis, CPM — Critical Path methods, which are basically same are used for reviewing jobs such as contracts, projects etc. which have time schedules, with respect to activities involved in these schemes. Networks L_1, L_2, L_3 are corollaries of these types of analysis made simple for convenience.

GANTT charts, which are of another form, are akin to PERT charts also depict the activities split up in a job, with reference to time.

While the usage of these charts in actual contracts have been illustrated in detail further, the explanation of these charts and the terms used are explained, starting by taking simple examples for the understanding of the readers. First the meaning of the terms used in these charts are explained and later actual charts are also drawn as used in various applications. These are universally used methods of monitoring big and multiple activities, contracts and projects. Since the jobs are generally done at different places and at different times to suit the sub activities as also overall projects, the segments showing various activities are interconnected into an integrated network. These charts use small circles and lines to describe the activities. In a chart a line will have an arrow on one-side. It indicates the duration and end of an activity.

Float

It is the difference between time available for an activity and time actually used. The difference is otherwise cushion time for completing the activity.

Total float : It is latest finish time for an activity, minus the earliest start time for it, minus its duration.

Critical activity : have zero floats. It indicates tight time duration without any cushion built in it. Any delay, spills over the activity time.

Free float : Earliest start time of following events, minus the earliest start time of proceeding events, minus the activity duration.

Critical path : It is the longest duration path. Chain of critical activities that cannot be started till the finishing of an event. Any delay in an activity/sub-activity delays the project.

The task is what is to be achieved. It has a definite starting time and a definite ending time. In the early stages Gantt chart, which is more or less same was most popular. From this as an extension networks came up which is a refined bar chart. In this network arrow shows the direction in which activity goes on. The tail is the starting point and tip of the arrow is the ending point. Circle is a task completed or to be completed. The total arrow also tells the duration in time may be hours, days, weeks etc. One thing to be kept in mind in this network is the succeeding activity starts after proceeding activity is completed. Some times several sub-activities will be there in a network and a bunch of sub-activities need to be completed before starting next activity. There is a critical path in the system. This is the maximum duration that is supposed to be allowed for completing the chain of activities, may be done before stipulated time but till all the connected sub-activities are completed next main activity will not be able to start. Dummy activities are some times shown in the network, the path of dummy activity is shown dotted. This activity is given zero duration. This dummy activity is shown to satisfy logic in the various activities of the network. One thing about the critical path is the authorities executing the project are responsible for the project as owner or contractors take care to see the timing of the path in the critical path is not slipping. They are satisfied as long as the events shown in the critical path are going on as per schedule without panicking. If events are going on as per the critical path that means project is going on as per schedule. The shortest time taken for sub-activity or total project, whenever it is evaluated is the longest duration path in the network from start to finish. There is no time left for delay in this path. No slack time is left in this path and any delay will delay in completing this activity will delay the project. Slack time is also called float. If slack time is available, it means float is a available. In other words difference between earliest and latest start time is float. There is no slack or float in critical path.

LONG DELIVERY PRODUCTS AND PROJECTS

In case of very long delivery products and total projects the activity curve with respect to duration takes the above shape. Initially, when product is ordered or project is conceived the activities will be less. Say upto 10% of the time. This time is consumed in conceiving the project, preparing the working plan of the project, ordering and procurement of material for the

LONG DELIVERY PRODUCTS AND PROJECTS

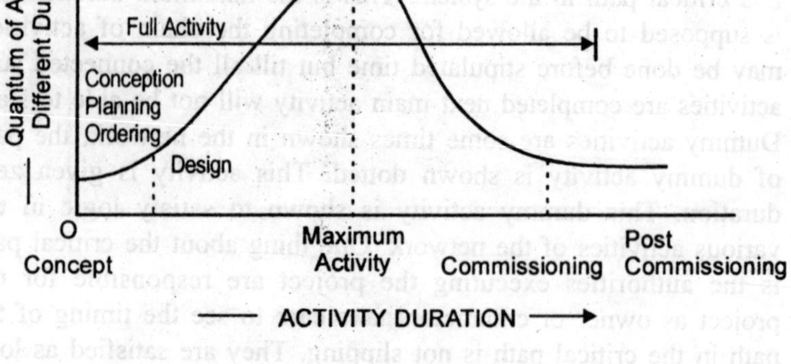

product, or projects. After this the quantum of work picks up with a peak time when different activities will be at their peak. After this the completion of individual jobs, commissioning after trial run takes place. At say 95% of the total duration of the product supply time or project execution time, all the activities except post commercial organization jobs will be completed. In the last 5% time, the operational checks after commercial operation is over and plant give full output and will be in continuous operation. Plant giving operation, successfully its operation is declared as completed in all respects.

Delay in an activity/sub-activity delays the project.

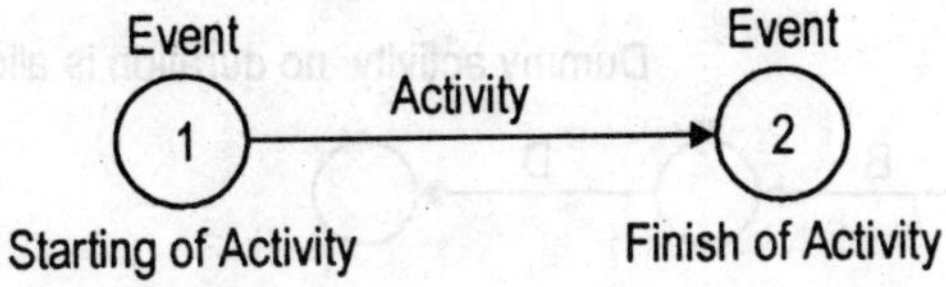

It happens in a sequence :

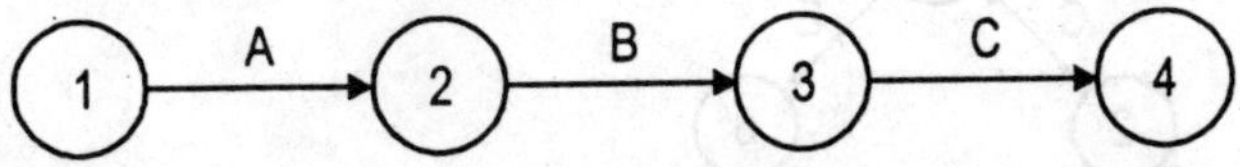

In this case the next activity is linked to previous activity, unless, the previous activity is completed, succeeding activity cannot be started. The activities are interlinked.

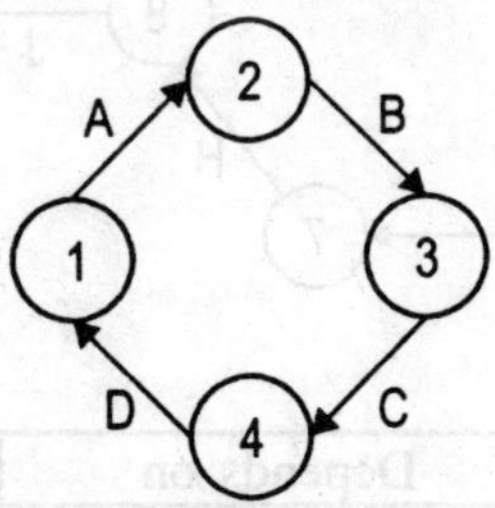

Parallel path for same activity. Here B cannot start till A is completed. C cannot start till B is completed. D is interlinked to the completion of A, B and C.

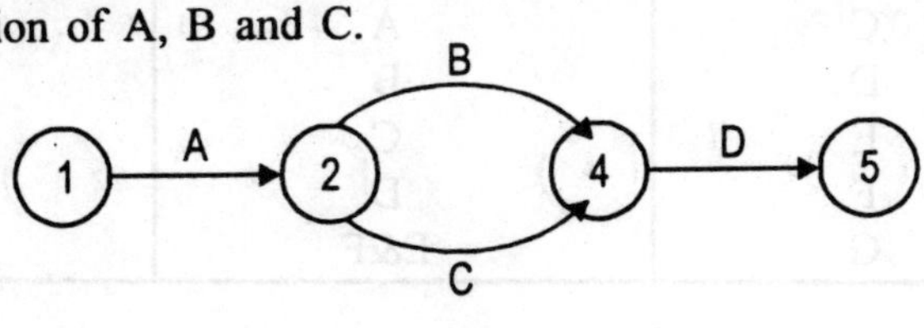

This is a case where there is a float. Activity 4 is linked to 2 which has linked B and C.

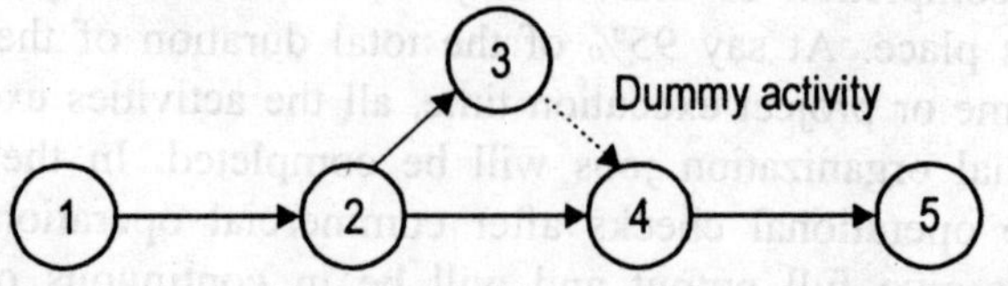

No duration is allotted for the activity shown in the dotted line between 3 and 4 activities.

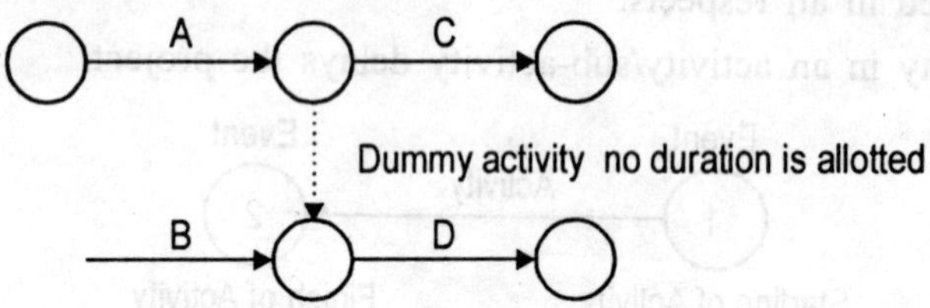

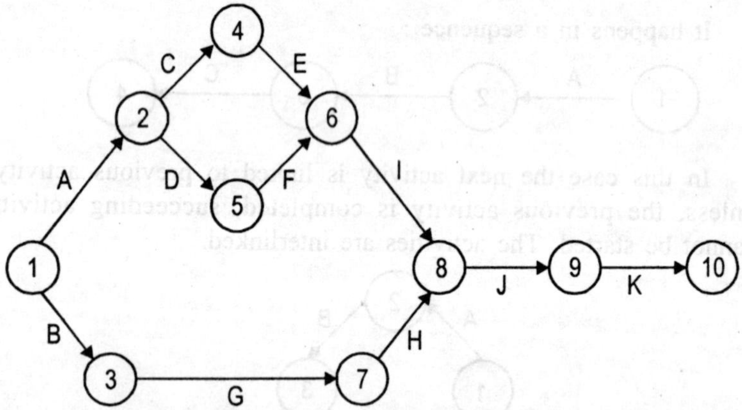

Data for timing

Activity	Depends on	Duration
A		3
B	—	2
C	A	4
D	B	3
E	C	2
F	D	1
G	E&F	3

As an example by following ways 6 activities can be involved in a system which can be represented in the following ways :

1. 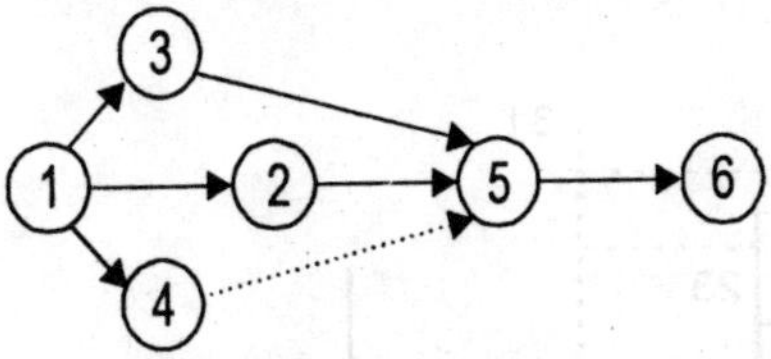

2. 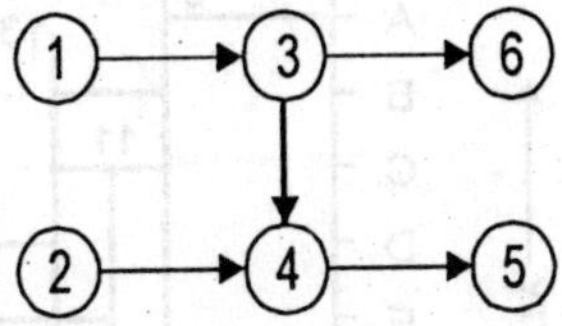

3. 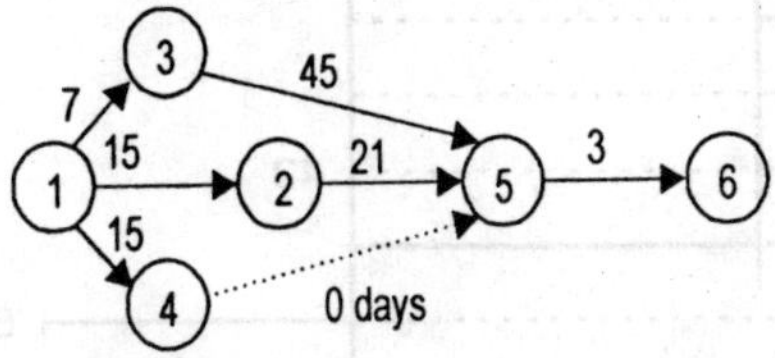

In this 3rd example Time in days is also shown.

Gantt Chart

Activities Plotted against time

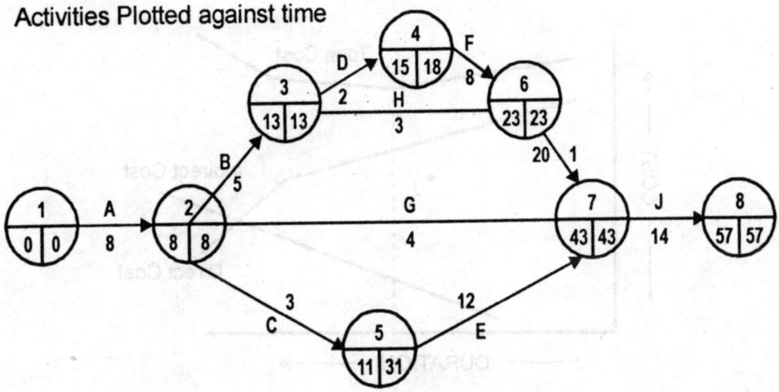

Machine Installation Example

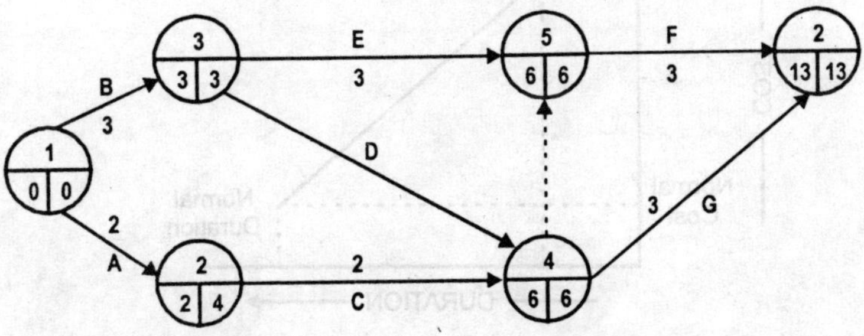

Example involving Dummy Activity

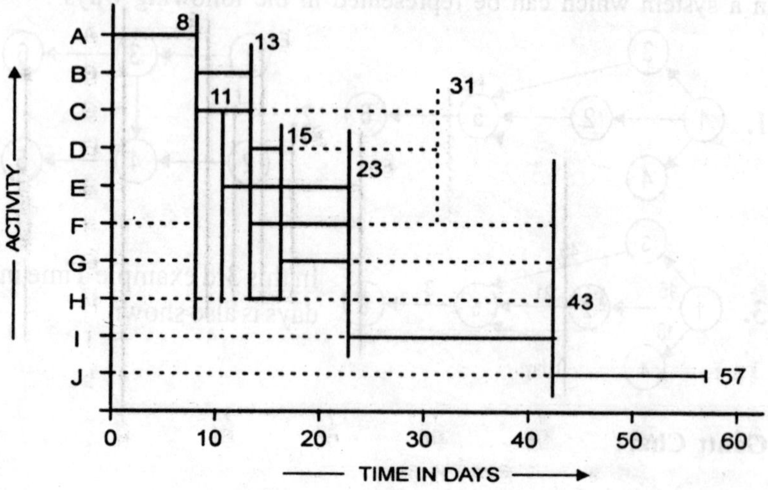

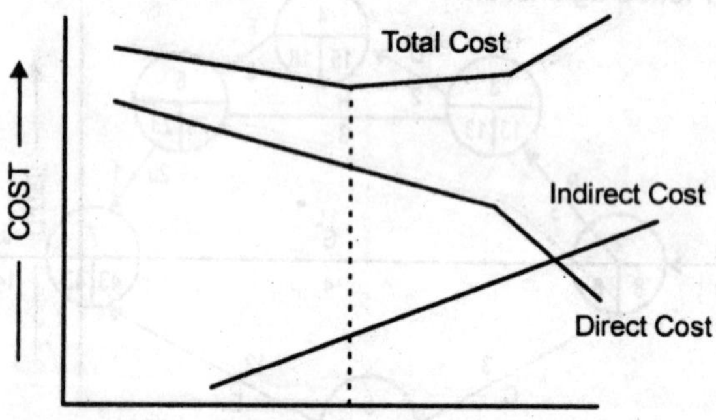

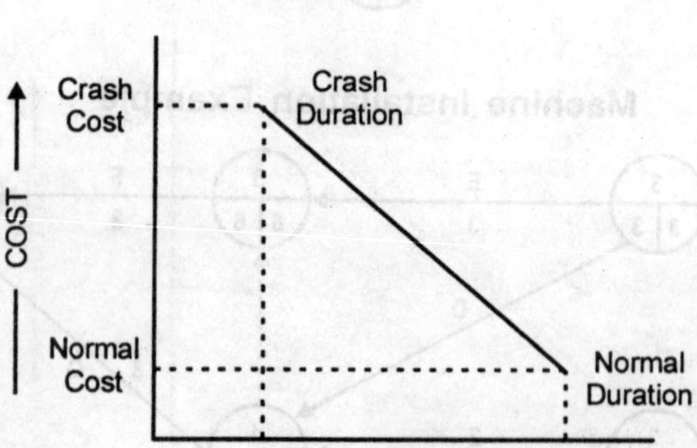

Costing Example

Activity	Normal Duration	Normal cost	Days that could be sowed	Cost of saving 1 day
A	2	180	1	100
B	4	300	1	150
C	3	300	0	—
D	6	600	2	120
E	2	400	0	—
F	4	900	1	250
G	2	200	0	—

Example giving data for timing

Activity	Duration	Earliest short time	Latest float time	Latest short-time	Latest finish time
A	3	0	3	0	3
B	2	0	2	3	5
C	4	3	7	3	7
D	3	2	5	5	8
E	2	2	9	7	9
F	1	5	6	8	9
G	3	9	12	9	12

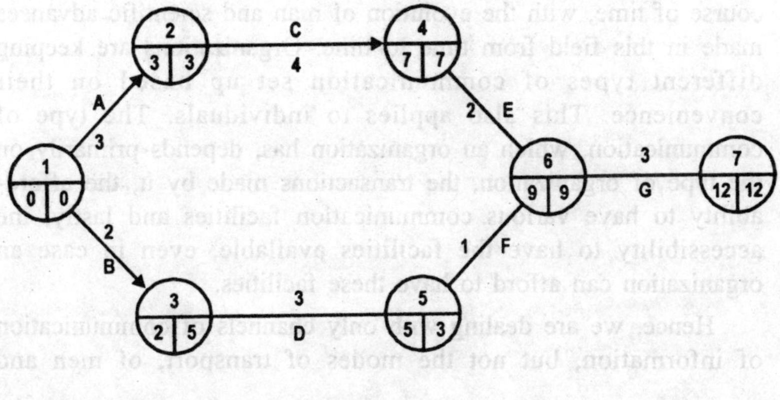

17

Communication and Customer Service

COMMUNICATION

Communication is the lifeline of an organization. It is more so, with commercial organizations. For, the organizations to be alive and kicking all available channels of communication have to be kept open. No organization can show its mobility, or keep working at its optimum levels, if communication channels are not active. People in the organization have to communicate, on all organizational activities, with its own people, and with people and the agencies inside and outside its premises, in their areas of working and activity or activities the organizations undertakes :

There are many ways of communication open to an organization which the organization avails depending on its economic resources and proximity to the type of communication channel available in the surrounding area, some are continuing from good old days effectively, and some have got added, in course of time, with the evolution of man and scientific advances made in this field from time to time. Organizations are keeping different types of communication set up based on their convenience. This also applies to individuals. The type of communication, which an organization has, depends primarily on the type of organization, the transactions made by it, the affordability to have various communication facilities and lastly, the accessibility to have the facilities available, even in case an organization can afford to have these facilities.

Hence, we are dealing with only channels of communication of information, but not the modes of transport, of men and material, to and from the organization, to outside places. The various communication facilities used by the organizations, with their advantages and disadvantages are discussed below :

Sl. No.	Mode of communication	Where used	Advantages/Disadvantages
1.	Person to person conversation across the table	In all spheres, of activities, within the same organization and outside.	Best and most authentic way of communication. This has all the advantages in that there are no chances of missing any issue to be discussed. Unless it is not intended. However, only the participating persons know what transaction was done. For purpose of legal authenticity, the discussions have to be followed in writing by way of minutes or confirmatory letters.
2.	Telephones	Person to person within the organization or outside the organization, this all takes place through telephonic lines, communications satellites and micro antenna.	It is the most commonly used mode of communication. In effect, next to only to person to person conversation across the table. In fact it is two way. The subjects can be put across on on either side for effective information evaluations, decision, etc. However, it has the disadvantage it makes persons talking to tell their opinions, views or decisions then and there. This helps in knowing things directly but the decisions, or views, pros and cons cannot be decided then and there. Many points are likely to be missed as there is no time available to fully evaluate the questions that transpires commit any thing easily on issue, proof of what has actually transpired in the conversation will not be available, except based on the credibility of persons who do the conversation. Hence this talk has to be followed up in writing by the concerned parties to give proof on record or for legal authority.
3.	Letters/dummy official letters	These are most authentic and are legally and logically	It is most commonly used and highest transacted mode of communication. However, the time, the party

Sl. No.	Mode of communication	Where used	Advantages/Disadvantages
		accountable. However, it is limited to what is put in black and white and goes by common interpretation of the people concerned in common parlance of understandability. The matters are exchanged mostly with the help of postal department and in some rare cases through representatives of the organizations concerned.	at the receiving end takes to get the contents of the letters depends on the availability of fatest communication service, which can deliver letters. It is logical and legally authentic in common course of correspondence. However, the authority writing the letter carries the weight it can command in the organization to which it is addressed. This is the best mode of conveying whatever is wanted and the way it is wanted to be conveyed and the impact, it is supposed to have at the receiving end. All transactions in commerce, governmental agencies private dealings are all done in this mode whether for condensed or bigger communications. Cheaper and contents will be available to all concerned parties physically.
4.	Record note of discussions/ Minutes of the meetings	This is gist of communication to be carried between concerned parties. It is the best way of pin-pointing issues addressed in the record exchanged. The communication is mostly with the help of postal department sometimes the representatives of organization physically carry them.	This has all the impact and authority between the discussing parties, who have transacted. Time of reaching of the notes to the concerned parties is dependent on what mode of conveyance is used to deliver the documents. This is one of the best authentic records for taking action at the desired places. It has full legal and logical impact, depending on the authorities that have participated in the discussions to those levels in the organization which have delegated authorities to make these discussions.
5.	Inter office memorandum/ circulars	These are normal ways of communications, Authentic	Used where it is practicable. Not fast way of communication but legally and logically authentic. Assuring receipt of correspondence at the required place is necessary. Matters put in these will be clear as to what can be seen physically.

Sl. No.	Mode of communication	Where used	Advantages/Disadvantages
6.	Audio, Visual aids	This is the best illustrative way of communicating between concerned agencies, effectively, next to personal discussions. Most educative and simple to understand, the message put in there. By the physical help of the representatives of the communicating organizations for whom this is done.	It has all the impact of letters or documents exchanged. Sometimes more demonstrative of what is to be conveyed. The time being put to use and amounts spent on these documents depends on time taken to get it delivered to the concerned agency to whom it is intended. It however has to be personnel after they are certified by persons involved in the transaction. It serves as logical and legal record. Also more demonstrative than other communications. But the authenticity of the parties credentials are best judged by the party being addressed. It is a costly communication technique.
7.	Computers, floppies, internet, e-mail	Latest and best mode of visually conveying the contents to the addressed party. It has with it the authenticity of the physical vision on computer. It is done through a telephone line and electronic media such as satellites as are to the made available to the parties by the Government.	It is one of the best and fastest type of communication irrespective of distance involved. It needs similar facilities at the end to whom it is addressed. This is a fast way of communication. It is a costly communication technique. It is legal and logical. Because of cost, available of facilities at the required place, discretion has to be exercised by people using these mode of communications.
8.	E-mail/ internet	Best and fast way of communications, however limited to the message contents conveyed therein.	It is fast communication and can be communicated very elaborately. Costly but fast and authentic. It has utility, only at places, where it is feasible at the sending and receiving end. For legal purposes it has also to be followed up by the documents and communicating authority certifying the contents sent.

Sl. No.	Mode of communication	Where used	Advantages/Disadvantages
9.	Fax	Fast and best way of communication limited to the contents put in the paper. It is done on a telegraphic line. As telephone communication using original paper which gets copied.	In all occasions, where important messages have to reach the concerned parties. This is good. It is a costly mode of communications. Where communication details run into more than one or two pages. Authentic can be used where facilities are available both with sender and receiving agency. Legally authentic as original message comes in postal system with confirmation copy.
10.	Tele printer and telex messages	Fast reasonably costly, but the contents are specific and to the point. The sending and receiving parties become partners in talking importance to the extent, the message is conveyed.	It is used where communication has to go fast, but what is to be communicated is to the point. The equipment facilities should be available at both ends for sending and receiving the messages. These messages also should be followed by certified originals of the connected authorities. Full information and details by post or other modes of communications or in person helps in having a record.

Clearly communication is very vital. It is necessary; authenticity of communication has to be maintained. If there is any action taken without the concerned authorities agreeing for those activities, series of repercussions will occur, which will have far-reaching consequences. The issues at stake may not be only money, precious time, delay in supplies, manufacture, erection, commissioning of the equipment or projects, may get affected if these are involved. The money spent and time and resources used, will never be able to get compensated as originally planned. If there is serious miscommunication since many problems arise responsibility will be very delicate when transactions are made. They become problematic, no authority would like to own wrong outcome, losses, failures, lessening of results desired, unanticipated lowering of output and remuneration's. These also may lead to misunderstandings. Authorities will feel very uneasy to get involved in unpleasant bickerings that might crop up due to miscommunication. Chances of wrong jobs being done, wrong priorities getting allotted, unscheduled completions and critical areas or critical activities not getting completed create losses and problems to organizations and authorities concerned with these transactions.

Care in communication has to be taken in the following areas to avoid losses, complications and attendant, misunderstandings. Such issues are :

(1) How to communicate? It is necessary the mode of communication, is selected properly for timely communication chances of communication getting lost, distorted or delayed, origin, the people to whom it is not intended. Ensuring that communication goes correctly to the right parties at right time is necessary.

(2) When to communicate? The timing of conveying a communication is important. If it is too early, there are chances of people forgetting the contents to act as was needed. If the communication is sent late or reaches late or does not go to the concerned agency, to whom it would have been addressed at a particular period, the consequences may become bad. Some time certain things are likely to be missed. It may not be possible to repeat that activity at all at a later state. As an example if an equipment is supposed to have certain auxiliaries which give certain facilities, if communication to provide these facilities does not reach the concerned agency, before the activity state has passed, that facility or provision may not be available in the product and the project may miss that facility, once and for all, as it may not be possible to provide that feature will all efforts to incorporate them.

(3) In every organization, either with supplier or user, a hierarchy exists certain powers will be vested with certain persons in the hierarchy, depending on the position, he or she occupies. So it is necessary, the issues are referred to the correct authorities to get correct response. If it also necessary, simultaneously various other agencies see a particular communication in certain situations. Even though this might involve additional work. If some agency

is left out inadvertently, what is expected of that agency, that contribution will not come, because that agency being in the dark will not get involved in the activity at the proper time.

(4) In commercial organizations, other than minor and very routine transactions, instructions are necessary, in writing, as records have to be maintained, since transactions go on for long periods, ranging from some weeks or months to more than a year or two. Some times to check the past activities, records are necessary. In organization people change and when a particular issue crops up, if concerned people are not correctly aware how things should have happened, it is not possible for concerned agencies to justify how a particular thing has been done and its consequences. Even when oral communications are exchanged by person to person discussing, telephone talk or meetings, it is better formal written records follow for guidance and correct interpretation.

(5) There are possibilities in critical situations, when some big amounts are involved or responsibilities are to be fixed things might deliberately get distorted by the affected agency to avoid facing possible vindication. Letters, dummy/official letters, legal written signed documents, by authorized representatives telexes, followed by signed copies of transmitted information, confirmation copies of telephone or telegraphic matters, minutes of meeting, record note on discussions, are always correct and undisputed modes of communication.

(6) For urgency telephonic conversation. E-mail, computer or internet communication, will help in taking action required or get to know of things. These need to be followed by appropriate signed copies from authorized persons on both sides to avoid any party backing out. In reputed organizations of sellers or buyers such instances are very rare and in most situations the information by responsible authorities will always be honoured. Inter office memorandums are authentic documents, however signed circulars will also receive authenticity. In cases of confidentiality care is taken to see that letters and documents are exchanged with full care. The appropriate authorities also preserve important discussions with authority attached to it.

(7) It is thus clear communication is a very vital sector in commercial transactions. All documents need care and proper approval by correct authorities particularly whe.. big transactions of far-reaching consequence are made.

CUSTOMER SERVICE

One of the areas, of vital nature, for a supplier is customer's service. In essence customers service means, coming to the rescue of the customer, in various times of need. Wherever a customer is using a particular brand of goods, supplied directly from works or from an authorized dealer or distributor, who is supposed to be at close proximity to the customer, either geographically or by easy communications. Next comes, the producer, who makes the goods, his agencies, and the original designer, consultant or collaborator, of product manufactured. They are also supposed to help the user contractually.

Generally, the service expected from a seller of a product or producer of the product, is to advise the user, timely and properly, in keeping the product give the performance, expected of it, without trouble as agreed in the contract.

There are two categories of suppliers or sellers of goods.

A manufacturer, who makes abundant quantity of equipment and the user either physically or contractually, is nowhere in the reach of the manufacturer or seller. For various reasons it is not practicable for the supplier to be easily accessible to use some time it may not be economical for supplier to attend to all needs of customer. Commodity-wise, many basic goods of daily use by a customer and consumer non-durables are examples. Here, the items are manufactured in bulk, to cater to wide areas, covering huge population. The cost of these items may not be much. Further there will be a wide range of agencies, between manufacturer and user. Like wholesale distributors, for a region, smaller distributors, who percolate down to user? Here, the distributor, or sub-dealer, can do very less, to help the user and manufacturer will be too far away, from the user, that the value of goods, do not find it worthy, to approach the producers. These items become items of use and in this category producer is not approachable, when they are asked, fully or when trouble comes.

Graphic Representation of a Computer Network used for Communication Inside and Outside an Organisation Information Utility

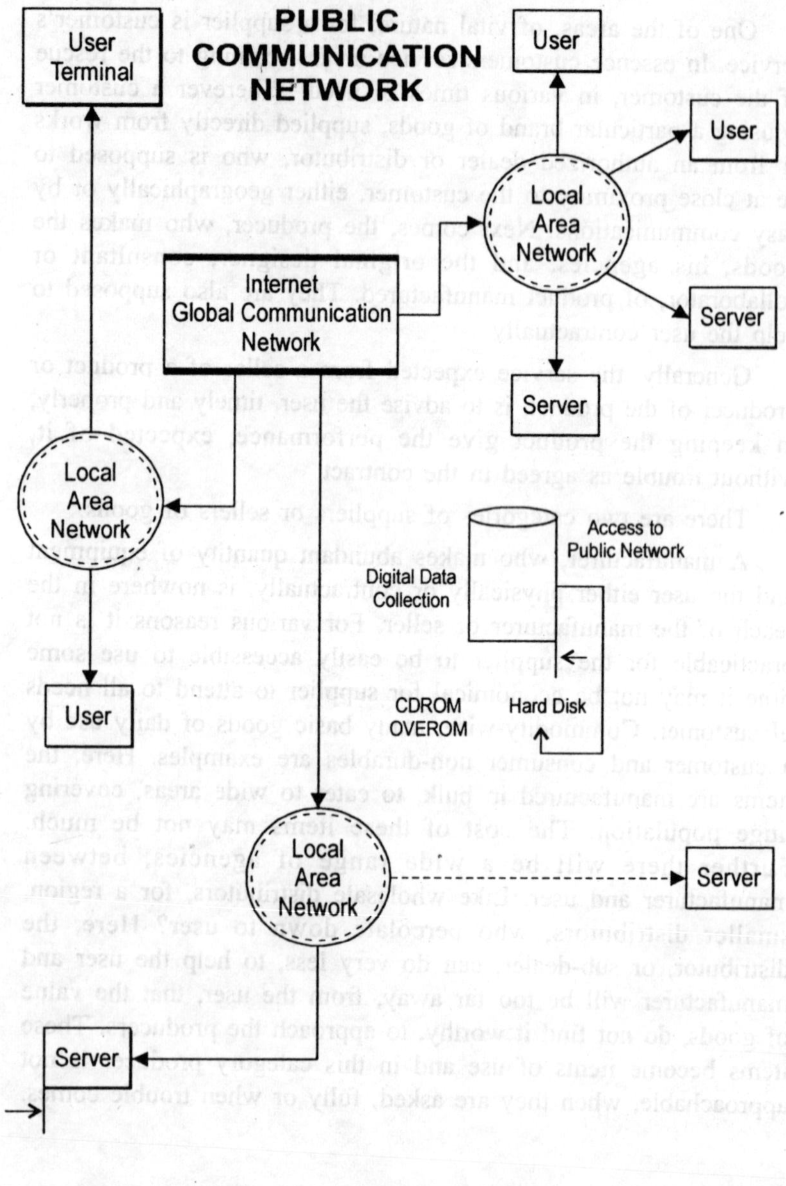

However, buyers go to these products by compulsions of price, quality, availability and better useful life, than perhaps similar commodities, which give much less, service.

Another category of suppliers, who come in this classification, are producer is not at easy reach of the user and various agencies are separate and the manufacturer and the user have no alternatives but to go to the same supplier or provider of service, even though, the user knows, these limitations, just for reasons of monopoly and as no alternative source of supply or service are available to users.

The user has to put up and feel content with what quality of product he gets or what life that product gives or what service the supplier of product gives to them. Examples in this category are public utilities such as electricity supply, water, sanitary services, roads, public transport, postal, telephonic, telegraphic services in communications sectors. Such examples are quite many in number in several monopoly areas. Users have no alternative and keep content with what they get. Now-a-days nationalized banks and insurance are also tending to dilate their services to customers.

In case of certain basic goods, consumer durables and capital equipment, the user has some times choices, with more producers, different brands of items, being available in the market. Here, some areas are there, where suppliers are interested in expanding their markets, have higher growth, get better profits. These organizations compete with each other in giving better service and attract customers. In basic and consumer goods users do not have much choice in items like milk and milk products, petroleum products, coke, coal, steel many basic metals.

Where supplier have a stake in market and want to woo customers, the discussion on services, which they can render and users can expect to get the following :

1. Quality products, which give long trouble free service.
2. Cheaper goods and services.
3. Availability of material in plenty and at easy access.

The kind of action that the supplier can take to satisfy the customer in services are the following :

1. Keep giving prompt and timely service which the customer wants, to the best extent possible so that the customer gets the feeling that the supplier is doing his best to give the service in the resources available to him and he is sincere about it.
2. Give good advise to users in advance about storage, erection, commissioning and operations of equipment and project educate the customer so that he knows these procedures properly to put them into proper use at the right time.
3. Attend to after sales services such as proper advise when customers ask for proper and timely repair to enable plant and machinery give trouble free service so that the user can get best returns from the items supplied.
4. Supply recommended spares, maintenance spares, literature drawings along with main equipment or project erection.
5. When trouble is reported from customer acknowledge the problem and suggest ways how to go about inputting back the equipment to correct use.
6. Advise customer on periodic maintenance so that the customer will get optimum output with trouble free operation in the useful life of equipment or plant.

There are areas where customer knows what precautions he has to take but due to other pressures working on him he will not be able to do the required thing to maintain the equipment. Here the responsibility goes with the user but the seller cannot be blamed. The examples of such situation are :

(1) Customers are highly skilled persons. They know how to maintain the equipment enhance its useful life take maximum returns from the plant machinery and project but because of the high demand in the market for the products coming out of the plant, the user will not shout down the concerned system or the machinery or project for regular maintenance. This results in accumulation of wear and tear and sudden failure of equipment. Some times plants run beyond the rated capacity owing to heavy demand. This also results in failure of plant or machinery being unable to take more than the rated capacity. Examples are loading

generating equipment beyond their rated capacity. Using water supply systems with more loads so that purified water cannot be supplied. Loading telephone exchanges with more connections than they are intended to. These cause failure to more equipment and loss of service from them. Some times passenger aircraft are run without break in service for maintenance to cater to passenger or cargo load or due to availability of less planes. This results in failures, which may be major in character.

(2) In certain plants certain work centers are very vital, in production. It is difficult to put additional plant in that work center. Some times because the organization cannot afford to invest or putting another facility parallel to that will not be practicable due to constraints of space, plant lay out, difficulty to get similar machinery from market, affordability, change of technology etc. This results in loading that work center to maximum extent. Failure due to over load or not shutting down that machinery for routine maintenance results in major failures. This result in inability to meet customer's commitments by supplier, repairs, new equipment and so on. Many customers will be inconvenienced and made unhappy due to this situation. Knowing these constraints in production still orders will be booked heavily due to good market demand. Ultimately this will result in bad customer service and dissatisfaction. The organization will loose its image.

(3) In such situations a compromise has to be worked out. Long deliveries have to booked even though, fear of losing orders are there. The customers must be directed to other alternative sources telling the true constraints in executing the jobs as per commitments.

Other examples where even though supplier has the capacity of skilled manpower, plant, machinery, technology and other facilities, reasons beyond the managements purview make the customers to feel unhappy due to not getting proper service. Examples of such case are :

(1) Raw material will not be available due to various constraints. Customs cannot get their plant and machinery because of material constraint. Some times in sophisticated plants if both

indigenous and imported materials are involved, imported material may become scarce due to stoppage of inputs temporarily or permanently for reasons beyond suppliers control. There may not be indigenous substitutes available or the standard of these materials may not be up to the desired level. Using such material in helpless situations might result in failure of end product and customer dissatisfaction. Even indigenous material may not give proper service though it is used knowingly as material mix. This situation gives trouble at different stages with failures and the supplier incurring customer's wrath.

(2) In case of transition where technologies are changed from old to new one, in spite of skilled manpower and good machinery problems arise in end product. The customer might find the products not giving rated outputs or failures occur frequently. This transaction results in dissatisfactions to customer, which the supplier has to invariably put up with.

(3) Some times customs will be unhappy in having to put up with high prices for spares, repairs or service, the reasons for this high charges may be unavoidable to the supplier. Customer will find using the plant and machinery with high operational cost by using costly spares and services results in less returns to him and uneconomical. Customers will become unhappy on this account and suppliers have to put up with these situations helplessly.

(4) In case where there are few suppliers or only one or two suppliers due to items being manufactured by them as a way out in such cases to give the best service practicable the manufactures or supplier should follow these courses of action.

(5) Repairs are mandatory as there will be no other source for customer than from whom he has purchased. Here the supplier should accommodate the user by phasing out his supply of main equipment use his vital work center for repairs also to an extent and do the repairs slowly if not in the time in which the user expects them to do. Offload the parts of repair work to other reliable suppliers and share the work as a compromise thereby satisfying customer partly at least than making them totally unhappy. Also try for alternative sources to do repair so that best thing can be done in the prevailing circumstance even though the supplier may loose some of his income.

(6) In order to see all repair jobs, major and minor, do not come to works, only facilities of site offices should be improved and augmented to attend to possible repairs and service at site. As next step, sub service and main regional service centers, should be opened or their capacities increased, so that load gets diverted and customer can bank and count on their service count, instead of going to main works all the time. Ways have to be found, and organized such service centers and technical service offices should guide the services and supervise the work done by others. This way, the main factory can concentrate on regular production, major repairs and making strategic spares.

(7) Warranty obligations have to be accommodated, even if, new jobs get delayed. Old jobs, which come for services, can be given subsequent priorities. Material, resource, work centers, should look first for these obligations and then do old jobs or new jobs of regular production. This will make the user use the new equipment bought by him; give more trouble free service and output, with minimum down time. The factory staff should be trained and motivated to do jobs as far as possible at sites so that the supplier need not necessarily send them to works where these jobs have to work for continuous periods particularly when sufficient equipment's have rolled out of the organization and are in operation at various sites. Customers get relief in such help coming from supplier.

(8) In case of failure of major sophisticated equipment which are highly capital intensive, even though sites can carry out the repair for mandatory tests the equipment have to come to main works where special facilities are installed. In such cases arrangement must be made to quickly conduct these tests by giving incentive to people in those work areas and doing the required tests to satisfy the customers instead of prolonging the jobs, without allotting priority.

(9) Quick procedures and trained manpower must be available to identify faults suggest remedial actions. Resorting to long trial and error methods should be avoided which delay the repairs.

(10) Quick identification of material content, procuring them by emergency methods and completing the repairs where the

problems and quantum of work and material is identified, helps in disposing off backlogs and accumulation of pending works satisfying customer.

(11) Methods to reorient at various work places when more jobs get accumulated or good revenue fetching jobs are on hand should be accommodated and production and other work areas should be eased as far as possible. This will result in customer satisfaction and getting revenues for the organization.

(12) If jobs are not in warranty and are not going to give returns for the work done or resources spent on it they can be directed to other areas by suitably advising customers, than undertake these jobs helplessly if there is more load on jobs which work centers cannot cope up. This will help in satisfying clients who pay more and genuine in asking for services unless there is enough time and resources available to do all varieties of jobs easily.

(13) Sprees, repairing and services are a very delicate area. Here caution has to be exercised in delaying with jobs of customers. Allotting priorities have to be done with proper deliberations. While helping us to get more orders and revenue, care should be taken to prevent slogging of jobs for comparatively unrealistic problems. Customers will be more unhappy, if they have other alternatives if jobs are delayed.

(14) For a customer, who makes high value transactions particularly buying equipment, machinery, construction of a project, insurance is an important area, where customer has to give lot of attention. Customers do insurance to cover several exigencies from procurement of material to product commissioning or project commissioning as also operation. Customers will generally make insurance for a liberal amount to cover all agencies even though he will have to pay high premiums. Insurance will be for handling, transport, storage, and unforeseen damages to equipment up to and during operation.

(15) Here it is essential for sellers and distributors and manufacturers to help the customers. On behalf of customer the seller complies with all insurance procedures if necessary for taking the policy and later for settling the claims on behalf of

buyer. The exigencies may warrant repairing goods, replacing goods, make good the loses due to down time of the machinery products or project. Whatever expense the customer incurs till the products or project operate normally giving the stipulated output cover on the insurance company. This help to the buyer in making his project operate normally is the responsibility of the supplier if the buyer has procured the equipment from a particular supplier.

(16) If customer has entrusted observing the insurance formalities to the seller or manufacture, first after a policy is taken by the buyer or on his behalf, the supplier whenever goods are dispatched from a particular place to site or where the goods are installed and used as the buyer desires the supplier has to give the details of goods, value of goods, date of dispatch, transporter, mode of transport, place where goods are loaded, where they will be unloaded and stored, erected, commissioned project will be in operation. The number of packages, packing list details, delivery note, details giving material in each package, which materials were sent in which carrier, how they were packed etc.

When there is damage during handling, where it has happened how it was handled and by whom value of damage, liability value of damage for the insurance company. In case of trouble with equipment or machinery, the charges for repair reasons for repair any agency responsible for such damage, loading. To repair jobs also similar details have to be given for unforeseen damages during erection testing and operation. The contract reference, dates details of orders placed their value have to be furnished to the insurance company.

Insurance companies generally appoint surveyors to assess damage give a report on the liabilities of the parties in the transaction, fix responsibilities, settle any differences that may crop up as to whose account the expenses have to booked and who does the repair or give replacements.

Care has to be taken to see claims are made immediately in a specified time giving all the claims in full. Subsequent claims on the same job at a different time or for new liabilities will not be accepted, if there is time lag and any controversy over the sequence of events.

The process of settling claims is very laborious, compensation will not be paid easily on the basis of claims only, but how the insurance authority gets convinced of its liability to the customer. Many a times the claims will go to several stages. Lot of effort to satisfy the surveyors and insurance company has to be made as otherwise the buyer will have to bear the amount incurred.

One aspect, which the insurance goes through, is the record, which has been maintained by the supplier, the user and connected agencies for the various events, where the insurance company has to compensate the loss.

Situations are not wanting, where suppliers or users or insurance company, try to avoid their role, in the occurrence of losses or damages since the stake involved is generally huge money. All the agencies try to free themselves from compensating for the losses.

18

Renovation and Modernization of Products and Projects

The philosophy of commercial organizations, all over the world is to have growth, accompanied by profits, on investments made by them, in their respective enterprises. After the elapse of a certain time, when the organizations stabilize in their operations, and when they have established certain markets, they look-forward to further growth. It is at this juncture, that they think of indulging in various permutations and combinations, of options for growth open to them. They think deeply, about the pros and cons of their moves before venturing into any major growth areas. The options that are normally open for growth for such commercial organizations are the following :

- Renovation
- Modernization
- Diversification
- Expansion

All business organizations big and small, irrespective of the kind of business undertaken by them/handled have to undergo a process of demand, recession and stability, as a cycle in their operations. Very naturally, the organizations have to gear up to this cycle and time their transactions accordingly. When a management, has to take a decision to alter their structure and make changes in their above prevailing operations, a thorough study of markets will be made by them taking the environment around them, the strengths and weaknesses of their competitors and evaluate, how they will be relatively placed, after taking recourse to one or more of the above available options open to them.

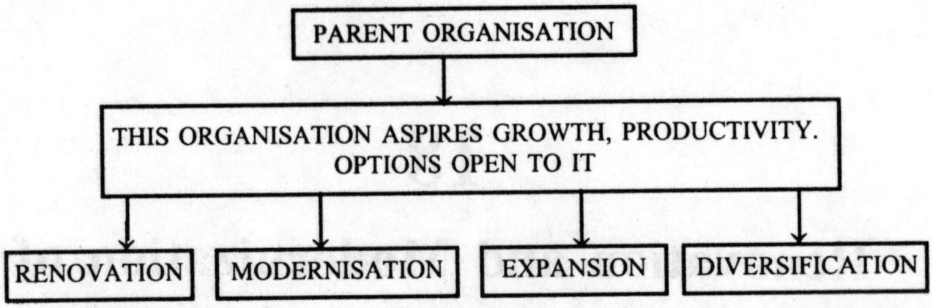

Business organizations are generally classified under the following headings based on the work carried out by them. Most of the examples are the following :

- ➢ Engineering consultancy of various products and various projects.
- ➢ Inspection agencies of projects and various products
- ➢ Construction activities
- ➢ Purely sales and marketing activities
- ➢ Service activities such as large repair jobs and renovations jobs.
- ➢ Mining and metallurgy operations
- ➢ Onshore and offshore drilling and refinery operations of petroleum products.
- ➢ Power generation, transmission and distribution
- ➢ Transport sector, such as surface transport, say roadways, railways, sea transport, civil aviation, space research and space satellites.
- ➢ Communication sector, information technology
- ➢ Defence and security
- ➢ Process plants like paper, cement, chemical and fertilizers, drugs and pharmaceuticals, textiles, foundry and forge, building materials, rubber, jute, tea, coffee, food processing, soaps and detergents, cosmetics, jewellery, metal and non metal industries, coke, coal, mica, beverages, milk and milk products, agriculture, horticulture, forestry, decorations, fashions technology.
- ➢ Archaeology, education, film industry, hotel and tourism,

sports-material, sports stadiums, arts and crafts, handicrafts, cottage industries.

➢ Financial and insurance sector. Real estate.

Each activity, namely renovation, modernization, diversification and expansion are distinct activities. These give different results. The actual work required to be done in each of the above areas are not same. The benefits that come, after carrying out these activities are also different in each case. Further, the resources to be employed, financial and manpower deployment will be different in each case.

Each activity of growth, are discussed separately giving details as to what each activity means, *modus operandi* and extent of benefits that can be expected are discussed, separately under each field and is an art in itself.

Renovation is carried out in the following cases, in their respective areas :

- Products renovation
- Project renovation
- Technology renovation
- Plant and machinery renovation
- Service renovation
- Operational renovations of plant, machinery and product

Now it is more than 50 years since, we got freedom. Our freedom has come to us in the post industrialization era. In the field of engineering and scientific advancement, across the globe, 50 years is a long period. Several changes have taken place in products, projects, services, operation of plants, machinery and technology, in this period.

RENOVATION

In renovation, the main plant layout and its machinery already installed will generally remain same, but the life of this plant and machinery will be improved, to give, more useful life and maximum output from product or projects as was intended, when plant was originally installed, and during various subsequent periods of use, over the years. Each product, plant, machinery and project, have specified life of optimum output during operation at various periods, calculating from the time of first new installation, to years of usage. In some cases, the plant or machinery, might start giving trouble, every now and then, require frequent repairs and shutdown. The measured output for certain rated input, might slow down, or tend to become totally uneconomical, from the time of commercial operation. It may even be better at some stage, to change and install new plant and machinery, than keep using the old machinery from economical and longevity point of view of these machines.

The factors, which are to be taken into consideration, in renovation, be it a product, plant, machinery or total project, are the following :

1. What is the condition of the plant presently, when compared to how it was, when it was originally installed?
2. Has the performance of plants slowed down, in its giving rated output over a period of use, as was originally intended, or has the deterioration been fast?
3. What is the life left in the plant, machinery etc., at the time of recurring and what are the methods, which can be employed to arrest or slow down the deterioration of life and increase its working life?
4. What is the capital to be invested for renovating the plant and machinery or total project?
5. What is the cost if a totally new project is brought in its place, instead of doing renovations?
6. What are the relative expenses to be incurred in both alternatives?
7. What is the return that can be expected after renovation in comparison to the condition in which it is presently lying and what is the capital outflow to renovate? In how many years, the outflow can be recovered, when compared to leaving the plant run as it is in its present condition?
8. What is the total period of shutdown of the plant, for undertaking renovation? What is the loss in revenue as a result of closing the plant?
9. Whether shortcuts in repairs can be resorted to, instead going for total renovation of plant, to reduce the capital

outflow, incur less losses due to closure of plant for renovation? At this stage of recurring is there enough margin of life left in the plant to operate the plant for more time and get returns out of it, considering the expenditure likely to be incurred?

10. A clear economic analysis of costs, to be incurred, returns being obtained by these several operations are worked out and best advantageous alternative have to be selected.

Consideration of options of using new technology *vs* exising old technology already adopted has to be considered.

1. If new equipments of similar nature, have come up and become operational, is it worth, renovating an old plant, than put up a new plant, with latest technology and get better returns for longer period?
2. How much plant should be renovated, depending on the life left in various parts of the plant and its machinery and investment to be made for it when compared to the returns by total renovation of plant and expenditure incurred. Is doing only renovation of a part of the plant already installed, sufficient?
3. If some supplier has supplied the plant and machinery, it may some times be worthwhile, to go to another organization or use another new technology, in renovation, than stick to old supplier and old technology. The benefits may be more in adopting new technology and methods, compared to using old renovated equipment, with old technologies.

Following are classic examples of renovation, where management's prefer to opt for such renovation for various considerations and reasons detailed above.

Civil construction is one area, where renovation is most common and equally, benefits are obtained, which are of varied nature, other than just utility. In some buildings life span is less, those buildings become old and depleted quickly, some times they have to be abandoned. Renovation at comparatively early stages, prolong the life and aesthetic value, utility of buildings increases, roads, bridges, railway tracks, airport terminals and buildings, runways, ports, give more life, after renovations. Public utility buildings also give more life. Renovation costs will be less than going for totally new premises. Some examples more preferable for renovation are educational buildings, offices, hotels, recreational centers, monuments.

How much to renovate and how much building can be left as it is, is a matter of opinion, and utility. The management can decide better, based on the financial status, as also monumental value, technical considerations such as safety, return on investments and several such aspects are to be properly considered.

Renovations are many. Examples of product renovation are the following :

(1) Use of synthetic/plastic material for loading cement in bags, in place of jute bags. Jute is a scarce commodity. It is costly, synthetic or plastic material used is cheap for using them to load cement and for handling, storage and transportation. The production of cement has gone up enormously, in multiples of millions of tonnes and proportionately the consumption, compared to earlier few decades. The number of container bags required now are more. Synthetic bags are cheap. Raw material used for these types of bags is easily available. These bags can be thrown away after emptying due to their low price compared to price of jute bags. Because jute material is also in short supply and costly, use of synthetically made bags are popular and economical, in the field of storage and use. It has been the same case with certain chemical and building materials, where synthetic material bags are used, in place of jute bags. This renovation is of far-reaching consequence as a product in economic operations.

(2) Use of plastic pipes, in place of GI pipes or steel pipes or pipes made of other metals is a good example of product renovation. Plastic pipes are cheap, material availability is more. It is also easy to use, as GI or other metallic pipes are not free from corrosion. These pipes are used for transportation of all fluids, water and for electrical wiring in buildings such as for concealed wiring, in place of other metallic tubes. Availability of raw material, flexibility in use and also conservation of metals for other uses are major advantages in this renovation. Prices are also

quote cheap compared to metallic pipes and fittings, life is also quite comparable to metal.

(3) Another renovation that has come is in the movement of products by the use of containers for transportation, by road, rail, and sea, in some cases by air. These metal containers come in different sizes. They have more life. Easy to handle. Material put in containers are stored and transported, do not get spoiled due to rain, sun, wind or other atmospheric exposures. They are very compact, railway yards, wagons, shipyards, ships, give cleaner and safer appearance and each customer is free to use container of his choice to put his things, transport them to places of his choice, easily, quickly and without risk or cumbersomeness, interference by other parties reducing loss of material in transit and transporting material, over long distances for longer periods, without spoiling the material. Before containers became popular, material was occupying more space in transport operation, such as trucks, wagons, ships, etc.; they were getting stolen/lost in transit due to lack of proper supervision. These places used for storage were remaining dirty. This method of using containers for transportation is clearly a boon to customers, transporters and suppliers. This is a very good example of renovation, in transportation of material and equipment.

(4) One renovation that has come in the field of material handling, is the use of conveyors, for loading, unloading and transpiration by horizontal, vertical and circular conveyors, which are used to load and unload wagons, take material to heights. Examples of good, economical and bulk use is in coal mines and power stations. Metal ore at the time of mining and transportation is done by varies varieties and designs of excavators lifts, conveyors, dumpers, haulers etc. Use of conveyors are also in abundance at airports for moving baggage and for taking people by moving escalators, adjustable and collapsable corridors to the planes for boarding and alighting.

(5) In case of bulk transportation of liquids, like petroleum, crude, finished products like kerosene, diesel, petrol, pipelines are run exclusively over distances, for transporting these products. The products are transported quickly in bulk, exclusively, in this pipeline by agencies involved in transportation. Expenditure for

this type of transporation is less and economical. These are good renovating techniques, in liquid transportation in very huge quantities, all over the country and between countries across the world. Under sea pipelines, are in use in gulf countries for petroleum products. Though installation costs are extremely high, running and maintenance costs are very cheap and very comfortable and easy for operation. This is a renovation helpful in projects.

(6) Renovation of generator stators and rotors of large capacity in thermal generation is a classic example of renovation. Ratings up to 210 MW generators are renovated at site and at works to give more useful life. By renovating rotors and stators by using latest state of art technology is enhancing, the life of and other thermal power plants.

(7) Pumps of certain capacities, used in thermal and other power stations are renovated, to give more life, by using latest state of art technology of rotors, particularly in boiler feed pumps. This is a case which helps in project renovations.

(8) A very classic example of renovation of small products of mass use, is small dry alkaline batteries, used in torchlight. Pen cells used in varied applications, in the field of electrical and electronic equipment, particularly, clocks, remote control devices, used in TVs, VCRs, VCPs, etc. Earlier alkaline battery containers were leaking creating dirty surroundings eating away, the containers of equipment, and making them useless and were thrown away after short usage. Now leak proof batteries, have come which do not allow, the oxide material to come out of the battery containers, thereby enhancing battery life, bringing clean containers, where these batteries are used. Electronic cell operated equipment are now cleaner, with better life expectancy.

(9) Automobile industry have got a boon, in changing lead acid battery containers, by plastic containers. These are compact and are light in weight. Though they are to be thrown out after use, unlike previous acid containers, in the useful life period of these batteries, they are problem free, for owners of cars, small two wheelers, vans, small trucks, transport equipment used in factories like battery operated trolleys and lifts of smaller capacity.

(10) In power and telecommunication sectors, use of high quality, underground cables, in place of overhead lines are helping in disturbance free service, due to weather, wind, outer atmosphere. Steel and iron poles and tubes are getting replaced by cables. Less telephone interruptions and repairs are there now compared to overhead lines. This helps in project renovations.

(11) A good example of reducing pollution and keeping environment clean and having less cumbersome transport is by using liquefied petroleum gas cylinders as transport fuel, in place of petrol. This fuel has been very successful in case of auto-rickshaws, cars and vans of Bajaj make, Maruti, Premier Automobiles and vehicles of General Motors. Gas cylinders as fuel are cheap. Small initial cost for installation in the vehicles without changing the vehicle look, space for seating and also helping in reducing exhaust smoke. This is a good renovation from the point of view of easy installation charges, easy availability of fuel. Less maintenance, less running costs, aesthetic look of the automobile.

MODERNIZATION

As the word modernization implies, it means making things upto date and new. This is a comparative term. There is some contradiction in the word modernization. With passing of time, new things become old and again other set of new things appear on the scene. Change from old things to new things come fast, in certain areas. Old things become easily obsolete with time. In certain other areas, it is slow. New things do not come all the time, reason here being cost proven technology, less customer confidence to go in for new things, immediately, delays in the process of going for new things.

However, at the outset, modernization is a continuous on-going process. Always a balance has to be struck, when one decides to change from an on-going system or process, and changeover to new things. Some, processes, technologies, plants, machinery, input raw material, become old and obsolete. These also become economically unviable. Here, carefully, new things have to be introduced. Many occasions warrant, slow change, even when new things are good, more useful and productive to switch over to those products or systems overnight. Reliability, continuity of supply of new material is a vital consideration.

In principle, modernization means, changing over to new set up. It may be business premises, factory, pattern of use of material, efficiency of operations, better returns on capital, discarding old things, for several reasons of compulsion and necessity, to remain in the market and retain, market share of consumption and returns.

Business organizations resort to modernization to get the following advantages :

1. If old premises, has lost its aesthetic value, looks ugly, not compact, enough space for operation is not there and by using latest facilities, the old premises gives more comfort, space, better useful life, looks more attractive and enhances business by attracting clients.
2. The methods operated, process, technology, input material, inquality and quantity, give returns of high value and production of more physical numbers are possible by resorting to modernization.
3. If the demand for products made in a plant, has become dead, due to better products being available in the market, here modernisation helps. The plants need to be shutdown, then new plant, has to be built, with new product mix, which is in demand, more product or products have to be manufactured in same or less time, with same capital outflow.
4. In some cases, the size, rating of the product, will become uneconomical to the user. User goes for bigger ratings. Here to cater to markets smaller ratings, have to be stopped from manufacture, the plant has to be geared up to make bigger products.
5. Raw material, used for products become scarce, costly, may become totally unavailable, prohibitive to use, as the plant starts incurring losses, by using such material. Here, the plant has to be oriented to use new raw material.
6. The plant uses old machines, maintenance of which becomes costly. So new plant, which operates efficiently and gives better output, has to be installed reducing operating costs. Products coming as new outputs cost less,

give quickly higher production, with easy processes, simple supervision of new plant will suffice as compared to the high attention of old plant. This is all a result of modernisation of the old plant.

7. The layout of the old plant looks ugly, Management is unable to keep the plant premises clean. Plant is widely spread out, with less productivity. Here, modernization with compact and efficient plants, better marketable products, modernization has to be done here. The efforts will bring good returns and good market.
8. The products coming out from the plant are no longer used by customers, due to various reasons, such as size of product, output, value paid for a certain quality of the materials. Here disbanding old plant and instaling latest and best equipment is more preferable than to make good the likely loss of market. Compact, quality products, which are in demand, have to be made, to get good returns. This needs modernization of plant, processes, technology, skills, machinery, operation etc.
9. If plants are of manual operating type with slow output and uneconomical returns by more investment, to get compact, efficient, quality products, with more features, is best thing to do. Here restoring to modernization is necessary.
10. Many plants come up, which give quality products quickly, at lesser prices, giving more numbers, with better performance, than old, uneconomical, outdated and redundant production lines. These have to be discarded and new plants, have to be put up; which are efficient, economical, give more products better use of human resources, conserve input, material and operational costs, etc. in such case, suitable new plants should be installed, better products, have to be manufactured, which are more useful, give more user benefits by resorting to modernization.

The above are several examples, where modernization has helped, in creating better return on investment, more output, with comparatively less input cost. Keeps cleaner environment of plant and machinery.

Following cases of modernization give better output and other peripheral benefits. Operating staff work in cleaner environment, work with ease and comfort. Some such examples are detailed below :

1. A major modernization example is in the case of railways. Railways are using three types of gauges for the tracks. Narrow gauge, meter gauge and broad gauge. Narrow gauge is naturally the least productive, due to limitations of width of the track; the engines and bodies have small capacity. The passengers or goods that can be handled naturally gets limited by the small capacity of the train and its length. Except in very high altitudes, serpentine and slippery sections in north and eastern sector, certain area of south, some mining areas this gauge has become obsolete. In order to have one gauge for mobility, interchangeability, capacity to carry more load in each train, meter gauge is getting phased out and broad gauge is becoming the main track in railways. This has been helping in carrying more passengers and goods per train, use wider and longer coaches, use of more compartments and wagons to carry more traffic, in addition to running trains faster. More production of railway equipment because of less varieties of goods cheaply and fast have become possible. In railways, high productivity has been possible its infrastructure including railway stations, signaling equipment etc. This is a very big renovation in rail transportation, rail infrastructure, economy and growth.

1.2 The railway engines were made up of steam locomotives. Diesel and electric locomotives in traction have replaced these locomotive predominantly. Steam engines are very rarely used that too in workshops for small shunting and in some remote areas for certain technical reasons. Using electric locomotives have been bringing more standardization higher handling capacity of trains, more speed, clean environment inside the trains and outside atmosphere. This is a very big renovation since railways form a major surface transport in our country. In mountain tracks, deep and narrow curves are some constraint for using broad gauge. However great strides have been made in railways, both in gauge conversion and standardization, increasing capacity, speed and cleanliness associated with safety by resorting to modernization.

1.3 Necessity to store water and coal mid-way for steam engines oil for diesel traction has been giving place to smooth transportation by railway traction. It is increasing passenger comfort in coaches, more passenger and goods mobility take place in a given time. Maintenance is becoming easy and cheap, more trains driven by electric traction are introduced in each route safely as recourse to modernization.

1.4 Computerization in railway reservation is a big renovation. Major stations are using this facility for ticketing passenger transport. This has resulted in using less manpower, operation is quick, lesser or no mistakes, and faster transactions in booking centers. There were lot of manipulations, which has been avoided. Computerization is also helping in good planning of train movement, load distribution proper utilization of coaches and wagons in the network and also quickly is one advantage. This is very good example of modernization.

2. Another major modernization in the world and our country is in the case of civil aviation. Many airports have been expanded, terminals have increased the capacity to receive bigger aircraft. Boeing and airbuses are carrying more passengers and freight with higher frequency of operations and has resulted in more traffic movement economically for airways. More passengers are able to travel in less time with better frequency of travel in the increased plane schedules. This is a very good example of modernization and also expansion.

2.1 In big airports, where both national and international aeroplanes ply passengers are provided with time saving and other comforts by using air corridors which take passengers nearer to the planes parked by the side of the terminal buildings economising/lessening alighting and boarding time and bringing additional comfort.

3. In case of agricultural operations modernization, have brought very big growth in agricultural production. Not only pump sets are used for water supply, tractors are used for ploughing, inter cultivation, harvesting, transporting labour and agricultural yield and manure. Further, harvesting is done by using threshers, which separate the chaff and grains and load them into trailers simultaneously after harvesting. Major crops like paddy, wheat have become very productive because of this mechanization. In additions to quick agricultural operation, higher yields are obtained with less effort. Manual work has reduced with increase of production and performing several simultaneous operations from harvesting to transportation to market yards.
4. In offices, banks, design and engineering departments and production organizations computers are doing multiple functions quickly and easily. Work centres are compact with less people and working places are giving cleaner environment. This has been a major modernization. Use of computers is enabling to keep records in smaller racks, in design, technology, purchase, sales, planning, production centers. Finance and accounts departments, inspection departments, administrative departments, packing, loading, transportation areas are all getting simultaneous and quick information accurately and in bulk. This has increased productivity very fast by removing laborious comparatively very slow manual working. Machines in bigger operations are using computers to do multiple, sequential operations by setting up programmes. Here rejection and reworks are avoided. Jobs are done accurately and fast.
5. Computers are helping to do work fast in design, so that more modules can be tried fast to conserve material, process time, preserve records for avoiding repetition whenever new jobs come, which are of similar nature. This has reduced manufacturing time, deliveries of products and execution of contracts and projects in time have become

easy. In case of high value products, in short time several permutations and combinations can be worked and the most efficient and cost effective design and processes can be chosen without much effort.

6. In areas of printing technology, modernization has helped in producing big volume of work in short time. Several operations are done simultaneously in a chain and manual supervision is reduced to minimum. The output involving several operations are getting completed in short time from feeding the input to getting completed jobs controlling the various stages in the operation are done to give best performance and look of the surroundings.
7. Material handling is another area where there is big renovation. Loading, transportation, unloading is all done in major jobs like handling coal, mineral, ore, metallic and non metallic bulk items. There are done quickly in bulk and over long distances by doing sequentially several operations.
8. In the area of bulk transportation by haulers, dumpers, conveyors these have helped in using qualified manpower to get maximum output by using heavy equipment in less time and get high output. Coal, oil and other fuel used for conveyance have become relatively cheaper, quick and trouble free. Resources and time are put to best use.
9. Higher voltages in transmission of electric power have helped in evacuating power from place of generation to place of use, over long distances in less time and with less money. Even though more money is required initially to put up higher ratings of equipment for generation, transmission and distribution the power available is more, economical, effective with lesser inception time reduction in the breakdown of plant and machinery. Here also computers are helpful in generating plants, transmission and distribution of power.
10. Use of bigger units in generating power ranging from 200 MW, 210 MW, 500 MW are in common use. Transmission voltage up to 230 KV and 400 KV are increasingly used.

This has been facilitating availability of bulk power at user points, quick evacuation of power at generating stations.

11. Automation is a big modernization in the field of drugs and pharmaceuticals. Drugs and chemical manufacture are getting more and more automotive and bulk manufacture has become possible. The process from raw material to finished stage, such as bottling and packaging has been fast and highly helpful in manufacturing huge quantity of medicines, chemicals and pharmaceuticals and make them available to users across the country in short time.
12. Modernization in the manufacture of construction material is an area which is helping build multi-storied houses, colonies, big educational buildings, commercial complexes, offices, places of recreation, auditoriums, sports complexes, roads, bridges etc. at shorter time.
13. In the area of brick making good quality of fabricated bricks are used in constructions. Cement moulded bricks are replacing, big stone in building walls and separators. In the construction of pillars, mechanized cement mixers and conveyors are used. Roofs and structure are being built by prefabricated plates and formers, which are adjustable. This is reducing capital and time.
14. In building construction, one new trend that is fast picking up is in the area of mud bricks and cement bricks. In case of mud bricks they are made of different design with excellent external finish and architectural beauty the inside of the bricks are hollow. When these bricks are used in construction, while the outside gives good appearance because of hallow interiors there will be scope for air circulation. This helps in keeping the walls and interiors cool in summers. In winters, there is not much scope for inside houses or buildings to became cold as air acts as insulation from outside atmosphere. These bricks are also strong for constructions of buildings and not very costly to use, as building material in comparison to conventional heated bricks. In case of cement-fabricated bricks, these bricks are big. They have the strength of stones used in buildings and are of big size. The cement used in these

bricks is not much as the bricks are hollow. These bricks are made outside, in yards, cured and are made available as good seasoned cement bricks. While they make construction fast, because of size, with less bricks, strength is not sacrificed. The profile is rectangular. They are light because the interior is hollow and there is scope for air to circulate inside the bricks. Like the designed tiled bricks, these are not costly and act as insulating material suitable to keep interiors cool in summer and does not transmit, outside cold in winters because air acts as insulation. These are not breakable and easy to transport and use in construction of buildings without sacrificing strength and cost. They are easy and can be quickly manufactured in bulk at nearby places of construction. If necessary for aesthetic sense other shapes of bricks are also made if money is not a constraint. These two examples are modern processes used in the construction of buildings without sacrificing strength or cost. They are easy and can be quickly manufactured in bulk at nearly places of construction of big buildings. These are good examples of modernization.

15. One very important and vital area where modernization of technology is used is in laying and asphalting of roads. Roads are made with metal having plain surface. Bitumin (coal tar) is heated with jelly and mixed in huge quantities at an open place nearer to the places where roads have to be asphalted. The mixture is heated. By a conveyor this mixture is transferred to mechanical dumpers. Dumpers take the hot mixture to the nearby roads where asphalting machine takes this bitumen mixture and lays on the road. The depth of this tar and jelly is controlled by a road-laying machine which after pouring the material on the road spreads to the required thickness on the road very neatly. Here maintaining uniform thickness of bitumin, laying the road to required width, is all done by controlling the volume, pressure and quantity by the hydraulically operated road-laying machines. This process is fast; large distances of roads are laid in shorter specified time. The

quantity or material, in bonding is controlled and the road will be ready for use by traffic in short time. This process is very good. It lessens the manpower used, controls the material, its proportion and large lengths of roads are laid quickly, compared to old methods of asphalting which are also still being used parallelly. This new method is very modern, scientific, gives long life to the roads and work is done very fast.

16. Progress made in space technology and information technologies are very commendable. While, progress of information technology is open to public purview and use, space technology is rather a confidential area, since defense utility is involved. There is information block out due to strategic reasons. Governments are not willing to disclose the enormous progress made to public in various applications and development. However certain areas like photography, climatic study, utility as information carrier both audio and video is open to public. TVs, cable operators, computer users, Internet, e-mail are the beneficiaries. There is so much advancements in this field that millions of people across the world are learning to use the facilities of space satellites in the area of communication and information technology. The growth and development in this area is very vast and wide and is covering more and more spectrum of population right from school children to qualified scientists and technologists.

19

Diversification and Expansion

DIVERSIFICATION

Diversification means, change over to new lines of activity, from the activity, which the organization his already been involved in, at present. In effect, diversification activity means, entering into new areas of operation, from what the organization has already been associated with. A dynamic commercial organization always keeps looking into the outcome of its own present activities and in addition, takes interest in other activities taking place, in its surrounding areas of operation. There are several reasons for doing so. Every organization's main goal is growth and get better results for its efforts. In this process, the managements strive to look for grey areas, where progress is faster or better, returns are more than, in the activity, which that organization is pursuing. Always, business keeps changing with time.

The reasons are many. It is so if at a particular point of time some areas are lucrative and the bringmen start working in that area at a point of time later a change in business scenario takes place. At this time the management take stocks of its operation, when once a management starts a business with the resources at its command then, and feels on a review of its working of the results of the enterprise it is pursuing changes and goes in for beneficial pursuits, either totally retaining its old activities and taking part in new activities, or as an alternative, cut short, some of its present less productive pursuits, and enter into new pursuits, either totally retaining its old activities and taking part in new activities, or as an alternative, cut short, some of it present less productive pursuits, and enters into new pursuits, which become more productive. It is the discretion of the management to decide how it should go about, with its present ventures. This type of taking recourse to extra activities is diversification. This is one of the strategies, adopted by managements to get better returns for the resources, at their command, in various areas, such as finance, human resources and skill available, the plant and machinery, with which it has established, the technology and know how, it has got, capability of absorbing new technologies, capacity to undertake new ventures, new facilitates, it can capitalize, new markets it can capture, which prove to be beneficial, with the opportunities available to it at that time.

(2) An organization established in a particular field will have certain area of operation certain specified markets, certain known clients, with which it keeps pursuing business. With the change of options to new fields there will be change in markets, clients, areas of options. Obviously these new areas may be in addition to its old familiar areas or new venues depending on how the organization diversifies its operations and what its area of operations already are.

(3) In case of organizations dealing with one or two products the operations may be in limited fields. In multi-product operations the earnings will already be big and new areas get added and some might get deleted depending on how the organization goes about with its diversification.

(4) To cite examples, an organization dealing with construction activities of civil infrastructure, such as buildings, roads, bridges, aerodromes, shipyards, public buildings, sports areas, factory buildings, hospitals, water supply, drainage, irrigation dams, canals etc. might take up areas such as plant erection, in erection of factories, hotels and resorts, railway line constructions, mining operations, material handling operations, process plants such as cement, paper, brick manufacture and so on.

(5) An organization, doing the engineering work of transportation sector, such as roads, railways, seaports, aerodromes might enter into irrigation, construction of townships, factory layout design, processing plant design, oil exploration fields, information technology, chemical technology and so on.

(6) An inspection organization doing inspection of electricity generation equipment, transmission equipment, distribution

equipment might add to its scope of activities fertilizer and chemical plants and equipment for some processing equipment inspection, inspection of equipment in transportation field, space research, mining, material handling equipment, machine tools equipment, communication equipment etc.

(7) An organization, which deals with only sales and execution of contracts as distributors to certain products and plants or projects, might divert to other fields. Organisation selling electrical equipment in generating field, transmission field, distribution field might divert to transportation sector, instrumentation sector, process plant sector, oil sector, aviation sector, railways road transport sector, consumer goods sector and so on.

(8) An organization making passenger ships and goods carriers can shift to dredging operation, repair of ships on shore or offshore repair and construction of submarines, fighter ships, ships used for navigation in areas of weather forecast, coast guard, dry dock shipping, sea vessels which might construct ships in water and repair them.

(9) Organizations doing financial lending and allied areas, might take up sales and contract of projects or products. The areas where organizations diversify are illustrated below :

Simple Chart showing Typical Diversification

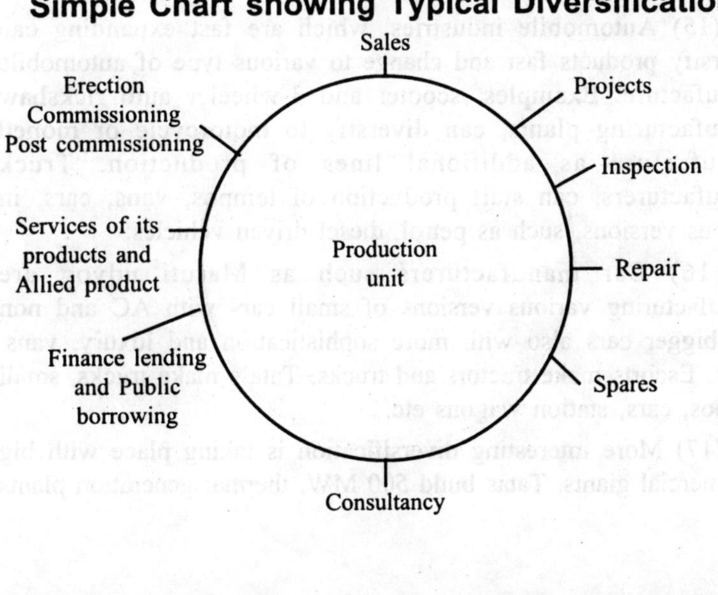

(10) An organization, which deals with the manufacture of machine tools, which are manually operated, may diversify to semi-automatic and fully automatic machine tool manufacture. An organization involved in mining of some metals might diversify to extraction of metals, sale of metals, also some finished products in that area. Organization dealing with coal mining, might take transportation of coal to various sales outlet and supply coal to them by organizing the expansion of transportation and sales.

(11) Organizations in the field of oil exploration of petroleum products might take to manufacture of other petroleum products, transportation to potential areas of consumption and distribution.

(12) Plants in certain chemical extraction and production of its products, can add pharmaceuticals and drugs to its production and take up its main sales distribution also.

(13) The organization in the field of power generation, transmission and distribution areas can take to construction of plants in generation, transmission and distribution, it can undertake maintenance of these projects. Increase capacities for these projects by constructing additional plant capacities for these projects.

(14) Organization in material handling equipment, production such as heavy dumpers, bulldozers, tippers, conveyors, can undertake projects, where lifts hoists, drilling equipment, haulage equipment, can be manufactured.

(15) Automobile industries, which are fast expanding can diversify products fast and change to various type of automobile manufacture. Examples, scooter and 3-wheeler auto rickshaw manufacturing plants, can diversify to motorcycle or moped manufacture as additional lines of production. Truck manufacturers, can start production of tempos, vans, cars, in various versions, such as petrol, diesel driven vehicles.

(16) Car manufacturers such as Maruti udyog are manufacturing various versions of small cars with AC and non AC bigger cars also with more sophistication and luxury, vans, jeeps. Escorts make tractors and trucks, Tata's make trucks, small tempos, cars, station wagons etc.

(17) More interesting diversification is taking place with big commercial giants. Tatas build 500 MW, thermal generation plants

and also undertake distribution and transmission of energy. They make chemicals, transport vehicles, soaps, detergents, and salt, sell refined coconut oil, telephones etc. Bajaj also, sell, in addition to automobiles, many consumer durables in electrical field, such as fans, heaters, geysers, and even coconut oil. Birlas make polyester fiber, jute material, cement, and chemicals.

(18) L&T make cement, electrical generating, transmission and distribution equipment, control equipment. They undertake major civil construction activities like roads, bridges, flyovers, and town ships.

(19) Organizations like ABB, GE, BHEL, English Electric, Siemen's, Kirloskar, have much diversity in their product range right from electric equipment to control gear, switch gear, transformers, motors, AC & DC generators, hydro thermal, gas turbines and matching generators, the area of operation ranges from selling small products, spares, tools, repairs, construction and design of plant, machinery, construction of projects to manufacture power, process material, erection of plant and machinery, testing, trial operation, post commercial operation.

(20) HMT make manual, automatic digital and computer operated machine tools, general lathes, multipurpose lathes, drilling and planning machines, boring machines, presses, watches, electric bulbs, which are valuing from several rupees to crores of rupees in the production field and sales, erection and commissioning fields as also service, repair and engineering.

(21) Some major utilities like railways are diversifying from manufacturing of engines, coaches, wagons to construction of lines for narrow gauge, to meter gauge and broad gauge. Diversification has come in operation, from basically steam operated to diesel and now electrical operation. They also undertake consultancy of electrical systems and construction of railway lines and infra-structural facilities to users in other countries.

These are some of the major reasons for going diversification, in fields of production, sales, engineering, technology, processes, testing, erection, commission and operation.

1. Catering to latest market requirements, so that they are having demand for their products and services and continue

to increase their capital and profit. Increase or keep their work force intact and with higher and latest skills.

2. Give customers less costly equipment, products and services without sacrificing quality.
3. Give cheaper and quality services and have market demand and brand names attractive.
4. Give quality and skilled products and services and at the same time maintain their growth and profit margins.
5. Where products or services are reducing in demand and become obsolete have alternative products, plant machinery and services to compensate so that the organizations do not incurr loss or reduce the growth rate.
6. When more efficient products and equipment are coming into market keep in line with those advancements by upgrading their products or change over to allied products of demand.
7. To keep the best use of plants, capital, and services available with them and get optimum market returns.
8. Capture new projects coming in their line of activity by diversifying wherever possible, production diversification, technology diversification, process diversification, raw material input, change over or diversification, change over to new ways of services in fields of repair, maintenance, supply of spares, tools etc.
9. Add in their scope of operation additional products of other manufacturers, which run in tandem with their equipment, supply accessories with their products procuring from other manufacturers etc.
10. New facilities are added to their manufacturing plants, to make different rating of equipment to cater to market needs. Such facilities are in areas of testing, like expanding the test facilities. Increase critical areas of machinery in production line, which may be constraints. Increase support service facilities such as steam generation, oxygen supply, acetylene, install extra generation equipment of small capacity generators in their plants, to augment power supply, without depending only on external supply.

11. Appoint recognized inspectors parallel to their own inspection team to induce confidence in customers about the quality of products.

One of the important criteria in diversification in addition to capturing markets is resource generation. Many diversification activities need hard work to attract customers where other competitors have already established. Here quality, superiority of products, market availability, proven performance base has to be established to gain the markets. When change over takes place, if some lines of production are discontinued, those plant lines become obsolete. Ways and methods of using the redundant machinery have to be found. When new markets come, new plant lines are established by extra investment by proper management of capital invested.

Generally diversification is done in phases, so that the return on investments already made do not get lost. New markets have to compensate for loss of discarded products. Good long-term planning, proper working, on plant resources and expenditure, have to be made carefully, well in advance before changes take place.

It is necessary to strengthen sales and services, outlet for new products introduced due to diversification and cater to new markets.

EXPANSION

Expansion is one of the vital areas of growth of an organization. As the term implies, expansion process is increasing, the present capacity of operations of the organization, by resorting to various progressive processes selected by the management of the organization by choosing the best alternatives available to it which can give most beneficial effects. Expansion can be in any of the following areas selected by the organization :

1. By expanding the capacity of the plant production, by retaining the same technology in the old plant and incorporating similar technology to the expanded capacity of the plant also.

It can be by retaining old technology to the old plant and bringing in new technology to the expanded portion of the plant.

Different Plant or Project Configurations and choice of Lines of production that can be adopted there

	Plant	Line of production			
I (A)	One Single Plant	Ist line of Production →	Input to old Plant same →	Output is same →	Old Technology
		2nd line of Production→	Additional Plant added →	Output same or varies →	Old Technology of old plant is used or new different technology is used.
(B)	One Single Plant	Parallely both lines of Production as in I(A) is used. →	Technology used is old technology of I(A) or New technology of I(A).		
II (A)	One Single Plant	Ist line of Production →	Input used same as earlier →	Old Plant only is used →	Technology used is also old.
		2nd line of Production→	Output from this line of production different →	New Plant is used →	New Technology in adopted.
(B)	One Single Plant	→ Both lines of Production as in II(A) are used.			
III (A)	One Single Plant	Ist line of Production →	Input to plant same old plant →	Output same →	Old Technology.
		2nd line of Production→	New plant input to plant different →	Output different →	New Technology.
(B)	One Single Plant	→ Both lines of Production as in II(A) adopted.			
IV (A)	One Single Plant	Ist line of Production →	Input same → Same old plant →	Output same →	Old Technology is used.
		2nd line of Production→	Input different → New plant →	Output different →	New Technology is used.
(B)	One Single Plant	→ Both lines of Production are used.			
V (A)	One Single	Ist line of Production →	Input same → Same old plant →	Different types of outputs →	Old Technology is used.
		2nd line of Production→	Input different → New plant →	different output →	New Technology is used.
(B)	One Single Plant	→ Both Parallel lines of Production are used.			

2. By increasing the capacity of the plant by using new inputs to the old plant as well as expanded portion of the plant by retaining the type of output same, which increases the total output quantitatively. Some times the quality of output is improved, to get more marketability of products made in the plants.
3. By bringing another product line into the plant, in addition to existing product line so that the quantitative and financial output of the total plant increases.
4. By putting another plant by the side of the old plant, with totally new product line and technology keeping the product of old plant same and changing the product line of new plant. In the process get more quantity of turn over by both plants and also more financial turnover.
5. Expanding the operation of the ageing plant by new ventures, in addition to present ventures so that the total plant gives more financial output.
6. If the present venture in the plant is production oriented add services to the plant so that more financial transactions and returns are obtained. If service sector is also there increase services to existing services and products so that there is more turn over and better financial returns.
7. If multi-products and multi-services are in the original organization, reduce unproductive products or services and improve the production of products or services, which are in demand in the market to increase growth.
8. If auxiliary inputs are there in a plant and they are sufficient to present turn over create extra auxiliary supply capacity and increase the overall product output.
9. If an organization is in the field of consultancy for certain products and projects, extend the same services to other products or projects of other areas. Increasing manpower, additional skills to the organization, can do this. Examples, consultancy in steel projects or products can be extended to similar metals like copper, aluminum, zinc, lead, etc., consultancy in setting up projects can be extended to setting up production product lines for the products which count for the projects.

10. Organizations in production or mining, extraction of metals, chemicals, have shifted in addition to these activities to refineries. Oil drilling in petroleum sector, information technology, financial management like leasing, for creating plant and service infrastructure.

The above are some examples where big plants extend in various fields their activities. There are examples in other sectors, where expansions have been successful and productive.

(1) Railways carryout expansion by improving electric traction by laying tracks increasing the fleet of passenger and goods traffic, in electric traction by putting more trains in this area.

(2) Roadways, which are operating in city limits, are expanding operations to muffusal areas by increasing the fleet of buses and catering to more traffic effectively.

(3) In the field of telecommunication more and more new capacity automatic exchanges are coming up, giving more telephone connections, catering to more communication facilities.

(4) Some plants in the area of chemical and fertilizers are using their by-products to make drugs, pharmaceuticals, pesticides and insecticides increasing their own plant outputs, in chosen fields and increasing the total plant output and markets of by-products.

(5) In thermal generation, co-generation projects are being set up increasing energy output and more returns. Hydro plants are adding thermal plants, side by side in generation. Irrigation projects are adding generation of electricity by putting hydro projects.

(6) In the process of expansion, the benefits that an organization derives are, the output increases, plant capacity increases, assets increase, and benefits increase, and more people will be employed. More investment will be mobilized. When new additions to existing plants are made, big plants and associated capital attracts more investments.

(7) Some times organizations foresee markets declining, in some fields. By putting additional investment; parallelly, new products will be started by additional investment. The products

so chosen give, better returns, on additional investments, and in the overall process, organizations gain even if old product markets decline.

(8) The growth of the organization, by additional expansion creates new facilities. These attract more investors, with collaboration and technology, resulting in increasing new assets and more profits by new schemes.

(9) The expansions result in reduction of product costs, service costs, and better technological and quality leadership resulting in induction of more skilled and new talents. The strength and reputation of the organization, goes up by these measures. The organizations establish well, with better base in the market.

(10) Much study has to go in when expansions of new types of production lines or service lines are brought in the same organizations. Often the consultants are so chosen who give best opinion in making various viable changes through expansion schemes.

(11) The expansion schemes, go on slowly and for a long period. The output, from new expansion schemes will not start coming out till new plants go into operation, and results start coming from market, only after this period. Financial management, asset management and manpower management have to be done carefully. The organizations have to absorb new productive investment, for a certain period up to which the product lines become operatable and give results. However, after the expansion scheme stabilize, organizations grow well and give very good returns on investment and profits.

(12) Market studies have to be made carefully for a fairly long period to take care of exigencies during the period of construction and production take off stage. Feasibility studies before taking expansion activities also have to take into consideration the activities of competitors, their future plans so that expansion becomes a profitable proposition.

(13) Expansion has to take into consideration latest technologies in the chosen field. Care to take new processes and technologies in expansion can only bring proper returns, otherwise losses may be incurred by not getting market for new products.

(14) Common expansions are in the field of power generation, information technology, petroleum refiners and oil exploration. Communication areas, automobiles, medicines and pharmaceuticals, Mining of coal and coke, atomic energy, space research, tourism, civil aviation, shipping, rubber, synthetic materials, building construction, paper, cement, education and research. Health, sanitation, water supply, manufacture of electric equipment, telecommunication, and using by-products in major plants to make the material from them. Non-conventional energy sources and environmental improvement schemes are also among them.

(15) In case of expansion of projects, equipment availability in the market for carrying out expansion, availability of raw material in huge quantities, with assured supply. Availability of services and spares for plant and machinery, assured market for the goods coming out from the plants are very essential.

(16) In power sector more emphasis is on bringing units with higher capacities in utilities. In machine tools sector, semi-automatic and automatic machinery giving trouble free service are used. Period of completion of projects is reduced to avoid cost escalations. Bringing projects in short time is a major consideration.

(17) In the block diagrams are shown the areas where expansion activities are taking place with their associated merits of expansion being highlighted compared to the practices in vogue till now in these fields.

(18) One very high production and resource generating area, which has helped the economic and industrial growth of the country is in the area of use of high voltage generation transmission and distribution. Though this growth and development does not attract the attention of the common man, who need not have to address attention to this phenomenal progress. Transmitting power at extra high voltage at 400 KV has been helping in the bulk evacuation of power generated and make it available for increased usages at farther locations. Generally in our country 230 KV is used for power transmission in our national Grid. To multiply this power transmission from heavy power generating centers to load utility centers at other places where they are

required, 400 KV transmission by both AC and DC power is used in western parts of generating centers like Maharashtra and Gujarat, northern belts at Punjab, Haryana, Delhi and UP as also West Bengal, Bihar sectors, in the eastern side. This higher voltage usage in transmission has enabled multiplying of power supply to user networks from sources of power generations to places of utility. This is an area of huge financial investment and taken several year to construct the total system and make it operational.

(19) This has necessitated usage of high voltage larger capacity transformers, switchgear transmission wires running over long distance, switching centers. This equipment is extremely expensive and very highly capital intensive. To off set this capital investment, availability of power easily at long distance from generating centers, again changing and using at lower voltages at places of utility enables companies to realise the capital used in generating more revenue at places of utility power is used at 11 KV, 6.6 KV, 3.3 KV, 400/440V and 200V in normal AC circuits. However for transmission the voltage ranges are in 33 KV, 66 KV, 132 KV, 220 KV and 400 KV. It can thus be seen by economics of electrical energy, more power can be created at users premises if voltage is high. Laying down 400 KV transmission lines in transmission with sub station equipment to give user voltages and also change over of transmission at generating station by stepping up from voltages of 11 KV to 400 KV is a very big expansion activity adding to more power availability.

(20) This; comes in handy where huge funds are deployed to transmission sector to enable power to become available in very huge quantities. The projects brought in this extra high voltage transmission are very major expansion projects. These have helped in making energy available to user with comparatively lesser-cost investment in transmission sector, neutralising by the advantages of comparatively cheaper operational and maintenance costs in longer years. 230 KV was maximum voltage used till nearly 2 decades back as against 400 KV today.

(21) The transmission of power at 400 KV has been a very big national asset in making the expansion of power sector and economic power availability has come as a booster to users and electricity supply agencies. It is one very good example where expansion schemes help, off setting the invested capital by bringing returns at many times the capital invested in return and also bringing with it many user advantages. To give the advantages off hand to the country, these are summarized below.

(22) The physical space along the transmission lines used for transmission of power is saved in several thousands of hectares of area.

(23) The space which is being utilized for 220 KV and below transmission lines and substations which are non utilized having become surplus and being conserved for other users 400 KV substations which are lesser in number, help in releasing large areas of space for other uses. The equipment cost is also saved by using less number of 400 KV equipment in transmission compared to 220 KV and 110/132 KV transmission lines, switching stations and transmission substations.

(24) Conservation of valuable material such as aluminum, steel, copper, insulating material, transformer oil, porcelain

SIMPLE DIAGRAM

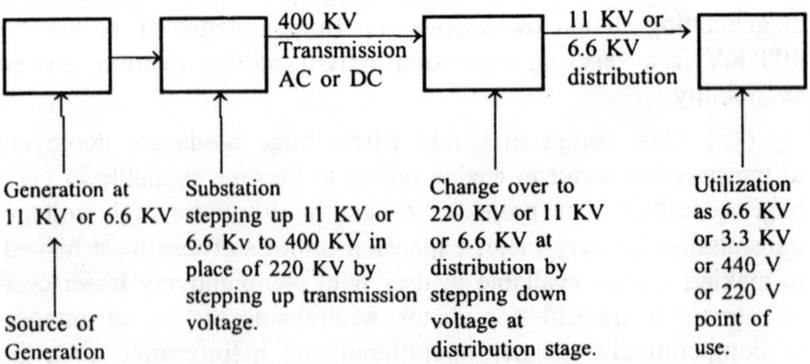

- Reduction of Transmission Space/Number of lines
- Reduction of Physical Numbers of transmission equipment
- Reduction of staff strength and number of substations

isolators, control panels, meters, cables, switching material is enormous and these materials are redeployable for using to constructing transmission lines to more deeper areas across the country at the points of utility. Expenditure on staff in EHV transmission area is reduced and they are made to comprise of more compact teams and extra staff deployed over a wide area. There are less maintenance problems, which would otherwise increase for the quantum of power transmitted.

(25) Example of expansion in the area of material handling and transportation is by using bulk container equipment for transporting material, to take to distant places on land, sea, by road, rail. Material Carrying capacities are increased by increasing the material containers, big capacity lifting and loading equipment, so that more material moves in a fixed time, with lesser, but which capacity carriers. Here also the economically use of less number of large containers for carrying a certain quality of material high are transported by using more number of small containers affects in savings number of transporting equipment like loading and unloading equipment which otherwise require transport vehicles move more smaller capacity containers used in bigger physical numbers. This also reduces manpower for operation by using less bigger containers than more of smaller capacity ones on road lines, railway wagons and ships for same quantity of material transported.

SIMPLIFIED DIAGRAM OF TRANSPORTATION

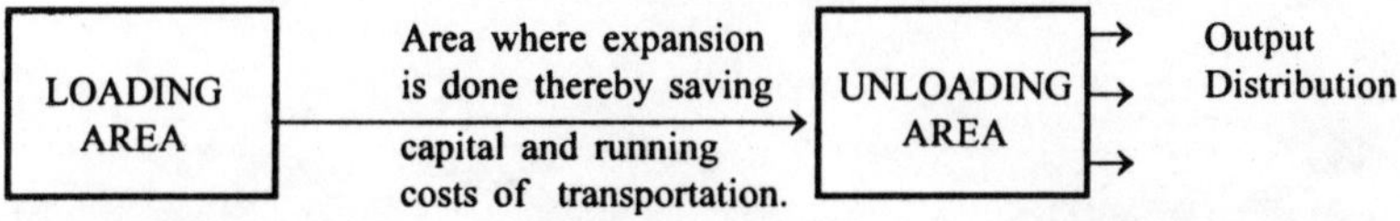

- Less/high capacity loading equipment and reduction in loading staff.
- Move number of vehicles on road, rail and sea which are of lesser capacity changed to less number of higher capacity containers and haulage equipment.
- Less number of bigger transport vehicles and large capacity containers
- Less staff
- High capacity unloading equipment.

Diagram depicting transportation of material by using less high capacity transport vehicles in place of more number of small capacity transport vehicles.

(26) Expansions schemes in the existing plants, or starting parallelly, other plants, retaining existing plants and entering into new areas by starting new plants, without discarding old plants, are very common. In some cases, new activities will be started in the same plants. With new tie up, to certain customers and satisfy markets, increase operations, better yields, better returns on new capital instead. These are done in expansions schemes. These expansions, result in multiplying their outputs, bringing new assets by employing more manpower, installing more machinery, entering into new technology/engineering and processes, with allied organizations, in the field, by mergers or market expansions. These are done very commonly.

(27) Where wide customer outlets and service outlets are available in the country, expansion and diversification become very profitable. They can quickly market new products, in addition to existing products and retain old markets and also increase, new markets by new products and services which they start employing.

(28) Cost reductions will occur resulting in more markets and help get less costly products for customers.

(29) Cheaper services by giving better services and quality services, in as many areas as possible.

(30) Better quality leadership of products, projects, better skills and better knowledge base, to help the organization to sustain their reputation. Capturing customer confidence and better operations in the market.

20

Acquisitions, Mergers, Liberalisation, Privatisation and Globalisation

ACQUISITIONS

In generally big, popular, well-established, geographically well-connected commercial organizations, where the organizations have achieved good maturity, good capital base, a well-conceived, well-planned, strategic proposition, comes up for consideration of the managements. This might involve some two or more than two organizations at a time. Generally this process takes place in organizations working for similar objectives from professional angle. This general process is thought of for the organizations to come closer to achieve the common objective of making major profits. This process of coming together of the organizations come under a major heading acquisitions and mergers. The line of demarcation between acquisitions and mergers is technically very thin but operationally very different in practice.

What prompts organizations to go for acquisitions and mergers can be categorised under the following broad headings or objectives :

1. To increase the capital and asset base.

2. To increase bigger markets of operation.

3. To earn more profits and give higher dividends to the share-holders.

4. To grab new emerging market, social, technological and scientific opportunities.

5. To equalise the strengths and weaknesses of the organizations as they exist before acquisitions or mergers and after emerging as better entities dress up the operations and jointly get higher benefits such as predominance in market, technological and scientific eminence, wide area of operations geographically capital wise and reach pre-eminent positions and if possible monopolise trade in certain products or projects, countries and retain that position by good joint expertise.

6. Another very scientific reason could be the organizations involving in acquisitions or mergers, might be losing ground in markets, demand for products, plant and machinery might be getting old, outdated requiring huge deployment of capital resources of other kind such as raw material, qualified technical manpower, latest technologies of processes, etc. Here one organization on its own may not be able to do but more than one organizations together could achieve these objectives.

The above in general are some of the reasons to think of acquisitions and mergers of organizations. There could be many more explicit and implicit reasons.

Now diverting to acquisition part acquisition process could be in parts or in full. That is to say two or more organizations A, B and C could be entering into the process of acquisitions with the following alternatives :

1. A may be the biggest of the three organizations among A, B and C. B and C might be smaller organizations in comparison to A. A might take dominating role in the process of acquisitions. B and C might also fall in line and agree. Now question comes whether A takes over total activities of B and total activities of C also. Then after acquisition the total entity becomes A + B + C. This will not be the case.

2. A remains as it is. It acquires the rights of B in some areas and rights of C in some areas. B and C will lose the identities in those areas where their wings get acquired by A and becomes part of A. For example A may be a production organization. It might be carrying on all its activities by itself including marketing and services. However, A remaining as it is, might take over the marketing and distributing activities of B and C which also may

be production organizations pursuing all their activities independently including marketing and distribution. Now the new picture will be A will remain as it is the marketing activities of B and C get added to A but other activities of B and C with B and C as they were earlier.

3. Second example could be A, B and C might continue with old activities of production independently however A might club marketing and distribution of B and C and make this marketing and distribution of A, B and C as another part of A. The advantage that comes from this type of acquisition will be markets A, markets of B and markets of C will all be together. They can have common policy. Physical locations of the marketing and distribution offices of A, B and C will now be available in a big way. They will get big infrastructure, new customers, more trained staff in each office owned by them. They can bank on all assets of these offices and also do better business of all products of A, B and C in a bigger area.

4. A might have big capital but B might have better and latest technologies in the fields of B's range. Same thing may be with C. If A acquires the latest technologies of B and C, by reorganising its staff, operation machinery and markets the overall technologies of A, B and C might become very strong. Better products can come out from A, B and C. All three can be benefited. This combination might become a bigger technological entity with latest technology available in the world. That way this combination emerges as a very big modern and highly powerful and competitive entity with other similar big competitors in a particular country or a group of countries or the world as a whole. Thus, lot of examples can be given where benefits will be reaped by organizations by acquisitions.

5. This process of acquisitions might become effective from a particular date. The process might start getting benefits immediately or in phases or it might take years to stabilise to give optimum results.

As practical examples power generating plants carry on transmission and distribution. By process of acquisitions a big company with only generation as motto might come into existence.

Another company might emerge doing only the activities of transmission and distribution. In the new system power generation company might become very strong, get a big capital base, human talent resource base, technologically update its working. Later this power company might increase its production capacity, operate its plants very efficiently. Get very high profits. This might enable the new company to expand its base further. Same thing can happen if distribution systems and transmission systems are pooled up. The new setup with big capital and human resource base can very well organize and become a very efficient highly profit-making enterprise. Before these acquisition processes many loop-holes might have existed resulting in poor profits, inefficiency, etc. Another advantage that will crop in will be that the talents in these fields can organise to do their duties more efficiently and bring good name to the new setup and good returns to the organization, better remuneration and growth to employees.

In the field of oil sector in addition to exploration of petroleum production if the petroleum producing companies join with refinery and distribution of its products or of similar companies the new setup might bring good returns as a full entity. Losses made in one area or difficulties encountered could be overcome as bigger entity.

Lot of planning, deliberations, market studies plant configurations before and after acquisitions take place in the organizations going for this change. With full satisfaction the organization after satisfying with advantages and disadvantages clearly known to them go for this change.

After acquisition profitable sections of the organization will be reorganized and strengthened to give renewed profits and better dividends to shareholders. Decisions whether to close done some non-profit-making wings of the organization or make them improve by depleting capital organizing the resources markets will be carefully done. After acquisition the new setup will go higher up in the ladder. It will acquire more venturing capacity with more capital and resources at its command. The new competitors give new experiences to reorient the organization. The customer confidence in the new setup will increase. They will become more secure. New markets will increase. Flexibility in working will increase. Slowly over a period with better management the bigger enterprise can earn more money, make more products, give more service to customers. Improve quality of its products and services overall by very careful deployment of facilities at its command.

The assets of the total organization increase. The total liabilities of the total setup decreases in comparison to the new size of the enterprise. Scope for totally nullifying the liabilities in course of time and improving better remunerative profit base will come to the organization. This new setup can expand its operations by entering into allied areas of operation such as taking up new production bases, improve working of the organization. Staff in new setup can be given more remunerations, they can be shown growth in their careers and made to give their best efforts to the organization and benefit themselves at the same time bringing better image to the organization.

The new management will have at its disposal more area in all spheres of its operation. Meticulous working and step by step concentration on growth as also the inherent problems which slow down its operation and growth can be addressed in a big way. It is left to the bigger setup to utilise the optimum resources and come out successfully with better results.

MERGERS

The case of mergers of organizations doing merger is different from organizations which go for acquisitions. In mergers it so happens that two or more organizations decide to merge from a particular date. From that date onwards, the organizations which merge lose their complete identity. Lot of discussions, deliberations, feasibility studies, advantages and disadvantages, later status of organizations, managements, people working in the organization, various resources at their command all will be evaluated threadbare from major to micro level. People in the merging organizations know fully well how things will be after merger takes place. Everybody will be prepared and hardly any surprises except for unforeseen reasons happen as it is a planned activity. The managements merging, their past ideologies, future course of action, ideologies to be adopted will all be clear. The merging organizations whether they are two or three or more will become one in every sense of the word. The managements became one. How the management has to be like would also have been decided. Another thing that happens in this case is before merger the organizations will have their own chosen company/ organizations names. After merger an agreed new name will come into vogue. Generally bigger of the organizations merging will keep the name leaving the name of smaller oganization/ organizations. Sometimes there will be names of two organizations structured suitably. As a third alternative a totally different name discarding the old names will be used. Apart from names total assets merge, total liabilities merge, total manpower, physical resources, all come under one management.

Here assets will become big. Liabilities will become positively less in comparison to assets and become insignificant and might get wiped out totally, in course of time. Since the new organization takes one identity, the identities of old organizations as they existed cease. The future operations will be in the name of new organization. The size of organization as a whole having gone up, as bigger concern, its status goes up in the ladder, in comparison to other organization. It takes appropriate place in the organizations of similar capital base and operation. Market value goes up. Customer confidence becomes high. Dividends declared to shareholders improve.

With mergers new set up acquires many rights of the merging organization, patents, design data, process information and management strategies adopted by the organizations will be used to best advantages. It is the practice, if different product mix is there in the merging organizations, new setup will retain more profitable products, increase the production of products which have more demand and generate more profits. At the same time, less profit making products or products which have less demand or likely to go out of markets will be reduced or discarded. The areas where less returns are coming will be developed to suit better profit generating products. These activities take a lot of time and cannot be made immediately. In the intervening period a lot of care will be taken for growth and reduce investments on unproductive activities.

In some cases, one organization will be having good markets. It will be generating good output. There will be optimum utilization of capacity. In the other cases, the organizations may not be working to optimum level because of lack of markets, less efficient plant and machinery, outdated technology. Hence, knowing such a situation, best capacity utilization by more investments, deployment of staff from profit making organization will be used so that the new bigger entity will give comparatively better returns. What would have been total loss in the merging organization, will be converted to making profits.

If a plant makes certain equipment, with smaller capacity of equipment (ratings) but market demand is for only higher capacities, the renovation of the plants will be made to cater to higher ratings which are in demand and which will have assured markets in future. If there are certain chemical or pharmaceutical plants and if there is no demand or profit in operating them, the loss making line of production will be phased out and profit making products will be strengthened. The same can happen to a consultancy or inspection or construction organization. If the demands for the line which they are pursuing leads to loss and demands change to other fields, the organizations can be oriented to profit making lines, discarding projects or products which they were looking after earlier.

Organizations prepare to change overnight to work in new areas in every line of activity where there is demand and cast off activities in areas which have become redundant. With mergers bargaining strength of organizations increases, with augmented resources. The management will start taking stake in higher value tenders and execute jobs of higher value than their earlier lesser value markets. Merging organizations will have a lot of knowledge base in their field of operation. If organizations are the venturing capacity increases. A lot of flexibility in operation will come to the new management. Talents of employees will be pooled. Better skilled and experienced people will be used in operations, which generate more profit and to improve the operation of less productive or even loss making lines of operation. Other staff will be deployed for areas where other operations have to be looked after. The emoluments, benefits, status of the employees grow.

While some top slots in the job might pose competition and bickering due to pyramid shapes of the organizations, other jobs will all become productive creating employee satisfaction enabling them to give the best output they are capable of. Mergers in the organizations take place generally when the organizations have become quite mature. Each merging organization would have established its own name and standing in the market, in the fields of individual operations.

The reasons for mergers could be many. Some of the examples are :

1. Each organization which decides to merge with another will generally have similar lines of operation so that they encash on the experiences and markets of merging organizations. If a banking organization merges with an insurance organization, staff in both organizations work in similar ways. They quickly absorb the working of the new organization and orient to that setup.

2. A manufacturing organization, if it merges with another organization of similar standing and quantum of operations, size of operation, markets, philosophies, then the merging organizations quickly orient themselves to the new change. The advantages and disadvantages having been identified earlier, they quickly settle down to capitalise on the advantages, find ways and means of eliminating the inbuilt deficiencies quickly, make the organization in the new setup to grow fast and bring higher outputs.

3. If organizations with certain technological background or scientific background join, they quickly adopt new technology in the overall organization, discard effectively and beneficially old and outdated technologies and grow fast.

4. If more markets are there for certain organization in a particular country and another organization has certain other markets in the same country or other countries with all markets put together, the operation of the new setup will be best where markets are good, and where they are not upto the mark, they make efforts to improve or totally discard some and strengthen the profitable markets. The sales outlets also will be used cumulatively with similar strategies. As an example a steel plant

of long standing knows what was the process available certain decades back, the utility of end products, information on competitors source of various raw material markets, plant and machinery mark, the R & D available to all organizations, the type of products that existed in the past in the markets, the demand position now, how the demands will change in course of next 5 to 10 years. How their infrastructure is geared for future years to cope up with the demands ? What profit or loss it has been making and what will be position later ? This field of activity with all similar competitors, producers, consultants, markets dictate the plans for future. Same conditions will exist in other sectors say power, petroleum, cement, paper, building construction activities, latest fields like information technology, communication, defence equipment, educational and scientific organizations. It is this knowledge and experience that drive organizations to keep watch on the developments in the field and make proper moves of mergers, with managements which also look for broadening their bases, strengthening the weak areas in their organizations. Otherwise the weak areas might slowly result in less productivity less dividends, sometimes losses or even closing of business. This merger phenomenon is partly aimed at arresting negative trends that might set in and grow at early stages itself to safeguard the interest of the shareholders or capital advancing agencies.

The organizations after merger quickly organize their production strategies, expansion strategies, market strategies, capital, human resources, etc. when things are well within their control to manipulate things to their advantage. In many cases organizations quickly start adding and strengthening their bases such as plant, test facilities, markets, use of raw material bringing good marketable products. They quickly remove loss making lines of operations by phasing out of market tactfully and absorb the inventory that would have accumulated in several areas.

To strengthen their organization strict controls on operation after mergers will be enforced. Increase cash flow, reduce debts, bring more quality goods, enter aggressively into markets. These are the implications of mergers in general and reasons for going for mergers.

LIBERALISATION

Liberalisation word means getting imported things such as raw material, finished good, technology, process techniques, several trade transactions with foreign countries, their organizations in trade, commerce and other areas easily. This is today a very popular word used by all people and organizations in our country, as also in other countries of the world, who have the enthusiasm to know the developments taking place in our country.

Till early 90s, the import policies of our country were so formulated that import of majority of commodities from other countries was totally stopped if not to use words more emphatically prohibited, except in strategic areas such as defence, core sectors like steel, coal, petroleum products, power production equipment, atomic energy areas, cement and food items, till we became totally self-sufficient in food. There was freedom to get spares which are vital for infrastructure industries and also in industries and areas where foreign equipment and machinery was installed provided of course, those spare are so vital and important that using indigenous substitutes was not reliable or risky or the quality of the indigenous spares was not acceptable for usage as substitutes, for fear of spoiling the main equipment, plant and machinery and at the same time put up with, shut down of these plants. Same thing applied to services also. One uppermost consideration was, our foreign exchange reserves were very meagre and heavy trading was going on in this area. Another consideration was, government wanted to protect indigenous undertakings fully in infrastructure areas. Government gave same consideration for foreign firms and investors in this area which was obviously right thing to follow in those circumstances. The restrictions imposed on imports were such the procedures involved to get import licenses was made so lengthy and complicated that people would get totally discouraged even to make attempts for importation, unless there were some parties who knew that after following the procedures meticulously they would get permission to import what they want. Life-saving drugs and priority sector commodity items at the discretion of government, were the only exceptions. It was made a rule and not exception that last word had to be said that indigenous sources could not meet with the commodities and services, which the parties wanted to import. The facilities were in the form of price differential, relaxation of deliveries, meeting fully certain standards and clauses of technical specifications, sever relaxations in commercial bids like EMD, Bank guarantee payment terms, performance guarantees to name a few. This policy had given total protection to indigenous manufactures and suppliers as also foreign collaborators, who were operating in India, catering to indigenous consumers. However, with the export market it was the reverse and wherever exports could be made, after satisfying indigenous needs fully or sometimes partly, were totally encouraged to build foreign exchange reserves, in every area of operation, where it was practicable. This policy gave room to monopolistic tendencies. Almost all public sector and monopoly sectors of economy, had higher hands and were totally dictating terms to the market. Sometimes, a lot of hardships had been created by delays in getting commodities and services from the organizations and people suffered many times without getting their requirements from the market. Quality, accountability, prices, availability, were all at stake.

This scenario got changed by liberalisation due to various compulsions that were forced on the market.

1. The demand for commodities in our country increased in multiples, compared to installed capacities in our country. Even by over-stretching production, it was impossible to meet the market demands. Growth and developmental activities began to suffer. Foreign exchange trading was not in the reach of ordinary users and they could not totally afford. It was not possible to rely on indigenous suppliers, even after long periods of waiting beyond the promised deliveries. Quality, adherence to standards and important specification became questionable.

2. The technological development across other countries of the world, began to grow at a very rapid pace. The gap in technological advancements in several sectors and other global organizations, in other countries began to become very wide. Realisation came that it would take long years to catch up with rest of the world in many vital areas, even after liberalisation and liberalisation was becoming a dire necessity. This field also

included education and technology where wide gaps existed. Necessity for huge investments in the enterprises in our country became necessary, which we could hardly do, with our limited resources. Tendency of our country falling back to other economies of the world in comparison began to show up very glaringly.

3. We could hardly ill-afford to continue with old practices, by restricting imports and flow of knowledge, technological advances and superior and latest commodities coming to our country, from developed countries. The tendency of developed countries not to part with new technologies was also very clear unless those countries got benefit from our trade and other benefits asked by them of their choice. The cost of commodities with latest advantages of use, was costly to bear for our country. After living in this situation for a long time, knowing the disadvantages of restrictions on imports, which began to have a telling effect in several vital areas, our country started allowing imports in phases, first in priority sectors and important areas of economy and later to less strategic areas by arranging foreign exchange by pursuing every possible efforts, open to the government. Permitting goods to come to our country from surplus sources in other countries started giving good results in developing our trade and commerce. Economy started growth in many areas.

4. Some developing countries and developed countries, started using our liberalisation policy in aligning with organizations in our country, in sharing know-how and start joint cooperative ventures. Some companies opened offices, started production and consultancy organizations in our country which would help them and also our people to have access to advancement in other countries. This brought more employment avenues to our people.

5. Sense of dynamism and vibrancy began to grow in our enterprises which started making more quantity of quality products so that they could compulsorily compete with developed, advanced and more sophisticated organizations outside. Sense of competitiveness, started helping us as these organizations began to improve their operations, against the onslaught of competitors from outside for their survival with organizations trying to shed their old practices, acquire new technologies, install and operate

latest state of art technology, machinery and plants, aid and soft loans from international lending agencies, like World Bank, Asian Development Bank, Commonwealth countries, starting supplementing our capacity, since they began to get confidence in our new policies and outlook *vis-a-vis* earlier policies.

6. For example talents and improvements in information technology and software in our country has been comparable to outside developing countries. There have been areas where we are better equipped in this area than outsides. Today export of software and systems, have become an appreciable part of total exports. These exports are not only to less developed and developing countries, but also to developing countries. Surprises are taking place in this country, in the area of information technology, software, e-commerce, internet infrastructure, that many global companies are putting up plants and offices either on their own or in association with Indian partners. Developing countries committing their finances, have eased our foreign exchange and we are having surplus foreign exchange and for sometime to come with the anticipated progress, foreign exchange will not be a problem to our country. We are noticing this growth in other areas, and many areas of our country are self-sufficient in commodities. Our knowledge reserves are comparable to outside world. This is one surprise, that liberalisation which has become an accepted policy of our country, has been bringing to our economy.

7. Development in the nuclear field and the know-how we possess in the area of radar, missiles, space technology has brought our country in the list of top few countries of the world, as a nuclear power. Our governments at centre and state, have made import policies simple. Exports, where we are already having some traditional percentage of world commerce, such as in the commodities like tea, coffee, jute, cotton and polyester garments, steel, certain food items like wheat, jowar, condiments such as chillies, cashew, rubber, have now spread to engineering goods such as railway engines, coaches, signalling equipment, electrical generation, transmission and distribution equipment, certain fruits, flowers, jewellery, certain automobiles like two wheelers, cars, trucks, buses, some area of civil aviation

equipment. Our Indian companies are operating in the fields of construction activities abroad, such as in railway line construction, construction of airports, townships, building factories, power plants, laying pipelines for transportation of petroleum products, supply of iron ore. Many of these changes are attributable to liberalisation. In the area of intellectual know-how, our youth are settled in many developed countries like, USA, UK, Singapore, Germany, Gulf countries and some African countries where software engineering knowledge of our people is in very great demand. Software and information technology talents of our country has made a big mark as an asset where our people are working. Devotion to work, talents and knowledge, hard work put in, has been bringing extraordinary recognition to our country in information technology. Companies in software business are selling products and systems abroad, at highly competitive environments. This area has been giving employment to our people to a considerable extent compared to other areas where there are hardly any openings and surpluses are declared.

8. The era of waiting for supplies from indigenous suppliers is getting over. It is easier to get essential spares, equipment and services from outside countries, easily at short notice, with better quality, reliability and better working life. Foreign suppliers are coming forward to supply items with long credit, less interest and easier terms as desired by Indian users. Governments have started giving counter guarantees easily to organizations which are coming up in infrastructure areas such as power, water supply, roads, housing, sanitation, health, to improve our capital and employment base. Monopolistic tendencies in public sector in banking, insurance, civil aviation, power sector, machine tools, construction fields, mining, processing, automobiles, communication, steel, cement, paper, heavy machinery and almost all engineering and technology fields except defence and core sector which government would like to identify.

PRIVATISATION

The literal meaning of this philosophy of privatisation is allowing organizations run by Central Government and state governments, to be managed either partly or fully as governments decide, by private individuals, private organizations, employees of these organizations or any other organization of total Indian origin or an organization of foreign origin, operating in India independently or in collaboration with individuals or organizations, non resident Indians, non resident Indian organizations, operating in India or outside India or Foreign organizations operating outside India, big multi national foreign organizations, for that matter any organizations, individuals or combination of these. The point in mind in going for this change is that the central government or state governments, some times where both central government or one or two state governments as partners, surrender their capital, partly or fully as they decide at that time, in each case, under their management, ownership and financial control, of the concerned governments and money invested in these organizations will come to them as cash. Here, the governments in some cases want to totally withdraw all the capital or money invested in these organizations. In some cases, the governments want to withdraw part of their investment. How much share, the government or governments want to withdraw is a matter of choice and to every extent, the prerogative of the governments. Cases are not there, except perhaps with some exceptions, where government does the management of an undertaking/organization, which is not a direct government organization, without having any financial investment from government's side. Generally, commercial undertakings, which are in business, are free from governmental control, if financial stake of governments is not there, in that enterprise or undertaking, or a group of these undertakings. Governments, as is generally known, only exercise control on all categories of commercial organizations, if it is not government owned, either as per company laws of the day or controls incorporated in the constitution of our country, as on that date, in addition to maintaining general law and order in the region surrounding the understandings.

In other words, barring routine and some exceptional cases, where government at centre or states manage a commercial undertaking, government undertakings have this type of stake in them, to be called government undertakings.

1. Governments have hundred per cent investments in it and no other individuals or organizations have any financial stake in it.

2. Governments have majority financial participation, in its capital and all other partners, have a minor participation compared to government.

3. Governments have small investments in it and majority of financial participation is by others, say private individuals, employees, private organizations, cooperatives, Foreign companies, Foreign nationals etc. or a combination of these. Further in all above cases government representatives head the organization, other partners will be on the management below this representative.

As of now, there are about 245 central government undertakings, where centre has financial stake and invested capital. In case of state governments, the number is different.

During independence, our country was mostly an agricultural country. The former rulers had some undertakings under their control and private Indian or Foreign nationals or organizations were owned by others. However, the overall economy in commercial sector was primarily agriculture. Other small economies were with government. Our people, depended on traditional agriculture, fisheries, poultry, cattle rearing, sheep breeding, pigetry or other traditional handicrafts, cultural enterprises and small miscellaneous occupations, including business for their living. Some people also were in jobs under central and state governments, local bodies etc.

After independence, it was decided, that India should shift its economy, from agriculture, to industry, at the same time, retaining and improving agriculture also, so that country becomes self-sufficient in food and also develops, agro based industries. Government first started some big major infrastructure projects after independence. Investments on these undertakings was 100 per cent from government's side. These were in the areas of irrigation, power, steel, coal, petroleum, machine tools, power generation transmission and distribution industry, including consultancy, construction and inspection of these products and projects, heavy machinery, communication, railway infrastructure, civil aviation, road infrastructure and such industries which promote other industries in either infrastructure or non-infrastructure areas. Such industries were fertilisers, chemicals, pharmaceuticals, building construction items, education, health, water supply, sanitation, textiles, cement, paper, mining, refineries, processing and extraction of petroleum products and other metals. Refineries were also started. These industries were to bring up and develop the expansion of several, major, medium and small scale industries and in a very big way, defence installations and infrastructure industries. At that time, the policy was to make the country self-sufficient/reliant in as many areas, such as food, clothing, health, education, housing, communication, water supply, sanitation etc. It was also intended to cut down dependence on other countries for our country's basic requirements.

With this in mind, when projects, industries and undertakings were started, they were few in number. These were totally owned by governments at centre or states or both. The concept was to run these undertakings with minimum profits at the same time, governments not incurring additional expenditure from their side, except for some genuine reasons. These organizations being few, with high capital investment, long gestation periods, served the purpose, for which they were started. Here the governments took the help of friendly countries, foreign organizations, who could volunteer capital, knowledge technology, skilled manpower resources, to build and operate these enterprises and run them and see that in course of time these organizations live up to thc values for which they were started. Another major objective was, to provide direct and indirect employment to a good section of people, improve their skills and enable them to help in the overall growth of the country's economy and diverse entrepreneurial base. It was also intended that technological skills of our people improve in other productive areas, other than agriculture.

In course of time, many industries were started, which were of similar nature or different functional areas in public sector. These undertakings under public sector went on increasing in numbers and capital invested also grew. At the same time, as mixed economy, private sector enterprises, joint sector enterprises, co-operative sector enterprises also grew in infrastructure and other feeder areas, parallelly.

Upto a point of time, this concept worked very well. However, government at centre and at states began to fed the burden of managing these organizations. The staff employed in these organizations began to cross several lakhs in public undertakings itself. In addition, governments also have departments directly under their control, who do administration of the country, under their direction. This figure also began to grow, with more work under governmental purview, such as P & T, Defence, Atomic energy, space research, nuclear power, satellite communications, defence research and development organizations, central scientific research and development organizations, electricity boards, water supply and sewage boards, directly controlled autonomous universities and institutions etc., to name a few. Very naturally, administering and maintaining the undertaking controlled by central and state governments has become a gigantic task. In addition staff and maintenance of direct governmental controlled departmental staff and totally government aided institution staff, have made the problem most complicated, and disproportionate to the returns which governments in general and public at large, are able to derive from these establishments. The salary bills and establishment expenditures themselves, including welfare measures for these staff have now been running into several tens of hundreds of crores of rupees, per annum. The very process of administering complex undertakings and different categories of staff is in itself, a gigantic task in addition to effectively administering the country through its direct staff.

Bank nationalisation and nationalisation of general and life insurance companies has further added to the intensity of this problem and its magnitude particularly the big staff working in these areas. The number of people to be managed as human resource management, increased tremendously by this process of nationalisation of various economic sectors.

Now the working of many organizations have slackened due to huge work force at every work centre in every organization. One factor that contributed to lessening of returns from public sector organizations has been the policy of including organizations which were hither-to with private sector or joint sector or co-operative sector, on grounds of retaining work force in these organizations even though they had become less productive or sick and a drag on the economy. It is not just the salaries of staff and other welfare expenses on these people keeping the organizations running by incurring huge investments from general revenue resources of the government towards quantum of losses incurred on them renovation expenses, interest on capital, depreciation maintaining idle plant capacity due to lack of demand etc.

One other important factor, which has also been putting lot of strain on the working of public sector organizations is, there has been competition in the market for these organizations from private and foreign organizations which are operating in our own country. Generally the overhead charges of public sector undertaking products or projects are higher than other sectors in the field. There is reduction in demand for these products and projects for several years. The financial backing for making these organizations to be operating in the markets is on the governments. Plant and machinery get spoiled totally if they are kept idle including other infrastructure such as buildings and support services.

The physical number of organizations in central public sector is around 250 now compared to around 50 to 60 in 50's, 80 to 100 or so in 60s, 140 or so in 70s and 80s around 160 to 180 in 90s. The undertakings in state government public sectors have also gone up in the same for similar reasons and these governments are also having same kind of situations as at centre.

In a nutshell the reasons cited above are the dominating factors, which are forcing governments at centre and states to take to privatisation and shift the responsibility of ownership and maintenance/running these organizations to non governmental agencies. It is the proposal/policy to keep defence undertakings, core sector undertakings of national importance and security to be run by government and leave the rest to others hands. It is also thought that the resources that get generated by total or partial privatisation of these balance organizations could be used for strengthening the direct administrative agencies of government and plough the resources to welfare activities of the people of the country in the areas of water supply at all places including far off villages, in scarcity areas of towns and cities including metros, provide people proper medical facilities, educational facilities, communication facilities, housing and venues of employment and enable people to improve their lot. Many social welfare activities in other areas such as sanitation, proper all weather roads etc. are also in need of development.

In the category of privatisation the industries come under following classification :

1. Industries, which are well managed which have good track record and which are continuously generating profits. There are few in this category.

2. Industries, which are not making profits but some how are sustaining on their own without being problematic to government. Quite a few organizations are in this category.

3. Industries, which are not making profits and generally making losses and need governmental financial support to sustain in market and keep operating. This number is presently more.

Another classification is, organizations have such fine infrastructure, that many bidders would come to take and run them effectively, without problem to government or staff working in these organizations. Some organizations have become old, lot of money is needed to renovate them and look after the staff interests and welfare. In these cases the organizations one not coming up with proper remunerations to sell. Another category of organizations are such that the products they make have become obsolete, technology is obsolete and around the countries of the world they are lacking in markets and very low prices are likely to be offered in the take over.

Some other more important considerations are each organization has some book value, some market value, if they have to be built afresh now. Some organizations have neutralised their interests on capital, depreciation and there are no liabilities on these plants. In some cases, there may be the possibility, over the first lock in period is over these organizations may shift to other lines of manufacture or other trades, that country might lose that kind of infrastructure which it has today. Most important factor in addition to these is the condition of the staff and welfare, which might create issues, once privatisation takes place and managements change.

GLOBALISATION

Of all the philosophies in trade and commerce across the world, one philosophy which has been talked about and widely debated all around the world and round the clock, as on today, is the philosophy of globalisation. In layman's word Globalisation means opening the gates of each country's trade and commerce, technologic, scientific and logical commercial intelligence, to other country or countries or group of countries across the world, to the best advantage and benefit of that country's people as a whole and the government of the day of that country or countries in particular.

As on today, over 186 countries of the world are participants in this process. Debates are going on within other countries among its policy makers, whether to participate in this group or not and if yes, which is the most beneficial time to do. Our country is a member signatory to this agreement, which is shortly designated as WTO, World Trade Organization or GATT, generally agreement on Trade and Tariff. Round the clock discussions are going on each day at Davos the present capital of WTO, in Sweden. China, which is one of the major developing country is debating whether to join or not, if yes when. Japan and USA, who hold 40 per cent of world's economy are the leading partners of this organization. Each day agreements are signed with countries, after detailed deliberations about areas of agreement as to how much of the participating countries commerce is open to the other country in free trade. As far as our country is concerned, which is already a member of WTO, already all items except 786 items are included in free trade agreement even on these balance items quantity restrictions in free trade will go, with effect from 1st April 2001. It means import restrictions will not exist on all goods quantitatively.

There are three types of countries in the world, from the point of economic growth, technological and scientific growth, defence potential, per capita income, rate of GDP growth, quantum of assets owned, trading and commercial potential, education of masses, basic facilities of life, which they possess in abundance, bargaining power in the world, knowledge potential, standard of living of people, natural resources available in the countries and such growth potential. They are mostly as follows :

1. Developed countries, USA, UK, France, Japan, Germany, Russia.

2. Developing countries, China, India, Pakistan, Middle East and Far East countries, petroleum rich resource countries such as Iran, Iraq, Isreal, Saudi Arabia, Quatal & Kuwait, Canada, Norway, Belgium, Sweden, Spain, Italy, Netherlands.

3. Underdeveloped countries like Bangladesh, Tibet, Sri Lanka, Indonesia, Philippines and bulk of other world countries.

This categorisation has been just made to illustrate how these countries are placed in influencing world markets in various commodities. There are other category of countries which are traditionally rich in some commodities from the beginning and they carry on their trade with all their friendly countries on the surpluses of these commodities and in turn obtain other necessities for their daily requirements and augment their defence potential.

There are several advantages and disadvantages in this globalisation process, for the participating countries. To cite examples in this cadre :

1. When once a country makes a free trade agreement with another country or countries, for those items the participating countries have easy access to the extent the items are available after these countries fulfil their own internal requirements and priorities made with other countries. While quantity of items is one factor which gives assured imports some conditions are put in this trade on the periodic imports based on internal consumption and from other sister countries from whom they get similar commodities based again on the availabilities there as per the above parameters.

2. In case of agricultural products, countries like USA have edge in quality and quantity and price, with respect to other countries. The basic reason being this country has enormous potential of natural resources of all kinds. In industrial products,

because of the leading scientific and technological advances made in the process and quantum of production, the country generates abundant money in these fields. It has too much surpluses which enables the country to give the highest subsidy in the world, for farmers, so that they produce the best and highest quality of agricultural products and processed goods from them cheaply. These goods are easily exported to countries, who need them at the most competitive prices in the world. This country takes off the advantage of commerce from other countries and dumps major commodities at a small premium to other countries. Countries who at a small premium to other countries. Countries who cannot afford giving enough subsidies to agriculture there the farmers have the disadvantage of exporting these goods at cheaper rates, because of the inability to compete with surplus producing countries.

3. Where India is having an edge in traditional exports, which are in abundance, after meeting India's requirement the country's markets can use the returns for procuring scare commodities, which are in demand in India and make profits and enough capital. In this way to the quantum of money obtained by these exports, our country gets the benefit of bargaining and getting latest technological products in the order of its choice and priorities and improve in that area in Indian market. This is a very genuine and non controversial gain to the country, from the trading countries in the respective categories.

4. Our country has reached self-sufficiency in several core items/commodity such as food items, milk and diary products, poultry and meat, fish, several varieties of steel, coal, common machine tools, information technology items, several communication equipment, building materials besides steel like, cement, wood and wood based products, horticulture items, flowers, most of railway infrastructural products, automobile products, certain mining and material handling equipment, infrastructure equipment for constructing airports, shipyards, equipments for putting up production units in areas of paper, textiles, cement, copper, zinc, Aluminum, quite a number of latest defence equipment, several nuclear power equipment, health care, education, water resources, sanitation, beverage inputs like coffee,

tea, cocoa, sugar, most of agricultural equipment for small and medium farming, polyester, resins, several domestic appliances, such as refrigerators, TVs, washing machines, VCRs, almost all varieties of utensils, cookers, furniture, upholstery, foot-wear, leather and resin goods, handicrafts, ivory items, jewellery items, sandal wood items, several chemicals, pharmaceuticals, medicines, infrastructure for Radio, television and cable operation, power cable, power conducts and power and tele-communication equipment, taking and execution of turn key jobs in power sector in thermal, hydro, gas turbine areas, and many other items. We are having excess capacity to export these items, we have received international standard certifications to compete in these markets. Only we need, price and facilities to improve our markets in export areas. By being signatories to WTO we can use countries where these items are needed and gear our capacities to supply them and earn money. Since, this process of globalisation is a recent phenomenon, lot of study and practical experience by our organizations and our friendly countries' help has to be taken to improve our markets slowly. We have the main difficulty of financing these projects and need outside investments to help us.

5. One disadvantage or consequence in globalisation of markets is surplus producing countries of several products vie with each other and dump their products, even though our own indigenous products of equivalent standards are available in plenty. Antidumping restrictions of exports to our country in these areas have to put a blockage by imposing customs and countervailing duties, so that the outsiders will find their commodities costlier and prevent making inroads to our own manufacturers domain and block their business. These are very wide areas and lot of study is required at market and commerce ministry levels to encourage our imports and bring profits.

6. There are areas where developed and developing countries try to sell their most advanced products in our markets. Here, continuity of supply price, availability of spares and service, easy access to these organizations foı settling transactions have to be looked into, before hastily introducing costly projects and products in our country. Some suppliers come with packages of production units, consultancy units, marketing and service units. These could

be promoted to get foreign investments employment opportunities to our people and learning new advances made to be absorbed by us in the process. In taking this offer, we get latest knowledge available in the world which that country is offering which we can take. Our people get opportunities to learn in the process fresh capital comes to our country in the form of investments. It brings with it jobs scope for providing facilities to them where our people in concerned market areas will get new jobs. This is how investments come with new technology and job and profits for our people who use them. Available talent in our country get opportunities to earn money and improve their living conditions.

7. When transactions are made with countries the heads of organizations who participate in them to get those products, projects and markets negotiate with the exporting countries on deliveries, prices, technical parameters, advantages of using their technologies and process, if they are not already available in our country. Here the suppliers open offices for engineering, sales services and construction operation etc. These investments stay for considerable time and people in our country can use it. We can also get opportunities to start and operate joint ventures in the fields beneficial to us in markets where these commodities are in demand. Information technology, fields gas turbine technology are some examples where our country's talents and resources are used in third countries in joint ventures in executing projects there. These give opportunities to exhibit our talents and know-how in other countries with organizations who join us with their superiority of expertise and bring us benefit.

8. Thus globalisation process is comparatively a new phenomenon in which our country is participating. It is opening opportunities to our industrialists, consultants, educated and talented youth in specialised fields are getting promising avenues to start and build careers and earn bring benefits to our enterprises including traditional commercial trade including agriculture to grow as profit producing centres. Our participation in other new venues of trade and commerce and reciprocally, other countries interaction with our trade industry and commerce will bring slowly but steadily growth and development. But this is a process, where

we are learning and in the learning process we have with us organizations of other countries, also in similar situations and in the overall process in the long run we have got opportunities for growth and development.